IN WHOM I AM WELL PLEASED

Edward T. Byrne

En Route Books and Media, LLC

Saint Louis, MO

⊕*ENROUTE*
Make the time

En Route Books and Media, LLC
5705 Rhodes Avenue
St. Louis, MO 63109

Cover credit: Edward T. Byrne
using a photo of Matthew Edward Byrne

ISBN-13: 979-8-88870-152-2
Library of Congress Control Number: 2024935480

"The road to hell is paved with good intentions."

Spuriously attributed to St. Bernard.

PREFACE

Your child's suicide feels like the biggest parental failure of all. Any parent wants to be prepared for the worst, but no one ever anticipates that horror actually happening until it is too late.

Although it's still shocking to me, this is a true story, as told from one observer's perspective. I apologize if I've gotten any details wrong or misstated the timeline by misplacing some events before or after others. I believe the essence of what I have written is accurate and the opinions expressed valid, whether you find them harsh or indulgent.

I want you to know that I could not even start this project until two years had passed since The Event. At that point, and despite being advised against telling my son Matthew's story, I felt destined to do so. My wife, Patti, and I believed that too many of the good memories were being lost as we forgot the bad. Unfortunately, you can't be selective. If you don't remember the entire story, you may not recall any of it at all, or end up with a distorted version of what happened. Suicide is just the end of someone's life story and shouldn't be permitted to overshadow its beginning and middle. Those parts deserve to be remembered, too.

As I tried to recall all that happened, my narrative morphed. It became no longer just Matt's story but, perhaps necessarily, an abbreviated history of our family, through good times and bad. In some of the background episodes, Matt plays only a minor role, yet these vignettes reveal the interrelationships within our family and its unique dynamic, all necessary to understanding how each member suffered, both before and after The Event, and in ways we still may not fully recognize.

I offer this as a cautionary tale. Plainly, many well-intentioned mistakes were made along the way, which I will not try to defend. But if you don't think something like this can happen to you, rest assured it can, and don't be surprised how quickly it happens if you turn out to be the unlucky ones. If this book gives just one family the heads-up it needs to change its luck from bad to good, or some additional strength to survive its loss, it will have been worth the effort.

I.

August 24, 2014, began as perfect as a late-summer day could be, like September 11, 2001, just a bit warmer. The people whose lives were affected by the historic events of that earlier day, already a decade past, had no idea what lay ahead that beautiful morning. Neither did we. Sunday began so normally, disarmingly, that it disguised the fact that it would be our personal 9/11, orchestrated not by Osama Bin Laden, but someone we knew and loved.

Paul and I had left early to go fishing. For days we had been pestering Matt, my older son, to come with us. He had been out of the hospital a few weeks, and I'd been with him nearly every day as his mother and I took turns shuttling him back and forth to doctors and out-patient sessions. We'd done nothing resembling a fun activity, however. Matt had always loved fishing, but he kept putting us off for some reason, trotting out one excuse after another to stay home. I had even taken one last shot the night before, when he said he was going to bed, to convince him to join us.

"No, not this time. But I'll go next time."

"Okay," I responded from the couch as he closed the family room door behind him.

Seconds later, the door reopened, and Matt walked back in. Thirty-four years old, he was unshaven and unsteady, hopefully just from the heavy medications the doctors had been prescribing.

"I almost forgot to tell you I love you," he blurted, waiting for a response.

I got up from the couch, walked around the table and spread my arms wide.

"I love you too, Matt."

We hugged, longer than men do, and I think I kissed him as well. I hope so. He just said "Goodnight" and walked back out the door.

The following morning there wasn't even a ripple on the water as Paul started the boat's engine at the marina. My younger son was twenty-nine at the time. Unlike his slender brother, Paul is powerfully built, and wore the wraparound sunglasses and faded Yankee cap he always takes fishing. He cast off from the dock, and we glided through the series of canals leading to Reynolds Channel. We turned for the Atlantic Beach Bridge, eventually passing the tip of Far Rockaway, then headed out several miles into an ocean that was as flat as a lake.

The fishing was not bad. Fluke were still in season, and Paul always catches a couple of legal-length "keepers" while I'm typically limited to undersized "shorts," sea robins, and other undesirables you throw back in the sea. But I love being on the water, especially on a calm day like that one with the sun shining down and the water gently lapping against the side of the boat.

It was probably around 11 A.M. when the cell phone in my pocket began ringing. Patti was crying. She had caught Matt trying to steal the pills for her rheumatoid arthritis and back pain again, and they had had another major fight.

This cat-and-mouse game had gone on for years, despite

Matt's four stints in rehab facilities and two more in what you would have to call psych wards. This particularly bad habit had generated some of the harshest words I ever used on Matt, along the lines of "How can anyone stoop so low that he steals his mother's pain meds and leaves her without any?" This had to stop. I knew I finally had to throw him out of the house this time and not relent, like I had once before, after he had begged to stay because no one would take him in.

The ocean's spell was broken, and I stewed the rest of the morning and into the afternoon, anticipating what would happen when I arrived home.

Maybe we should have given up right then, but Paul and I kept going through the motions, fishing without much conversation as we listened to the Yankee game on the boat's radio until midafternoon when we finally headed for shore.

We had taken two cars to the marina in Oceanside because Paul would always stay to clean the fish he was sure he would catch while I would head to the supermarket to pick up whatever was needed for the evening's meal. I honestly don't recall if I called Patti as soon as I got in the car, or whether she called me. I'll never forget the conversation that ensued.

She was hysterical. "Matt hanged himself," she wailed. "He really did it," somehow making clear that she had already called 911. I could hear my younger daughter, Ann, yelling at Patti to help her. They had just found him in the backyard and were desperately trying to get him down. Although the cellphone must have dropped to the ground, I could still hear their voices and footsteps in the background as I tried to race over what was maybe two miles to our home in Rockville Centre.

The waits at the two major arteries were endless. I kept searching for some gap in the passing cars I could dart through, but the traffic was too steady to attempt to cross. The phone call had kicked out for some reason, so I was no longer eavesdropping on my wife's and daughter's panic. I dialed Paul and told him what was happening as I begged the stoplight to change. When I finally got across Sunrise Highway, nothing could slow me down the rest of the way.

When I made the left onto Dorchester Road, there were so many emergency vehicles and volunteer firemen's cars that I had to pull over down the block and sprint up the sidewalk the rest of the way. I ran down the driveway, right past my crying wife and daughter who were being detained on the patio by policemen, then down the path that led to the yard behind the garage.

There were half a dozen firefighters working on Matt, who had on only board shorts. He had been lying in the wood chips beneath the swing set we had installed for our grandchildren. Under the direction of Big Ed, the head EMT whom I knew from playing basketball, the responders had moved him onto a backboard and placed a collar around his neck.

They were giving him CPR, and I started yelling, "C'mon, Matt, don't give up," as though I were at one of his swim meets back in the old days. His color wasn't bad due to his deep tan but, as hard as they worked, he was not responding. As I watched him lying there limp and lifeless, wood chips still clinging to his body, the awful thought entered my mind for the first time: "If he's going to stay like that, let him go."

At some point, I was recognized as the victim's father. I don't recall being escorted out of the backyard to the patio yet wound up there. Nassau County detectives had already arrived, and had taken over the questioning of Patti and Ann. The cops had them seated at the large wrought iron table set in the middle of the red patio that adjoined our house. I sat across from them. Patti was crying and looked bewildered by everything that was happening. Ann, our twenty-five-year-old daughter, had her head down toward her lap, weeping. I couldn't see her face, only her dark brown curls.

I began to learn what had happened. When Patti caught Matt trying to steal her pills, he begged her to share them with him. She properly refused, and it got ugly. When she threatened to call the cops on him, he responded cryptically, "Don't worry. You'll have to call them later."

Things apparently calmed down, somehow. By afternoon, Matt and Ann had decided to take some sun on the patio. They talked until Ann eventually fell asleep in a chaise lounge.

When she awoke, Matt wasn't there. Maybe from a premonition, Ann went searching and found him in the secluded, fenced yard behind the garage where he had gone with a rope Paul had bought for the boat. Matt had hidden it in the garage, at the ready when he decided to act on his plan. I'll never know how Ann managed to get him down with minimal help from her mother.

The detectives wanted to see Matt's room, and that posed a new problem. Portia, our fiercely protective Cane Corso mastiff, was going nuts inside the house from all the people milling outside. I can only guess that Paul had arrived home and taken her out because somehow the detectives made it to Matt's third floor bedroom and determined he had left no note.

When they returned to the patio, the detectives continued to question us about Matt, his background and his recent past. While the girls cried, I tried to stay calm and answer their questions completely. Yes, he had been depressed. He had been a New York City firefighter and had to quit after he got PTSD and began abusing alcohol and drugs. He had been a Jones Beach lifeguard for many years but had also lost that job weeks before.

At that point, the paramedics wheeled Matt out of the backyard on a gurney. Despite the tubes and apparatus, he showed no sign of life. The initial terrible thought, God forgive me, turned into an actual prayer: "Lord, please take him rather than leave him like that."

The EMTs continued to work on him in the ambulance they had backed into the driveway. I walked to its rear and watched them attending to Matt's propped-up body. Big Ed was in charge, kneeling to the right of my son's head. When I asked him, "Is he going to make it, Eddie?", he just stared at me, and I knew what the outcome would be. Within minutes, the rear doors of the ambulance were slammed shut with finality, and the ambulance pulled out of the driveway, transporting Matt to Mercy Medical Center.

The police and detectives could not have been nicer. They did not want us driving ourselves to the hospital and insisted that a young officer would take us in his squad car. Patti, Ann, and I walked with him to the vehicle and got in while Paul remained behind to lock up the house once everyone had left.

I can't recall much about the ride; very little conversation, just palpable dread. What I do recall is how much police cruisers had changed since I was last in one. The rear seat is just a molded plastic bench, constructed not for comfort but, like the similarly constructed floor, for hosing out the blood, barf, and other bodily fluids occupants in custody often leave behind.

The officer pulled right up to the emergency room entrance. The detectives had somehow beaten us there. Paul caught up soon enough, and we were ushered into what we soon realized was the "break the news" room.

There was a fortyish doctor in scrubs, tall and dark, who had tried to revive Matt, a nurse who apparently specialized in "informing" families, and a grief minister, assigned to this Catholic hospital by the Diocese of Rockville Centre, who let us know she was already supposed to be gone for the day. They had us sit around a conference table and told us officially what everybody already knew: Matthew was gone. The confirmation triggered another outburst of emotion, and the girls began crying hysterically all over again. The middle aged nurse was saying all the right, sympathetic things with a sing-song catch in her voice that I later learned had driven Ann crazy. The grief counselor, very prim, kept telling us that Matthew was with God now, and she had never seen someone look so peaceful. It was supposed to be comforting; it wasn't.

After a while, we were led out of the room. Our son, the kids' brother, was being prepared for a viewing. The detectives were in the hallway as well, still asking questions, very gently, while we waited to see Matt. One detective confided in me that he had lost his FDNY brother. I'm not sure what his story had been but, like Matt's, it hadn't been a good one.

We finally were admitted to another room where Matt lay on a gurney or table, something flat like that, all cleaned up and wearing a blue patterned hospital gown. He still had the clear plastic collar on his neck and one of the tubes that had been unable to save him dangled from it. They left us alone with him.

This scene was the worst. All the drama and commotion of cops, firefighters, and medical personnel was over and had been replaced by death, in its rawest, silent form. We had done this two years before when Patti's mother died, yet it was so different with an almost 90-year-old woman who had lived a full life and had done nothing to end it. As we touched Matt's hands, smelled his hair, one by one we lost it. I was standing up, shaking and sobbing uncontrollably until I turned away and yelled something I would have said as a kid: "Why'd you have to go and do that?"

After that initial wave of grief passed, because it simply could not be sustained, things settled down and we sat huddled around Matt, as if waiting for his explanation of what he had done. As much as I didn't like it, I had to admit that what the grief counselor had said was true: he looked extremely calm and relieved. I told the others that Matt had solved all his problems in a single afternoon, and I think we said a prayer together. At some point Paul, who was both extremely upset and extremely angry, stood up and announced, "We don't have to stay here!" He took Ann with him when he left.

I have no idea how long Patti and I remained in the room with Matt. A few years earlier, we had to put down our prior mastiff, Josephine. The vets give you plenty of time after the second needle to caress your pet that has just died and tell her how much you loved her. At some point you realize, however, that the staff is waiting for you to leave so they can get on with the business of caring for the living animals. It was the same thing with Matt. Knowing that we would never see him again, since he would be cremated just like Josephine, I eventually told his mother it was time to go, and we said our goodbyes. Physically supporting her, I led Patti from the emergency room complex outside to the hospital grounds.

It was already early Sunday evening, a time of day in late August when you just want to sit outside and enjoy the twilight. All the earlier bustle at the hospital had ended, at least until the next ambulance arrived. We had to ignore the quietude and get on with the very unnatural act of telling the rest of the family that our son was dead.

Ann had already begun the process with a call to Elizabeth, our oldest child, then thirty-seven, who has three children of her own. When it was my turn to get on with her, she was very upset, but like the rest of us, not surprised. As Matt's life had spiraled downward over his final four years, their relationship had become strained. His erratic behavior made her understandably reluctant to have him around her kids, and we saw less and less of them. We all knew that Matt was heading for a bad ending unless something changed. Taking his own life had been a definite possibility, although one we all desperately hoped to avoid. As I spoke with Elizabeth, waiting for her gasps to subside, I realized that Matt's preemptive strike had ruined any chance of the reconciliation I had hoped they might someday reach.

"Let me put your Mom on, Beba." I still used the nickname Matthew had hung on her as a little boy since his "Elizabeth" had been "Ebeba," then "Beba" for short. I handed the cellphone to Patti who sat on some steps, Ann's arm wrapped around her shoulder. Then I walked away from the ER entrance, across the lawn to Paul who was finishing a call with a friend.

Paul was five years younger than Matthew and had idolized his big brother when they were young. Just like with Elizabeth, however, Matt had practically destroyed his relationship with his brother, taunting Paul, who had cleaned up his act, for refusing to participate in the high-risk activities that had consumed Matt's life.

"What did Steve say?" I asked.

"That Matt never stopped digging the hole."

I nodded and began tearing up. Paul is a big guy and, when he hugs you, you've really been hugged. I closed my eyes when he did, grateful for that moment of respite.

I don't know how long we lingered on the hospital's grounds. The young police officer did take us home eventually to get our own car because we had decided that the next delivery of the bad news had to be done in person, not by phone.

My mother had turned 90 less than a month before. We had a nice party for her, and her friends who remained alive had pretty much all attended. It had been a fine day, except that one of her grandchildren was absent; Matt had been in Zucker Hillside Hospital, the psychiatric facility of what was then the North Shore-Long Island Jewish Health System. That time, we only had to tell her Matt would be missing her party; this time we would say he was gone forever.

I don't recall the short drive from Rockville Centre to Queens Village, where she lives at the Queen of Peace Residence. I do remember knocking on her unlocked apartment door. Patti, Ann, and I entered her living room; Paul had refused to come. My Mom immediately knew something terrible had happened; when I told her what, she wasn't surprised either. Just out of Zucker, Matt had come along a week or two before when I took her for breakfast, I guess to make up for missing her birthday party. He kept ordering food at the diner, more than any of us could eat, and she gave me a sideways glance as Matt moved from plate to plate, without eating much of anything as he rambled on through dozens of topics. She had known he had been in big trouble and cried quietly when she learned it was all over.

There was one more call that had to be made immediately, and we made it during the ride back to Rockville Centre.

"The Nephew," although he did not quite qualify, was the twenty-year-old son of Patti's late goddaughter, who had lived with us since he was thirteen to resolve a custody dispute after "The Father" had been imprisoned for the drunk driving that caused his wife's death. I had taken him back to college in Pennsylvania just the day before. The Nephew and Matt had a close relationship, although somewhat volatile, and he needed to be told what had happened.

When I told The Nephew that Matt had taken his life, he unleashed a torrent of expletives, cursing Matt for his "stupidity." The girls began screaming back at the dashboard, instinctively defending Matt's memory as I pulled off Exit 19 of the parkway. The shouting match continued as I reached the stop light at the end of the ramp. I tried to ignore them, shaking my head at the irony that, to cross Peninsula Boulevard and reach our house, you had to head directly back toward the entrance to the Mercy Hospital grounds we had left earlier.

I am very hazy as to what came next. We must have eaten at some point; I don't know when, what, or how. Maybe I took Portia out for a walk, as I usually would on a Sunday evening; perhaps Paul took care of that for me.

What I do remember was how silent everything had become, compared to that afternoon when it had never been busier with people, flashing lights and sirens. The house and yard where we had lived for more than twenty-five years didn't seem the same, and never would again. I had spent many a night wondering when Matt would come home: that night; the next day; the day after? This time, I knew he would never come home again.

At some point the phone rang. I was by myself; maybe the others had already gone upstairs, the kids to notify other friends, Patti to collapse in bed. It was the organ donor people. Either as a firefighter or lifeguard, Matthew had signed a donor card. Would I mind speaking to a representative? No. Maybe we could salvage something out of his death.

I must have spent close to an hour on this last, most exhausting call of the day, which could not be postponed if any of Matt's body parts were to be useful to someone else. I had to answer question upon question about his medical history, good and bad habits, everything you could possibly imagine. I didn't flinch at all. "Take whatever you might be able to use," I told them. I only insisted that nothing be returned, since I had handled a matter years before where the cadaver of a man who had donated his remains to a medical school was delivered back to the family three years later, an unexpected gift at Christmas that shattered them once again.

When the call finally ended, I sat alone at the kitchen table where we had all eaten dinner as a family practically every evening. I thought back to the night before when I said goodnight to Matt, never thinking that it would be the last time we ever spoke, much less that, facing an alternative he would hate, I'd wind up rooting for his death the next day, if he could not recover.

I began trying to sort all the conflicting emotions rushing through me. Shock, grief, loss, anger – plenty of it. For what Matt had done to his mother and sister. For how he had lied to me. He had tried to do away with himself a little more than a month before, but only wound up with a drunk driving charge and a trip to Zucker the next day. When he was released nearly two weeks later, he assured me that suicide "was off the table." I wanted to believe him, and somehow, foolishly, I truly did.

Matt's situation had been grim. He had fallen so far, his whole identity had been destroyed, and it was now clear that he hated the shadow he had become. Recovery is a process, and maybe not feasible for impatient people. Matt's task was difficult, yet not impossible until he refused to wait and allow his life's story to unfold further, cutting off any chance of a surprise happy ending.

Finally, I began asking the questions that would consume me

for a long time after The Event. Had all of this really happened? It seemed like it had, yet it couldn't have happened, not to us. This kind of thing only happened to other people; it was like something you read about in the newspaper but would never experience. You really can't imagine a "take your breath away" bad thing until it hits you.

But if this did actually happen to us, and it was starting to look that way, would we be able to walk away from Ground Zero and survive The Event like those people covered in ash in the photos of 9/11? Or would Matt's despair finish the rest of us, too?

I had known trouble before and had a few heartaches in life – but nothing resembling this. I searched my mind for one positive thought to cling to until morning, which had to bring a better day. It wasn't much, but I finally found something: at least I had not been forced to throw Matt out of the house. The more I considered it, though, I wasn't sure if that was a good thing or bad. It was one of the first "what ifs" I had to face. I began to play this most punishing game. If I had thrown Matt out years before, would he have pulled out of the tailspin and saved himself? Could we have avoided all this if Paul and I had simply stopped fishing and come home at the first sign of trouble in the morning? I knew I had to cut this type of inquiry off if I were even to survive that first night. There would be plenty of time for the "What If Game" later.

II.

Elizabeth was three when her baby brother was born. Patti insisted that he be called Matthew Edward. I thought it was one of the best ideas she ever had. The name Matthew meant "God's Gift," and he certainly was. Getting second billing wasn't too shabby either.

Patti didn't know how to have small babies, and Matt was another whopper, nearly nine pounds. As with Elizabeth, I was in the delivery room for the whole show, including the gruesome forceps process. I took lots of pictures of our newborn son. His head was molded and eyes all puffy like a boxer who had just lost a fifteen-round bout, yet I was so proud when Patti handed him to me. I had on one of those blue smocks that visitors must wear, and as Matthew lay his head on my shoulder, sleeping, I sat down in the easy chair next to her bed.

The after-birthing unwind is like a sweaty, postgame celebration, following the biggest victory of all. No matter how many times I watched it, I had no clue how it worked. Why is it that after a few gurgles, tentative at first, a child decides at that particular moment to loudly proclaim his or her arrival into this strange new world? We treat being born as a matter of course, something supposed to happen that's only shocking if it doesn't go smoothly, but it truly is a miracle, as anyone who has witnessed the first tenuous moments of life can attest. That afternoon's conversation with Patti had to be about all the dreams we had for Matthew and how excited Elizabeth would be when she met her little brother.

Matthew was responsible for two of the days of my life I recall most vividly. One I've already recounted; the other was the day he came home from the NYU Hospital in mid-May 1980. Elizabeth had been born there in December 1976 when we still lived in Stuyvesant Town in Manhattan, and we took her home in a cab on a frigid winter morning. This time, I picked mother and child up on a gorgeous spring day in a beat-up Chevy station wagon I was driving at the time. The air conditioner had not been tuned up yet for the summer, but I didn't think that would be a problem. Wrong again.

Patti's Mom, Lorayne, had knitted a beautiful white wool "traveling suit" for a newborn. Suitable attire for Elizabeth in December; way too warm for Matthew in May, but he was going to wear it home anyhow, hat and all.

I was insistent that we stop in Woodside to introduce Matthew to my Grannie, who had to be close to 90 at the time. When we parked on her block and checked the baby, facing backward in his car seat, he looked so hot that we decided to cut the visit short and get him home and out of the wool outfit. I left Matthew sleeping and managed to get Grannie down the two flights of stairs. The skinny old Irish lady climbed into the backseat of the car next to him, played with his little hands for a short while, and was happy as could be to meet her new great grandson, since, as she readily admitted, "I always liked the fellas."

When we finally arrived in Rockville Centre, it was like a scene from a Kodak commercial. Elizabeth came racing out of the house and rushed to her mother at the car. Patti bent down to let her kiss her new brother, somehow still wrapped in the wool blanket that went with the outfit, while I filmed them as they all came together down the driveway, Elizabeth chattering and practically running in circles. It was as though every bush and flower had burst into full bloom that mid-May morning, and it sounded like every bird in town had shown up to chirp its greeting to the new resident on Wachusett Street, which was already loaded with kids.

*

In view of Patti's nearly immediate return to work, since her maternity leave was eaten up when the pregnancy ran late, Elizabeth had been a bottle baby. Patti was determined to nurse this one. Matthew, however, was more interested in sleeping than eating, and he was not cooperating. Just when he'd start to nurse, he'd conk off to sleep again.

As soon as permitted, we began bathing him nightly in the kitchen sink. I've always been impressed with the sacredness of this ritual with a newborn. Everything gets very quiet, as though the slightest noise would ruin the bath. I doubt that would have been so for Matthew. From the first day, he seemed totally at ease with water, instead of having that panicked look you expect to see on a baby's face. We quickly noticed, however, that each night we stripped him he looked skinnier than the night before. He was losing all the weight he had brought home.

Patti became very concerned, even taking him to the A&P every day to weigh him on the old-fashioned fruit scale to see whether there were improvement or further loss. Fortunately, she soon brought him to the pediatrician, Dr. John, my friends' brother and the closest thing to a big brother that I have, who was in practice with his mother, Dr. Adelaide. They suggested an old-fashioned solution: a sandwich with a beer for Patti before bed, then sneak Matthew a bottle of formula during the night. For whatever reason, it worked. Matthew started to put the weight he had lost back on, began to thrive, and a crisis was averted.

This two-week period of tension proved significant. The fear of losing him had created a bond between Patti and Matthew that was different from that with her other children, whom she loved just as much. His siblings would often remind both Patti and Matthew that he was "the favorite," a proposition I never recall being outright denied. My own mother told me once that one of your children just needs you more than the others. I think she was saying that, in our case, that was my late sister Kathleen, not me. Maybe she was right.

III.

Just like it always does, morning arrived on Monday, August 25, 2014, ignoring the fact that our world had been shattered the day before.

I still wasn't certain that what I thought happened actually had happened, although there were many signals that life had changed forever. I sought refuge in routine: get up; walk the dog; do all the morning chores; get dressed. I had the feeling that maybe this was some sort of surreal test of the Byrne family's character. Somehow, if we could keep it together and pass The Test, things would go back to the way things were. It would be like all the many other times in recent years when Matt had gone away, only to eventually return home.

So, I went to work like any other Monday and broke the news to my colleagues and my assistants, Joanne and Linda, who are like sisters to me. Then I started making the phone calls that I felt had to be made. Each one would begin okay as pleasantries were exchanged, then my voice would catch when I finally got around to the reason for my call.

One of the first calls was to Leslie, the wonderful therapist who had been working with Matt on reassembling his life. I booked a session for the family that evening, the first of many steps to try to drag everyone off the ash heap.

A second was to cancel an appointment Matthew had with one of his many doctors. She supervised his outpatient group and had been switching him to one that was more psychiatric than substance oriented. He wouldn't be needing the session now.

The next calls were to our parish church, St. Agnes, and the undertaker, to set that process in motion. As mentioned, Matthew's remains were to be cremated, and a memorial Mass was scheduled for Thursday.

I knew I would have to speak at his Mass; it was plainly part of The Test we had to pass. That gave me three days to put aside all the anger I felt, sort through my other confused emotions, and come up with a fitting eulogy for my older son. It wasn't going to be easy.

I know I didn't accomplish anything at work that morning. My mind kept flooding with disjointed memories, alternating between the recent and distant past, bad times superimposed on the good ones.

*

Late Monday afternoon, armed with an axe, screwdrivers, and a shovel or two, Paul and Ann had dismantled the swing set from which their brother hanged himself. This effort must have taken them hours because this latest jungle gym was quite elaborate, with even more swings, slides, and ladders than its predecessors for the grandkids to climb and have fun on.

When I arrived home, there was just a void where the swing set had stood in the far back yard. I had been told it was gone, and I went to see for myself, expecting to at least see some remnants of the large structure. There was no trace of it.

At dinner, both Paul and Ann had very satisfied looks on their faces over what they had done. They had taken some anger and frustration out on the inanimate accomplice, although it wasn't to blame. We were all glad it was gone because we couldn't imagine watching the grandchildren playing on it ever again.

IV.

Matthew was baptized in St. Agnes Cathedral on July 13, 1980. This church has a curious history. Built by its parishioners in the depths of the Great Depression, it was such a grand structure that, in the 1950's, when Nassau and Suffolk counties were split away from Brooklyn to form a new diocese, St. Agnes was the obvious choice to serve as the new bishop's cathedral. Rome went so far as to call the new see the Diocese of Rockville Centre, after the village in which the cathedral is located, instead of a more sensibly descriptive name like the Diocese of Long Island.

There was certainly no debate about bringing Matthew into the faith; that was a given. Family traits cannot be denied – maybe they can't be successfully resisted – and there was no disputing that, on both sides of my family, the religious strain was a strong one. Two of my father's sisters had done stints in the convent, and his baby brother, my uncle, Father Tom, had entered the seminary when he was thirteen and never left the priesthood. My mother's brother, Uncle John, had spent years as a Trappist monk before leaving, getting a nursing degree at Boston College, then returning to run the well-equipped infirmary the Grace family had donated to the Trappist monastery in Spencer, Massachusetts.

Then there was my mother, Catherine. She at least qualified for the award as Catholic education's finest product. A woman of unshakable faith, whether it's because "Sister said so" a long time ago or not, she simply has no doubt. Everything, good or bad, happens for a reason in accordance with some master plan that will ultimately turn out to be correct. We just have to relax and remain constant, if unhappy, until God's providence is revealed.

I remember accompanying her to church from the time I was very small and being skeptical from the start about what she told me. The thing that really shook me up, however, was not her commentary, but a hymn I recall that was often sung, *Salve Regina*, a phrase of which hit me particularly hard:

"To thee do we send up our sighs, mourning and weeping in this valley of tears."

I objected to this imagery immediately, even though I was just a child. Life is a dreary trudge through a vale of tears? Impossible! Or, if that were the fate of those nameless "poor souls," I certainly didn't want any part of it and planned instead on a long, pleasant stroll through Happy Meadow.

I was never quite able to stick to the plan. Instead, I was like a moth drawn to Roman Catholicism's flame. Whenever I pulled away as a boy, something called me back, keeping me from getting too far off the path. The Jesuits I had in high school were the covert operatives of Christianity, subtly molding you into the person they wanted you to be without any crass appeal to religious authority, until you were theirs for life, a "man for others." Even in my most heathen college years, at worst I subscribed to a Buffalo Springfield belief: something was definitely going on in this life, but it's not at all clear what it is or who's in charge. I wound up taking religion courses at a nonsectarian school, finally concluding that, like a now unwanted tattoo, this Roman Catholic mark with which I'd been imprinted was indelible and could never be fully removed.

I doubt I recognized the implications of signing my son up for the same divine dance. Looking back, I may have been just a cultural Catholic at the time who scheduled a christening for his newborn with little or no reflection on what it meant.

Matthew was baptized on another bright and beautiful Sunday. He wore the same silken dress – there's no other truthful way to describe it – that his sister Elizabeth wore. Father Tom presided, and I don't remember Matt crying at all when his great uncle poured water over his forehead, welcoming him to the Church with a sign of the cross.

After the ceremony, the entire family came back to our house for a celebration, even several of Patti's cousins who happened to be in New York for a reunion the day before. It was a great party, but Matthew slept through it all and didn't meet anyone.

V.

Although he was hundreds of miles away at the time, Matt Byrne became another belated casualty of the terrorist attacks on September 11, 2001. He was a senior at Bowdoin College at the time, safe in Maine where he watched in real time on television as the Twin Towers first burned, then collapsed. Matt probably decided that very day that he would be a replacement for one of the 343 FDNY firefighters who perished.

Matt had known several firefighters as fellow lifeguards who worked at Jones Beach, and he always admired them greatly. When my childhood friend, Harry Ford, was killed with two comrades in an explosion on Father's Day of 2001, Matt had become directly exposed to the FDNY traditions and culture. I brought him along to golf outings held annually in Harry's honor, and he was clearly impressed with the men he met and their sense of brotherhood.

When he eventually voiced the idea of joining the Fire Department, neither Patti nor I were enthused. Frankly, we didn't see him as cut out for that job. Yet, it was comparable to having your kid inform you that he wants to join the military, which Matt never had. What do you say, "Matt, your Mom and I don't think you're suited for that"? Can you ever say that, even if you think it? You end up saying nothing and keeping your misgivings to yourself.

Matthew had never been a tough kid, and I guess our memories of him simply did not match up to his own self-image and aspirations. I'll never know whether we were acting like good parents or bad ones by keeping our shared opinion to ourselves.

*

Soon after his announcement, it became clear that Matt's dream of becoming a firefighter was serious, and likely exclusive of all other career options. He made no post-graduation employment plans, other than returning to Jones Beach for the summer and moving to Hawaii in the fall, the classic post-grad "year on the bench."

Matt returned from Hawaii in the spring, in time to take the requalification test and resume his job at Jones Beach. When that summer was close to ending, and the prospect of involuntary unemployment panicked him, he scrambled to enroll in law school in Ohio where a friend of mine was dean.

I was surprised by this decision. Matt had been a government major and taken the law boards while a senior at college, but there hadn't been significant follow up despite a decent score. He now faced years of waiting before he could become a N.Y.C. firefighter. If I were reading Matt's mind correctly, law school would be a great way of killing time, and keeping his summers off for lifeguarding, until he could do what he really wanted. Patti and I played along, because it was Matthew, to whom we rarely said no, and because we were half-thinking that he might actually get bitten by the legal "bug" like I had. By finishing law school and passing the bar before getting the FDNY call, which he had plenty of time to do, he'd at least have another career option to turn to then or sometime in the future when he might be looking for a second job to support a family or tiring of "humping hose."

Matt had the option of staying home and attending St. John's Law School at night. In hindsight, once again, that would have been a more sensible approach for someone who had not yet demonstrated commitment to what was a very serious project. He said he was afraid there would be too many distractions at home, which may have been true but would at least be something we could monitor. Matt convinced us to finance his enrollment at the University of Toledo.

During that aborted law school stretch – a one and done semester – Matt may have had his first serious encounter with depression. No one ever learned what happened in Toledo – how he spent his time or whom he was with – except he did mention he had been teaching autistic kids how to swim at a local pool. He certainly hadn't been occupied with classes and studying law books. Dropping out of law school was really the first significant failure Matt had experienced in his life, and the topic was placed off limits by all members of the family to spare him the discomfort of explaining what had gone wrong.

I think we always acted like that with Matt. Honestly, I don't recall that degree of deference to any other child's feelings. It wasn't just Patti and I, but his siblings as well who, most times – until he used up all the goodwill – gave him a pass in awkward situations.

I guess we all wondered, at some time or another, whether things would have turned out differently if he had liked law school or at least stuck it out. I don't think the subject was ever discussed again, certainly not the idea of his going back to give it another try.

When he returned from Ohio at the end of 2003, Matt turned his full attention toward executing his plan to gain entrance to the FDNY Academy. Against my warnings that it would come back to haunt him, he hit on friends and relatives to help him establish a bogus New York City residence address that would add a few points to his score when he was able to sit for the admission test. He held jobs as a real estate appraiser, waiter, and – of course – lifeguard every summer, but they were only intended to provide spending money until he reached his goal.

Despite our concerns, Patti and I resigned ourselves to the fact that firefighter was the noble but dangerous occupation our son had chosen. I remember being afraid of what would happen if he didn't achieve this goal. It sounds very funny now, but I wondered what was he going to do with his life if he failed again? I started to drop in on the 6:30 a.m. Mass at St. Agnes each morning to pray that my son got what he wanted.

This is a good place to bring up someone else.

From shortly after Elizabeth's wedding in 2003, one woman, whom I'll just call "GF" for girlfriend, was a constant presence in Matt's life, until shortly before it ended.

I won't say much about her for fear of hurting her, which I would never want to do. But anyone reading this should be aware that she was there and, as his life unraveled, Matt wasn't alone. I know she loved Matt dearly. She may have been somewhat complicit when things initially started to go off the rails, but she pulled back and tried to save Matt – something he wasn't willing to let her do.

Matt and GF were together, exclusively, for over ten years. I found it odd that, while we even exchanged Christmas cards with her parents, we never met them. GF and Matt informally cohabited for long stretches, but never really set up shop together. He seemed unable to pull the trigger, take that big risk, and make a commitment to GF. As he would eventually whine sardonically to counselors in the various rehab joints and psych wards: "I'm just a 33-year-old mama's boy, wah wah!"

Ultimately, GF wanted more than Matt could give her, and she realized she had to move on. Who could blame her?

As things were really spinning out of control in the last few weeks of his life, a large package arrived for Matt: the guitar he had left at GF's place. It wasn't intended to, but it put one of many final nails in his coffin.

What better place than here to pose the "What If" question. There's no doubt that Matt and GF loved each other throughout a rocky relationship. What if they had been less cautious, or less sensible as the case may be, and married? What if there had been a child? Would Matt have put aside his Peter Pan lifestyle and have finally grown up? Who knows?

VI.

Wachusett Street was a real throwback. Only one block long, running between North Village and Hempstead Avenues in Rockville Centre, it was populated with kids of various ages who played outside all the time, either in the street or in neighbors' backyards. After the usual period in a carriage or stroller, as soon as he could venture forth, Matthew was trying to catch up with Beba and the other older kids. He quickly made the acquaintance of Brian, who lived up the block and was the younger brother of Kevin, a classmate of Elizabeth. Starting with play dates, Matt and Brian became life-long friends – a phrase that is accurate but always bittersweet, in view of the subsequent Event.

Here's a good place to demonstrate how the "What If Game" is played. In 1984, I had a serious cancer scare. Some top-notch doctors were convinced I had Hodgkins Disease, and a relatively short life expectancy. I walked around for several weeks carrying the business card of my oncologist, a brilliant young woman in a wheelchair with her own serious health issues. It turned out to be a false alarm for me. Would Matthew, four years old at the time, have made out better had he grown up without a father? It's a legitimate question, because Brian and his three brothers, who matched up roughly in age to the Byrne children, tragically lost their father, Kevin, Sr., to colon cancer when they were still quite young. Kevin, Jr., Brian, Conor and Sean all survived and are going strong, a great credit to their mother, Carol, who had to raise them alone.

In any event, little Matt had no trouble fitting in and becoming accepted on the block. As you have probably gathered from the book's cover, his college graduation photo, Matt was an exceptionally good-looking guy. In fact, after he died, we received a note from one of his babysitters remembering him as "an incredibly beautiful little boy". I hadn't really recalled that, but it was true.

Patti and I recognized Matt's looks as an issue and always downplayed it as something he should never rely on, as opposed to intelligence or some talent. We brushed off suggestions that he should model and made a joke out of it. (I told his mother he had ears like Mr. Spock, the Vulcan, and that we should call him Lightbulb Head because, at one point, it seemed too large for his skinny body.) That didn't change the facts, however, particularly in his Mom's eyes. As a toddler, he had shiny blond hair reaching the back of his neck, and a habit of sticking his third and fourth fingers in his mouth so he could touch his face with his index finger and pinky of one hand. Simultaneously he would rub the silken tag of a stuffed animal between the index finger and thumb of his other hand. He could pretty much charm what he wanted out of us with a couple of flicks of the lashes hiding his hazel eyes. Before he could talk, which did not happen anytime soon because his sister would get him whatever he wanted in response to his grunts, Matt became a master of nonverbal communication. He used to do a pantomime shtick we called "Beauty Boy" where he'd pose like a little elf, toss his head to the side, and place his hand palm down under his chin. The only thing I recall him not finding funny was when Patti decided he was too old for the bottle. When she broke the news to him, at a time of day when he was accustomed to having his precious milk before his nap, he indignantly asked, "No baa?" and began crying. I don't recall if she relented.

Matt's sense of humor only surfaced more when he became able to use words. Whenever his shirt was off, he'd proudly point out his "puppy belly." He loved rhymes, stupid knock-knock jokes, and any kind of pun or word game. I would drive him to nursery school in Garden City each morning, and he'd sit in the back seat entertaining me while we listened to oldies music. One very favorite song was Buddy Holly's *Peggy Sue*, to which we'd make up new words to follow a nonsense introduction, such as, "If you knew, Honey Dew …." "If you knew, Babalou …." You get the idea.

The name I wound up giving him was Matt Byrne Raconteur, and he actually was pretty funny, even when he wasn't trying to be, like when he would grab a guitar to accompany himself when singing the theme song to the "Dukes of Hazzard," his favorite television show. He didn't seem to understand what I did for a living. When asked, he'd respond: "He drives a car and carries a briefcase." I became known as Auto Lawyer. Another instance was a fairly strong resistance on his part to toilet training. On more than one occasion, he'd stop his play in the family room and disappear behind the couch. When asked, "What are you doing back there, Matt?" he would respond, grunting: "Nothing!" Believe me, it wasn't nothing.

Matt found someone who shared his sense of humor – and, it would eventually turn out, several other traits – when, after a "sabbatical" from his marriage that probably lasted eight years, my father showed up at our house unannounced one day. I wasn't home, but I'm told Matt's first encounter with his grandfather was classic. Matt apparently answered the door. When the stranger claimed to be Grandpa Don, Matt informed him, "I don't have a Grandpa Don. I have an Uncle Don," his friend's grandpa, "but no Grandpa Don."

Their relationship improved immensely from that rocky start, and they became friends, trading quips and stories, such as Grandpa Don claiming to be busy every Tuesday night because that's when he attended his weekly "Liars' Club" meeting. Matt would try to match him with his own whopper in return.

I was pleased that my father had resurfaced after such a long absence, and I remember those as very good times. We still have a Halloween picture that captures it all, taken on our house's back deck that my father-in-law, Frank, had built, using me as his laborer. Elizabeth looks lovely in a Cinderella costume; Matthew has his face painted blue and is wearing white tights as Baby Smurf; and Patti, wearing a tall, pointed wide brimmed hat, was the prettiest witch you could imagine. I was a very lucky guy.

When the weather was nice, we spent lots of time on that deck, overlooking a small but private yard. We'd barbecue when I got home from work, and sit outside through sunset, often joined by a few neighborhood kids playing with Elizabeth and Matthew on the swing set, but sometimes just by Matthew alone, if Elizabeth had taken off with the older girls. He would roam the yard with a white specimen net to see what he could capture. Butterflies and lightning bugs were common, but a big ugly bullfrog was his all-time prize catch, and he displayed it proudly for the camera.

A few incidents and routines I recall, if not all the specifics. We had gotten Matthew a "digger" for his birthday one May. It was a contraption with wheels, a seat, and two handles that operated a backhoe sort of device. It probably wasn't the best gift; Matthew loved it, but he began digging holes and ruining the grass all over the yard.

This particular night, Matt was working very diligently with the digger on one deep hole. "What are you doing?" I asked. "Making a trap," he responded. I just nodded and went in the house. A while later, I went out to get him after finishing whatever chore I was doing. It was already dark, and I couldn't see him. "Hey, Matt. Time to come in," I yelled. "Okay," he responded, and I could hear sneakered feet running my way, followed by a thud, an "oomph!" then gasping. I jumped off the deck to find him.

When I located him, he was lying in the pit he had dug, doubled over the edge of the hole, wind knocked out of him. "What happened?" I asked. "I caught myself in my trap," he wheezed when he finally caught his breath, and I carried him into the house to clean him up.

We had once bathed the children together and they enjoyed it, always trying to prolong the fun by shouting, "Save water!" and trying to plug the drain with a facecloth or some bathtub toy. Elizabeth opted out of baths with her brother pretty quickly, but he never lacked company. Incredibly to me, who had never forgotten *Jaws*, his favorite bath toy was a ferocious looking rubber shark named Sharky. I never heard of a kid who wanted to share the tub with a shark of any kind, but I rationalized it as consistent with his favorite cartoon character, Mr. Jaws, a great white, well-dressed shark that would respond to the sensible suggestions made by his derby wearing sidekick, Catfish, "That's a very good idea I just thought of myself."

After their baths, we would get Elizabeth and Matthew into their pajamas. Story time was next. I confess I had my favorite stories I would read as often as they liked, *Ferdinand the Bull*, for one, and others I hoped never to suffer through again. When the story was finished, it was prayer time, typically my gig while Patti finally got some well-deserved time to herself.

One kid to the left and one to the right, all three of us would be on our knees, facing the side of one child's bed, alternating rooms for story time each night. Then we'd begin the litany of those we cared for. God should bless Elizabeth and Matthew, Mommy and Daddy, Grandma and Grandpa Murtagh, Grandma Catherine and Grandpa Don …. Since it meant postponing bed time a bit longer, Beba and Matt could get very creative about persons and causes for which we sought the Lord's favor. Invariably during the prayer process, Matt would very gently climb up my back so that, by the time we had finished our special intentions, he was draped over my shoulders with his arms wrapped around my neck. I never protested. After hugs and goodnight kisses all around, for which Patti would magically reappear, they were finally off to bed.

VII.

Either the machinations or prayers, or Matt's typically superior standard testing skills worked. He was selected by the FDNY
as a probationary firefighter – a "probie" – on October 30, 2006.
On November 13, 2006, Matt was processed into the Department
and began weeks of intensive training at the Academy, the
"Rock" on Randall's Island, below the Triboro (now RFK) Bridge
that connects Manhattan, Queens and the Bronx.

The firefighters' training is the equivalent of boot camp without the barracks. Matt did get to return home each night for food
and some sleep, but he would have been better off staying put, if
that had been an option. The quick turnaround time, coupled
with the pressure of a long, unpredictable commute to beat a
"drop dead" reporting time, left all the probies counting the days
until the ordeal ended.

But Matt was totally gung-ho, plus extremely physically fit,
and he had no difficulties in the Academy at all. He was very
proud to show us around the grounds on Family Day, one wintry
February Saturday in 2007, and we got to watch Matt and his
comrades demonstrate the climbing, rooftop teamwork, and other techniques they had learned, including putting out a fire in an
automobile hulk that could be reignited again and again. I remember Matt got to be nozzle man on the flaming car, and I
beamed with pride because he seemed good at it.

We have a photo that captures that day pretty well, just a
headshot of Matt and me. He's wearing his outer gear and hel-

met, Number 3279, and I'm bundled up in a scarf and wearing my Yankee hat. It's a nice picture but, as I look at it now, I can see that my eyes were welling up and my smile was a little bit off.

On February 22, 2007, Matt graduated from the academy at a ceremony held at Brooklyn College. Our family attended, even my mother who had flown up from Florida, and it was a grand occasion, as the photos attest.

There was one sour note, however. As I left the college's campus to fetch the car, I met a neighbor from Rockville Centre, an FDNY captain himself, who was there to attend his nephew's graduation. He asked me where Matt had been assigned.

"Engine 9," I replied cheerily. "On Canal Street in China-town," I added unnecessarily, since all FDNY members seem to know by heart the location of every unit and firehouse in the five boroughs.

For a split second, I saw a negative look flash across Dan's face. He quickly recovered and said, "I started there myself." I didn't inquire further.

VIII.

Maybe your mind glosses over things as the years go by, but I remember Matt as a very easy going and compliant little kid. He never asked for much and was content to let Elizabeth, who was extremely persuasive, take the lead and determine what they were going to do. In fact, the only time I recall him making a fuss was when Patti and I brought them along to my college reunion. We went to a local restaurant for breakfast before heading home on Sunday, and the waitress at the Chuck Wagon gave them both silly paper cowboy hats that they loved. Things went downhill rapidly between Matthew and the waitress, however, when she informed him we were too late for the breakfast menu and would have to order lunch. We have a photo that captures the whole scene: Matt with his paper cowboy hat on, looking like his world had just ended, and Elizabeth looking into the camera with her smile displaying a hint of a gloat over her brother's misfortune.

I'm not sure how soon after Matthew's birth that Patti had gone back to work, but by the time he was in nursery school and pre-kindergarten, she was teaching special education at The League School in Brooklyn to some very "involved" kids, the term then used. It was a rough trip from Rockville Centre, and she had to leave early. My assignment was to get Elizabeth on the bus to St. Agnes, then drive Matthew to Cathedral Nursery School in Garden City. Of course, this involved getting some breakfast in them, making lunch for Elizabeth, and all the other morning mania that families endure as the price for living together. It was fun stuff.

In early 1985, Patti was growing bigger as she entered the later stages of another pregnancy. My car rides with Matt to school each morning no doubt became less comical and more informational, as the prospect of having a baby brother or sister became more real. Almost five years had passed since our last child; I suppose we could have been done at two. Matt was very excited about becoming a big brother, and the questions wouldn't stop about what life would be like when the new baby came. I did my best to paint a picture that would be fairly accurate, but nonthreatening – even though I knew Patti and I would be "playing a man down" thereafter, and our old foolproof routine of "you take this one, I'll take the other" really wasn't going to work anymore.

A couple of days after Paul was born, I took Elizabeth and Matt to meet their baby brother for the first time. Patti had instructed that I make sure I shot suitable video, so I decided to have a test run at home before we left for the hospital.

Both kids looked a little tired, or maybe it was just the wistful look of children who have had to get by without their mother for a couple of days. Elizabeth was dressed in a blue velvet dress; her long hair looked clean and well brushed and arranged, which makes me think I had help because I had never been able to "do" her hair correctly. I interviewed her briefly with the video camera and, blue eyes sparkling, she very maturely explained where we were going and whom we would greet.

Then it was Matthew's turn. He had on a blue herringbone sports jacket, blue shirt, tie, and a tiny pair of gray slacks. As I filmed him, he was trying to button the slacks and fasten his belt.

He explained he had undone them when he needed to "go up-stairs" after breakfast. He worked on that pesky button and belt the entire time I questioned him at length about where he was going and who would be there. I finally put the camera down and helped him straighten his pants out.

After we arrived at the hospital, Elizabeth and Matt rushed their mother when she finally arrived in the lounge area of the maternity ward. As he grabbed her around thigh level, Matt ex-claimed, "Mommy, you look so skinny!" The boy really knew what to say to a postpartum woman!

Mom and Paul came home in due course and settled in. Within a couple of weeks, what was left of Paul's umbilical cord had healed sufficiently for him to have his first bath. Again a vid-eo occasion, I staged and directed this rite like Cecil B. DeMille, including an opening shot of the pocket door to the powder room sliding open, followed by Elizabeth and Matthew leading Patti with Paul in her arms into the kitchen.

The same hushed tones I had come to expect at baby's bath time were used. Unlike his brother, however, and in contrast to his future comfort in the water, Paul had a look on his face as Patti washed him with a cloth and new sponge as if to say, "What's this wet stuff you're putting all over me? Aren't you go-ing to help me out, Dad?" Matt kept trying to reassure him that everything was under control, speaking to his baby brother like he actually could understand, until he finally said, "Okay, Paul. I'll see you later. I have to go with Dad now for my own bath."

*

As Matthew was winding up his final year at Cathedral Nursery, a few noteworthy incidents occurred.

Elizabeth had been taking ballet lessons from a teacher affiliated with the school. Matthew got dragged along for drop-offs and pickups, and Miss Jean spotted him as a likely prospect to join her younger group. Probably because Miss Jean spoke with elegant, English accented diction and wore a black leotard with matching skirt, Matt readily accepted her offer to join his female classmates for ballet lessons. He would show up for practice in a tee shirt, little cotton shorts, white socks and black ballet slippers. At year end, when asked by Miss Jean to dance the role of Morris the Mouse in the youngest girls' recital, he again gladly agreed because Morris's mousy girlfriend Doris would be played by his own heartthrob, Laura.

This romance was pretty amusing, at least to me. I didn't take it seriously at all until we were planning his fifth birthday party. It was going to be held at Nunley's, a small, old-time amusement park in Baldwin with a historic carousel, plus the mini-Ferris wheel, duck boats, and little race cars you would expect to see. The usual group of kids from Wachusett Street and family friends were slated to come. In addition, however, Matthew insisted that Laura be invited too.

"Fine by me," was my reaction, although I left it to Patti to explain to Laura's mother that our soon to be five-year-old had the hots for her daughter. Patti made it happen somehow, and when the big day came Laura was in attendance.

It was a beautiful May day, and the kids all got along well, despite some steep difference in age among the attendees. Matt got to tool around the little racetrack driving a powder blue mock Corvette with Laura riding shotgun. He had the time of his life. Yet he was also careful to go on some of the two-passenger rides with Brian, his best buddy. It was interesting to watch how the birthday boy had not only managed to entertain his girlfriend. He was aware enough to spread himself around that day so no one else's feelings were hurt.

*

In September 1985, Matthew followed Elizabeth to St. Agnes Cathedral Elementary School to begin kindergarten.

The first day of school at St. Agnes was one of the most dangerous days of the year in Rockville Centre. For some reason, the new students had to be videotaped not only when they got on the school bus at the corner of Wachusett Street and Harvard Avenue, but also as they disembarked at St. Agnes. That almost requires being in two places at the same time, but Patti would leave late for work on this special day and somehow we always got all the mandatory film footage for each of our children, plus the still "porch pictures" under the front overhang of our house, which showed a little guy dressed in a seersucker short-pants suit, with a lingering tan and a recessed cowlick at the top of his forehead where Eddie Munster's widow's peak would be.

When Matt was asked that evening how his first day in kindergarten had gone, he said, "Great! My teacher's a movie star!" It turned out that she was an attractive young woman with blond hair, done "big" in mid-80's style, but her prior occupations may

have been flight attendant or restaurant hostess, not movie ac-
tress. In any event, Matt was smitten again, and Miss Jones was a
good distraction from the loss of his first love, Laura, the Garden
City girl.

The first day at school was indicative of what would follow:
Everything was "great." The older kids on the bus were great. His
classmates were funny and great. The teachers were all great. Life
at St. Agnes was simply pretty great. Miss Helen, the assistant
principal, described Matthew as a floater who was accepted by all
the various cliques of students without ever tying himself down
to any one group. He made friends very easily, and always would,
for most of his life.

*

The spring of second grade at St. Agnes was always a very big
deal. The boys and girls went through weeks of preparation for
their first Holy Communion, and the second grade teachers, Sister Kathy, the principal, and Miss Helen always had them ready,
totally versed in both prayers and songs when their big day arrived. I have no idea, and probably no way of finding out, who it
was that determined that second grade is when you can first receive Communion. I am certain, though, that whoever did made
the right call. The kids in that seven to eight-year-old range have
the perfect mix of innocence and understanding, as they come to
realize that there's a moment more important at Mass than when
you get to put the envelope or money in the collection basket.

The spring of 1987 was significant for another reason. Since

Matt's 7th birthday fell before the August 1 cutoff, he was eligible to play baseball in the Rockville Centre Little League, and I set out to teach him the sacred game, both as a fan and a player.

On April 29, 1985, I had painfully separated from my beloved Yankees. That was the day when, after having assured everyone that Yogi Berra's contract would be honored for the entire season, George Steinbrenner abruptly fired my childhood idol and replaced him with Billy Martin, whom I considered an emotionally unstable individual repeatedly used by "The Boss" as a pawn. Since I had always rooted for the Mets too, I threw away my Yankee hat and bought a Mets one. Two seasons later, when I needed instructional videos to show Matt how the incredibly complex sport was played, I sat him down in front of Mets games, then took him to a few at Shea Stadium.

We would try to put what he saw on television and at the ballpark into practice in our backyard. Matt would stand in front of the garage and want me to throw him pitch after pitch. After a while, I'd say it was time for him to put down the bat and pick up his glove. He'd say, "No, I just want to hit." I'd respond, "Matt, you have to learn to play the field." Disregarding the fact that the Mets played in the National League, he'd reply, "No, I don't. I'm going to be the designated hitter when I grow up."

I'd shake my head and keep pitching. After all, it was rumored that Edgar Martinez didn't even own a glove, so it was possible to make a living off your bat alone. I kept my doubts quiet, waiting for Matt to figure out for himself someday that, if you're going to play baseball, you'd better learn how to use a glove.

This early debate between us illustrates a special aspect of our relationship. Some fathers love their sons because they are so very much alike, the "chip off the old block" syndrome. I think I loved Matt even more because of the many ways in which we were so different. For example, if my father had told me that I had to learn to play the field to become a good baseball player, I probably wouldn't have taken the glove off for a week, and likely would have wrecked the garage wall by throwing balls against it so I could catch the rebounds. Even at seven, I could tell Matt was becoming his own guy, with a bit of a stubborn streak that made him insist on doing things his way.

Two years later, at the start of the 1989 baseball season, Matt made an even bigger move toward manhood. He informed me that he thought it was time I made up with the Yankees because, even though they were losing at the time, he would rather root for them, like his two grandfathers did, than for the Mets. I paused for a moment, then said: "Okay, Matt. For you I'll let the grudge go." It took Yogi another twelve years before he was willing to let bygones be bygones, and only after Steinbrenner's admission that firing Yogi was the worst mistake he ever made in baseball.

Matt became a rabid Yankee fan, an inherited affliction that delighted his grandfathers and, I'll admit, me as well. I guess I felt my point was made before Yogi did, or maybe Yogi's kids had never asked him to end his self-imposed exile sooner.

*

Some of the things Matt came out with when he was young shocked me. His barber, a sweetheart of a guy, was shot and killed one Sunday morning while driving on the Southern State Parkway to visit his daughter, who lived in a residence for the disabled. Apparently, the man took the same route at the same time every Sunday. This was certainly no accident; the police suspected a "hit" but were never able to bring anyone to justice.

One day, Matt brought up the shooting out of the blue. He then proceeded to tell me his theory of who did it and why. I just stared at him. I hope the cops investigated that suspect and ruled Matt's theory out, because it made quite a bit of sense.

*

Matthew enjoyed the school year, but what he really loved was the summer.

Shortly after he was born, we had joined the pool at the Rockville Links, and he literally grew up in the water, learning to swim at a very early age and modeling everything that Elizabeth and the older kids would do, like participating in the annual Aqua Show. When he was four or five, he fancied himself an accomplished break dancer, and signed up to perform with one of the teenage boys, John. When the kid didn't appear on the night of the show, with the aid of a microphone Matt called me with a plaintive voice to join him from the audience, which I did, no doubt after having had a few drinks. We probably weren't very good break dancers, but at least we didn't chicken out like John, the teenager.

By the time he was six, Matt joined Elizabeth on the swim team. That was no surprise; he was already pretty good, and would go on to join an all-year team based at Hofstra University. The surprise came when he informed us that he was also on the diving team, the main attraction of which seemed to be the teenage girl divers who fawned over him. I confess I had some anxious moments watching this skinny little guy in a Speedo plunging headfirst off the high board. I didn't regret it when, a season or two later, the Nassau County Department of Health determined that the Links pool was too shallow for diving, and the team was disbanded.

*

Saturday mornings in the summer were reserved for swim meets, which were loud and sweaty but fun affairs held at various pools throughout Nassau County. Once again, the differences between my son's personality and my own stood out.

I admit it, I was an ultracompetitive, borderline obnoxious kid. I couldn't stand losing and just wanted to win at everything. It didn't matter what the sport, contest or game was – I wanted to beat the other guy.

Not Matt. It wasn't that he didn't care, just that he kept his competitive spirit under much better control than I ever did. An example demonstrates this and speaks well of young Matt's character.

One of the boys at the Links had a physical disability, but he was always included on the relay team for Matt's age group. The race was 100 yards, consisting of four 25-yard lengths swum by four different swimmers. The leadoff man did backstroke, followed by breast stroke, butterfly, and finally the anchor man swimming free style.

The mother of the disabled swimmer believed he did his best at backstroke, and prevailed upon the coaches to let him lead off each relay. Problem was, the race was effectively over when he finished his length. The Links team was so far behind that I don't recall them ever making up the deficit, even against the weaker teams in the league.

If I had been on that relay as a kid, I would have gone nuts. I probably would have argued toe to toe with my teammate's mother that her son should swim the anchor length, so we would at least know where we stood against the other team at the end of three lengths, and be able to argue that we would have won if we had a faster anchor man. Matt said nothing and, as far as we could tell, although it persisted for years, this situation didn't faze him at all.

Matthew was a much better kid than I was. He just didn't have any mean streak at all. He always looked puzzled and extremely uncomfortable when he witnessed something unpleasant. He honestly couldn't understand why people couldn't be nice to each other all the time.

*

When the Saturday morning swim meet was over, we faithfully headed to my in-laws in Long Beach, typically spending an overnight at their house on the bay, just two long blocks from the ocean shore.

Those were great days. We have a favorite photo of Matt, a very young Paul, and me standing together on the lower dock at what my mother-in-law called the "front" of the Murtagh house on Reynolds Channel in Long Beach. My father-in-law, Frank, had a boat at the dock and was an avid fisherman. He taught Matt, then Paul in turn, to fish and operate the boat, and the boys loved being out on the water with their grandpa, Patti and me. Elizabeth was more Grandma Murtagh's girl and was always busy with her doing something around the house or in town.

When the fishing was over, the Byrnes took off for the beach, a place Grandpa and Grandma never visited. Sunday afternoon was a special time. We were in no great hurry to get to the beach, but boy did we hate to leave! All the kids were water rats, and would stay in the waves for hours. Patti and I would watch from squatty beach chairs until the lengthening shadows and setting sun warned us that we'd better get going or Grandma would start yelling that we were late for dinner again.

*

Summer was also vacation time. As if we weren't privileged enough, we always managed to take a week off and go away somewhere, usually with our friends, Jim and Kathy, whose kids roughly matched up in age with our own until they went on to have seven while we got stuck at four! Kathy and Patti had become great friends. Jim and I had gone to high school together, so I knew him since I was 13. I was fortunate to marry the best woman I ever met, and equally lucky to remain friends with the best guy I ever knew. On one of these joint, crazy trips we wound up at an amusement park, The Great Escape, near Lake George. They had a Wild West, Union Pacific type railroad ride, and the four adults took five or six kids on the train, which looked pretty tame.

What we didn't know is that the ride included a staged train robbery. Out of nowhere, a gang of four masked horsemen wearing chaps galloped up, forced the locomotive to a stop, then dismounted and boarded the train.

When the robbers reached the car we were riding in, talking loudly and menacingly with thick Texan twangs, Jim's oldest, Jimmy, got a little worked up as they approached him. "You'd better watch out," he warned them. "Matt here knows karate."

As if on cue, Matt jumped down from his seat. As his navy blue Keds hit the wooden floor of the train with a thud, he assumed the karate stance he had learned from watching television.

"Golly," the head robber exclaimed, "this one knows karate, boys. We'd better hightail it and skedaddle on out of here!"

As the robbers jumped down from the train, hopped back on their horses and rode off, Jimmy and Matt were totally convinced that Matt had saved the day. Jimmy was a year or two older, and had always been Matt's hero. Matt felt pretty good about himself that day.

Another "vacation" story took place when Jimmy and Matt were still little. I don't know whose bright idea it was, but Big Jim and I decided to take them on an all guys combo camping/fishing trip to Beaverkill, an upstate New York park known for its trout.

To say I'm not an outdoorsman is an understatement, but I'd been camping enough times, for better or worse, to have some idea of what I was doing. To my surprise, Big Jim knew even less than I did. He had gotten Jimmy a fishing pole and a pretty good Boy Scout sleeping bag, but he didn't bother to buy one for himself, assuming that he could get by with his older daughter Maureen's Strawberry Shortcake sleeping bag, designed for overnight stays in cozy pink bedrooms.

The campground was pretty far up in the Catskills, and when the sun went down the temperature plummeted. When Big Jim came out of the tent in the morning, I think his teeth were chattering, and he said he'd never been so cold in his life. To his credit, in typical fashion, he sucked it up and off we went fishing.

The boys only had fairly low-cut rubber boots, so we stationed them in the mud at the edge of the river, then demonstrated, as best we could, how they should cast their lines into the stream. I'm sure we weren't using flies, and I don't remember if we had gotten them any sort of bait at all but, remarkably, one of the boys got a trout on the line. (Their lines had tangled, naturally enough, so it was impossible to tell who had actually caught the fish.) They got all excited and both began frantically trying to reel it in. Just then, we spotted some guy in full trout fishing regalia – floppy hat, vest with flies pinned all over it, and most importantly, a chest high set of waders – winding his way up the middle of the Beaverkill river. "Trout Snatcher" walks right to where the fish is struggling on the line, grabs him, takes the hook out of its mouth, and sticks the fish in his creel.

Jimmy and Matt start yelling from the river bank, "Hey, you! That's our fish! Come back here with it!"

Trout Snatcher just kept wading upstream and never looked back. Big Jim and I couldn't stop laughing.

Big Jim recently reminded me of one final vacation story. It happened on a winter break in Florida, so that almost counts as summer. We had been with the Murtaghs in Venice, on the West Coast, and had arranged to meet Big Jim and Kathy's clan at the Polynesian Resort in Disney World for two days.

Day One went well enough. We went to the Magic Kingdom, then later into the Polynesian's pool, although the waterfalls and such were freezing. Day Two was a different story.

The girls had booked breakfast with the characters at the big riverboat Disney has docked, coincidentally, next to the Shoppers Village. The breakfast is a nice affair. We were all at the same big table, eating away, while Pluto, Goofy, Mickey and Minnie, Donald Duck, Chip and Dale, and all the other stars take turns working the room and posing for pictures with all the children.

You may recall from the Chuck Wagon incident that Matthew was always a breakfast guy, but he was really on his game that morning. He was eating everything that came his way, to the point that Patti and I warned him he really ought to slow down.

When breakfast was finally finished, the girls told us to have a nice time with the kids at EPCOT; they were going shopping. No problem. We were young but experienced dads who thought we could handle anything. So, we went to the park entrance where we could rent the couple of strollers we would need.

I'm not sure that we had gotten anyone in a rent-a-stroller yet when Matthew announced, "I'm gonna get sick!" He barfed right in front of the booth where you pay for the strollers, just missing their inventory. Little Jimmy suddenly appeared next to him, took a look at what had happened, then bent over and launched a huge sympathy puke.

Big Jim and I looked at each other, wondering what had just happened. Matt needed a change of clothes, and this posed new problems. The Byrnes had already checked out of the Polynesian, planning on returning to Venice that night. We had to go to our car, grab the suitcase with the dirty clothes, since Matthew had been wearing his last clean outfit, and piece together enough clothes so he wouldn't freeze to death since his jacket had gotten barf all over it, too. I remember changing him in Big Jim's hotel room, putting layers of previously worn shirts on him until it looked like he was wearing football shoulder pads. After doing the best I could, we gathered the rest of the kids and the trip to EPCOT resumed.

At some point, the girls returned from their shopping spree. When they asked how things had gone, I don't recall giving a very positive response.

Things settled down, however, and both Little Jimmy and Matt were fine after their respective purges. The day came to a fun conclusion at Fort Wilderness, where both kids and adults enjoyed the Hoop-De-Doo Revue.

When the show ended, we all went back together to the Polynesian Village, Jim and Kathy to stay another night with their kids and the Byrnes to pick up the rental car and drive three hours back to my in-laws.

As everyone was saying goodbye in the hotel lobby, I thought it best to make a pit stop before beginning the ride. I went into the men's room, took a leak, then pulled the lever on the urinal. The thing exploded, gushing cold water and/or warm pee, I'll never know the true mixture thereof, all down the front of my shorts, right into my sneakers.

Soaking and still incredulous at what had happened, I squished out to the hotel lobby, gathered Patti and the kids and began the long, wet ride to the Gulf Coast.

*

Throughout my career, if I had an opportunity to turn a business trip into a family vacation, I took it.

One such trip was to the Bahamas, where young entrepreneurs roam the beachfront yelling, "Jet skis, banana boat, parasailing." It's a pitch that's very hard to resist when you're surrounded by kids asking, "Can we, Dad?"

So, one time Patti and I succumbed. With Matthew and Paul, we went out on the parasailing boat.

Paul was heavier than his skinny brother, so he was assigned the bottom position. Matthew sat behind him on the deck of the boat, clipped higher to the rig that hung down from the colorful parasail. The native captain took us a bit offshore. When he gunned the engine, our two sons were launched, eventually climbing to what looked like one hundred fifty feet in the air. We could hear a lot of yelling going on up there. The captain didn't seem concerned at all. He just wanted to know if we minded if the boys got wet.

"Not at all," was our joint response. So he cut the boat's engine, letting the parasail descend until the boys dunked in the water, then gunning the engine again. He repeated the process a number of times before our half-hour was up.

When they climbed up the ladder back into the boat, Matthew was laughing hysterically while Paul seemed to be trying to regain his composure. "What was going on up there, Paul?"

"Matt kept telling me that the buckle was starting to come undone, and he was sorry he'd played with it but it looked like I was going to fall!"

There's nothing quite like having an older brother.

IX.

Matt's introduction to Engine 9, the Chinatown "Dragon Fighters," seemed to go well enough. He told us that the firehouse was populated with Staten Island guys because of its proximity to the ferry. He didn't seem too crazy about that group but liked his partner with whom he split shifts and time off. He seemed to be socializing okay, being recruited to pitch at softball games, bring food for special meal nights, like when families were invited to eat at the firehouse, and participate in the many other rituals the fire brothers perform, including making fun of volunteer firefighters, the "Vollies" who worship them.

On St. Patrick's Day, 2007, he was one of 343 probies carrying American flags up Fifth Avenue in memory of the firefighters lost on 9/11. After the parade, Matt went with some friends from the academy and his lieutenant to a reception held annually at Marymount School, which both Patti and Ann had attended and where Elizabeth had taught. The young firefighters were totally pumped after the cheers of the crowd, and I recall the lieutenant as a veteran and very kind guy. It was a fine day for the Irish, but especially the Byrnes, since Matt was so happy in his new role. He was beaming.

That attitude changed just a few months later. On August 18, 2007, the vacant Deutsche Bank Building in lower Manhattan, across from Ground Zero, went ablaze. A standpipe had been cut during the demolition and, without water to control the fire, the firefighters who responded faced nightmarish, near blackout

61

conditions.

Two firefighters, from another house, died of smoke inhalation and carbon monoxide poisoning. I never learned what Matthew witnessed that day when Engine 9 reported to the scene. Ironically, in the course of writing this chapter I stumbled on some news footage of him walking into the building. I do know he had some significant involvement because he had to give a formal deposition during the investigation of the deaths that followed.

After the Deutsche Bank fire, Matt disclosed very little about his life on the job. Although he was residing with us, he wasn't really living with us, and I remember telling friends and family that his comings and goings were like those of a cat.

It seemed to me that Matt was holding back from a full commitment to the FDNY. In particular, he refused to surrender his surfer/lifeguard persona, which really didn't mesh with his comrades' lifestyles. He wore his hair long and otherwise dressed the "surf dude" part when he arrived or left work.

There were some vague hints of hazing, perhaps directed at Matt as well as some of his minority friends who were also probies. I said little in response, figuring he'd just have to deal with it, but I did comment that, in an environment like a firehouse, to be different was to be wrong, and those who conformed – even if they did not agree – got along best.

Perhaps most annoyingly to his fellow firefighters, even as a probie Matt began banking his time off and working overtime and shifts for others so he could take the month of January off for a trip to the North Shore of Hawaii. His surfboard would accompany him for sure, and GF too, if she could get off from work.

This practice certainly contributed to his undoing, as did his refusal to give up moonlighting at Jones Beach in the summertime. I think it's difficult for anyone to master the art of working shifts. Firefighters work a particularly brutal kind of alternating shifts, not one steady one. I suppose to share the pain of time away from their families, consecutive nights on duty may be followed by a few days off, then revert to consecutive day shifts. Matt never seemed to get accustomed to this drill, which flipped night and day. When he finally did arrive home, he would watch television for hours, sometimes drinking beer in the morning because he was unable to sleep. The smell of burnt popcorn and beer at breakfast time was a not infrequent occurrence in our house. This insomnia persisted throughout his career and was exacerbated by the amount of overtime and extra shifts he was working for others. He tried to keep track of who owed him coverage on a monthly FDNY calendar that he constantly misplaced. The joke in our house was that when the time finally came for his annual January Hawaiian junket, he would never know who was supposed to pay him back or how much time he was owed for working their shifts.

I frankly don't know whether Matt was a good, bad, or indifferent firefighter. He had no desire to take the exams to become a boss, claiming he did not consider himself sufficiently experienced, nor did he want to try driving the engine through Chinatown's narrow streets. He also refused to consider transferring to a more compatible firehouse, even when it became clear that his bromance with the other guys at Engine 9 was over. But he couldn't have been too bad at the start. Matt did receive a unit citation for some noteworthy act on June 5, 2009, and a commendation for a rescue the following month, his lieutenant predicting: "you'll make a good truckie someday." Before he left the FDNY, however, his life was in tatters and Matt had become a menace to himself and everyone around him.

I think the problem arose from his fundamental misconception of what the job of firefighter entails. The term is a misnomer; it makes you think this person is constantly responding to blazes when he may not do much firefighting at all. The truth is that a firefighter is more like Death's caddy: he watches Death take its shot at another victim, then cleans up and tries to replace the divot left in the world when Death triumphs and that person is gone.

All indications are that Matt had little fear of the fire he occasionally encountered. On the other hand, since he was a teenage lifeguard, he always had a big problem confronting Death, which became his constant companion as a firefighter.

X.

Within six months of Baby Paul's birth, he had begun terrorizing his roommate, Beba.

Paul seemed to have developed exceptional agility for a child that age. He could get one leg over the end of the crib rail, hoist himself over, hang by both hands, then drop to the bedroom floor. Paul couldn't walk, but he would crawl commando style across the floor to where his sleeping sister lay in bed, then commence pulling Elizabeth's hair until she would wake up crying.

We couldn't stop Paul's escapes short of restraining him, a practice we had dismissed as both cruel and dangerous when we heard it had been applied to Brian up the block, who had been just as active as Paul as a baby. Mainly to preserve Elizabeth's well-being, we wound up moving hastily around the block to Cambridge Street to a bigger but rather beat up house where each of the kids had a separate bedroom.

When Patti refused to unpack her silver and china, it became clear that Cambridge Street was not going to be the final stop for the Byrne family. A neighbor had alerted Patti that a large stately house she had always admired, a few blocks away on Harvard Avenue, would be coming on the market before long. She started plying the owners with cookies at Christmas, 1987 to get the inside track. I think by the next spring we were in contract.

There were probably two reasons for another move. First off, Patti never asked for much, but she seemed to have her heart set on this place as her dream house. That was probably sufficient reason to move but, in addition, she was pregnant again and this new place would have separate bedrooms for four kids, plus one for Mom and Dad. I had been through the share-a- room-with-your-sibling scene with Paul already, and I was not willing to try that again. So I went along quietly, even though the size and price of the new house scared me.

I can't pinpoint why, but this latest pregnancy never seemed as smooth as those that preceded it. There were no alarms from the doctor and, as my old Irish Grannie would have said, Patti "felt life" all the time. Still, she just seemed a little off instead of glowing as she had in the past.

Then, one early spring Saturday afternoon, I was taking Matthew to his Little League game. He was playing for Miceli Brothers Pizza, and I was one of the coaches. Before we left, Patti told me she was spotting. Today I would know I should have stayed, but back then I saw no point in sitting home with Matthew waiting for something bad to happen.

We wouldn't have had to wait long. We were down at the field for a while and the game was just underway when one of Patti's girlfriends showed up. Again, in the pre-smart phone era, that's how you informed someone of bad news and that they had better get home quickly.

When we arrived, Patti was lying on the bed crying. Matthew went to join the other kids and left us alone. "I lost the baby," she sobbed. "Let me show you." She got up off the bed and walked toward the bathroom. I followed.

From wherever she had it hidden, Patti handed me one of the blue plastic containers that were usually filled with Wet Ones.

Then she went and sat down on the side of the bathtub. I did the same.

I looked at her, as she cried again, then opened the container. Inside, probably about four inches long, was a male fetus. I had never really seen a fetus before, and I kept staring at this one, who happened to be my son, just as much as Matthew and Paul were. He looked okay, but something had obviously gone terribly wrong and he would never get his chance to be a boy. Still, he deserved a name, and in my own mind I called him Michael. (This was a secret that I never revealed until years later.) When Patti left the bathroom, I baptized him, like any good Catholic grammar school kid would have done, because I now understand that, in times of sorrow, you revert to your most basic rituals to see if they will get you through.

We gathered the kids to tell them the sad news: there wasn't going to be another baby after all. There was a lot of hugging and kissing as they tried to console Mom. Paul, of course, didn't understand too much of what was going on; Elizabeth understood all too well; and Matthew, lying on the bed next to his mother, still in his green jersey, baseball pants and hat, was just so sorry for his mother and disappointed that he wasn't going to be a big brother once again.

The next stop was NYU Medical Center for Patti's D&C. It may have been an overnight visit, but the eventual departure did not compare favorably to those we had experienced before. No baby; no excitement; just an extreme sense of loss, as opposed to the exhilaration of bringing a baby home the other three times.

I was nowhere near distraught. To the contrary, it just

seemed like some bad luck had followed a great streak of good luck, and I felt we had nothing to complain about. Still, as far as babies went, I was done. To this day, I remember sitting in that bathroom, staring into that plastic container, wanting no part of something like that happening again.

I hadn't consulted Patti, the actual victim of the miscarriage. To my total surprise, she wanted to try again. Whether from competitive spirit (Michael would have been born around the same time my sister-in-law, Christine, gave birth to her first child, Kelly) or just a stubborn refusal to have her childbearing career end with a loss, Patti was ready to take her chances again while I was not.

On April 5, 1989, our beautiful daughter Ann was born. I gave her mother <u>all</u> the credit, from start to finish. Patti was one special, determined woman, and she did manage to have that last triumphant trip home from the hospital. Poor Michael had never been able to do anything in his short life, but he had been able to make something happen. Baby Ann took up residence in the spare bedroom of the large house that Michael, the big brother she would never meet, prompted us to buy.

*

Unlike our other children, Paul paid absolutely no attention to the television during the first couple of years of his life. That all changed when he watched *Little Spies* one day, and realized he had lots of catching up to do. He watched that one repeatedly for days in a row, then finally moved on to another Disney movie:

Mr. Boogedy. That's when things became really interesting, because Paul informed us that Mr. Boogedy, some kind of ghost, had taken up residence in his room in the new house on Harvard Avenue, specifically in the box that covered the radiator.

Paul wasn't afraid of "Boogedy," as he called him for short. He was an invisible pal, but mostly a convenient scapegoat, because everything Paul did wrong was either actually done by Boogedy, or admittedly done by Paul, but on the advice of Boogedy.

Like all other parents, we were always looking for an edge in the battle to get Paul to behave himself. We knew Paul desperately wanted to move to the third floor with Matthew, and understood that he was going to have to do so before the baby arrived. Maybe this presented a way of evicting Mr. Boogedy?

We had a heart to heart with Paul, informing him that we thought he was a big enough boy to sleep upstairs with Matthew, but that Boogedy had to go; he could neither leave him in his old room, nor relocate him to the third floor. Paul was not happy about it, but he made the deal and actually stuck to it.

The first night I put him to bed on the third floor, down the hall from his brother, his aquamarine eyes were wide open, darting back and forth over his chubby cheeks. He was so excited I thought he'd never get to sleep. "Hey, Matt. Hey, Matt," I could hear him yelling before I even got down the stairs. He adored his big brother back then, and their lights-out conversations continued, whether with affection or animosity, until the day Matt died. The topics were endless, from Project One Big Room ("why don't we knock down all the walls, Matt, except for the bathroom, so we can share one gigantic room?"), to get rich quick schemes. One winter it snowed so much that there was cash all over the floor from their snow removal business, which I supported with use of a snow blower provided they cleared our place first. As they grew up, the discussions turned to other adult subjects of which I was thankfully unaware. For the most part, Matt just let Paul drone on until one of them fell asleep.

*

The new house had a detached three car garage set back on the property, behind which was that secluded "inner" backyard, a larger rectangular space against which neighbors' yards to the north, east, and south abutted. Above the garage was a full legal apartment, much bigger than the one Patti and I had lived in as newlyweds in Stuyvesant Town.

We had been using a young moonlighting police officer, Eric, to paint the house and garage on his days off after we moved in. We became friendly quickly, as the job dragged on in fits and starts due to his "real" work schedule. Eric was very close to the Polish community on Long Island and in Queens, and he eventually approached us about letting a Polish family stay in the apartment until they could get settled. They were recent arrivals, and spoke no English at all. Given our backgrounds, Patti and I are soft touches for immigrants. Eric introduced us all and we agreed to have them move in. It wasn't entirely altruistic. The woman was supposed to babysit Ann while Patti was at work and help out with the laundry – which there was plenty of!

I introduced the husband to the man who owned the office building in Garden City where I worked, and he hired the husband as a maintenance man. I accompanied the couple to the local public school, established their residency in the apartment, and they enrolled their son in kindergarten. The newcomers began the assimilation process, and things were going well, with one exception.

Each Sunday afternoon, the husband's brother and his family came to visit. The Brother had been in the United States for many years and spoke nearly flawless English. I instructed my kids to be sure to clear out of the "inner" yard so that the two families could gather in private for their barbecue or other socializing. The swing set relocated from both Wachusett and Cambridge Streets was declared off limits, and they were told to play elsewhere on Sunday afternoons.

The problem was that The Brother was an omniologist: he knew everything about everything. He couldn't just come and go without fanfare. If he could possibly catch me in the driveway – or summon me with a knock on the door – he would lodge some sort of complaint about something that didn't suit him. If it pertained to the apartment, my response was simple: "Your brother's the handyman. He doesn't pay anything to live here. If something's not right, let him fix it." These exchanges had a bit of an edge, but were cordial enough, at first.

I remember one particular Sunday afternoon, however, when the brother sought me out and caught me at home.

"You know, Ed," The Brother began, "that older boy of yours is very impolite. He never greets me or my family when we arrive each Sunday. I expect better behavior out of the landlord's son."

It was the use of the term "landlord" that set me off. My Grannie had come to this country as a sixteen-year-old "greenhorn," and went to work as a domestic in Manhattan. Until the day she died, the word "landlord" was somewhat spat out of her mouth like a curse word, since it was the landlords back in Ireland who had subjugated the peasants for centuries and essentially forced the young people to emigrate, knowing they would never see their parents again. A landlord was something I never aspired to be.

I lost it. "Don't you ever call me landlord again, wise ass, when your brother doesn't pay a dime to live here, even for gas and electric. And don't bother commenting on my kid's manners either. He's never done anything except stay out of your way every Sunday, Mr. Big Shot."

Then it escalated, since I suspected the money he was making and flaunting over his brother was tainted. "And don't keep telling yourself how slick you are either. My people were throwing themselves off the trolley car and bringing lawsuits before your people knew what a trolley car was."

It was an ugly episode, which illustrates several things. First off, it proved that I was not as far removed from my own immigrant or playground roots as I might have thought; I still had what my Grannie had called "the wicked tongue".

More importantly, it shows my reflex to come to the defense of my son, despite all my claims of objectivity. I could tell Matthew was not happy about the entire living arrangement, much less the Sunday afternoon restrictions, since we never had any need to share space with anyone in our two prior houses. He kept that to himself, however, and although he may have been somewhat distant, he was never disrespectful to the other family or their weekend guests.

The way he was perceived by The Brother as aloof, however, was duly noted and something I obviously never forgot.

*

Paul simply refused to recognize the sizeable five-year gap in age between Matthew and him. He was big for his age and counted on being included in everything his big brother planned to do. He mostly got away with this tactic because his best friend, Sean, Brian's youngest brother, was the same age and shared the same mindset as Paul: "What do you mean we're not old enough to do that?" The age rules were often bent by me, not only because Paul was so persistent, but because he never whined if permitted to tag along and seemed to get on with all the big kids, except one we all hated because he mimicked Paul's stutter. Whenever I took Paul, I took Sean too because he was simply tough as nails and never said anything, much less complained.

A notable example was Matt's ninth birthday, which meant both Paul and Sean were four years old.

Patti was an expert at throwing kids' birthday parties. She wasn't extravagant, just clever, with a wonderful knack of making them fun for all the kids who attended, no matter what age.

Even by her high standards, however, this party was spectacular. She dreamed up a backyard sleepover party for Matt's school friends, plus all the usual family and friends who came each year. Her decree left me with an awful lot to do: get the far backyard into shape; assemble a new sturdy swing set so the kids would have something to play on; and procure and pitch sufficient tents to provide shelter in case it rained on the birthday night. In hindsight, the location of this party is extremely ironic, since this far backyard is where Matthew would take his life some twenty-five years later.

In typical fashion, I underestimated what it would take to execute my task: stake out a rectangular area with four by four pressure treated lumber; remove the top layer of soil and grass; fill the rectangle with wood chips; then assemble the new swing set with its various climbing devices, slides, and canvas covers.

My mistake was well intentioned enough: buying a few too many four by fours. This made the rectangle very big, requiring me to remove and dispose of a huge amount of soil and grass and leaving a tremendous void to fill with wood chips. I remember my first of many runs to Home Depot. I had emptied the bench seats out of our minivan so I could stuff it to capacity with bags of wood chips. I probably squeezed close to twenty bags into every open space of the vehicle. When I made it back, poured the bags into the rectangle, and took a look, I couldn't believe how little of the rectangle I had covered. By the time I had the rectangle decently covered to protect some kid who fell off the monkey bars, innumerable trips to Home Depot later, I had almost run out of time, as well as money.

It all got done somehow, and everyone showed up for the big party. I barbecued and fed everyone on the patio, then all the kids ran around like crazy catching lightning bugs and doing all the things young boys do at dusk on a mild mid-May evening.

When it was finally dark enough, I ushered them to the tents. We dispensed with all the pre-bed formalities. I think lots of the flowers back there were watered that other way. Matt's friends managed to allocate themselves among the various tents without too many disputes about who was bunking with whom. I had the pleasure of having Paul and Sean to myself in a small pup tent. They thought this was easily the coolest thing they had ever done.

I was surprised, but it didn't take that long for them all to doze off. It was like listening to birds in a tree falling asleep on a summer night. First, they're all chirping, then the noise begins to die down as fewer and fewer keep it up. Finally, there's only the last loudmouth bird left chirping, who can't understand why everyone else has already fallen asleep.

My surprise at how soon they fell asleep was at least matched by my shock at how soon they woke up. I think it was 4:30 a.m., maybe 5 a.m. at the latest, when I heard the first kids working the swings.

I came out of the tent and watched the eight or nine-year old, half-naked guests, all on the swings and climbing devices, with Paul and Sean racing to catch up to the big boys.

The funny thing is, I couldn't blame them. You wouldn't believe how bright it was, and how much noise the birds were making at that early hour. I think I started laughing, at least until I saw my neighbor, Marty, standing in his backyard in his tightie whities, yelling over the fence at the boys.

Somehow, he let me know that he had just arrived home

from Europe, was jet lagged, and considered the swing set an eye-sore in what should have been a passive French garden. I didn't respond. I just ordered the boys to get their sneakers on and got them out of the backyard.

Hempstead Lake Park was a few blocks away, so I led them up North Village Avenue to the footbridge that led to the park's hiking trails. I must have walked them until 7 a.m., when I thought it was safe to take them back and feed them breakfast.

*

I guess that party set the pattern for what was to come: Paul and Sean got to tag along with the big guys, who just took this as the natural order of things. Matthew, in particular, never seemed to resent the presence of his little brother and his pal and the loss of alone time with Dad.

Matt had been a Cub Scout, with Patti acting as his den mother, when he was in the lower grades. When he became old enough for the Boy Scouts, I would accompany him on camping and other overnight trips. This was fun stuff and, in contrast to all the youth sports in which Matt participated, very noncompetitive and attractive to all different types of kids.

One incident on a camping trip still baffles me. At dusk one evening, the leader scheduled a "snipe" hunt, and all the scouts formed a horizontal line in an open field where they would catch the elusive creatures their fathers would drive toward them. I cannot remember Matthew being angrier as a kid than when he found out it was all a hoax and there was no such thing as a snipe. I had figured he would laugh the prank off, like everyone else, but he was truly disturbed at being duped and, uncharacteristically, saw nothing funny about it.

After Sean had lost his father, the rest of the world was not inclined to enforce age restrictions that would separate him from his three older brothers. Once the exception was made, Paul always seemed to get to go along for the ride, too, like on weekend overnights and even to Boy Scout camp in the summer. He left with Brian and Matt, each of them with a steamer trunk, but without Sean, who had bailed out at the last moment, leaving Paul quite pissed. About halfway through their stay, we received a postcard from Matthew asking whether we had heard from Paul, because he had not seen him in quite some time. I guess Matt preferred playing the joke, rather than having it played on him.

XI.

In the Fall of 2009, Ann had taken off for a junior year abroad semester at the University of Salamanca in Spain. No doubt because his own car was out of commission once again, since he was constantly banging it up in unexplained collisions, Matt began "borrowing" Ann's car, an old but serviceable Chrysler Pacifica. One night, he drove the car to Long Beach but returned without it and went to work for days, remaining out of touch. No one knew where the car was, and no one wanted to tell Ann we had "lost" her car just weeks after she left town.

I asked Paul to come with me a couple of times to cruise the streets of Long Beach to try to locate the missing car. Paul resented these requests, despite my argument that we weren't helping Matt but his sister who had no part in creating the situation.

Within a few days I gave up. Concluding that the car might have been stolen, I went to the Long Beach Police Department to file a report.

The car had not been stolen, but simply towed from the no parking zone where Matt had left it. I don't understand why I had not suspected this from the outset, given the multitude of N.Y.C. parking enforcement judgments I had covered for Matt over the years. We negotiated the Pacifica's release with some towing company in Island Park and nobody let on to Ann what had happened.

Patti decided that, since Ann could not return from Spain for Thanksgiving, we should all visit her in Salamanca. She and I left first, with the boys to follow a day later after they finished work. The trip was a disaster.

My sons barely made the flight and battled most of the rest of the trip. It finally became so bad that Matt announced he would be back but was taking off for a couple of days.

"Where are you going?"

"Surfing."

"With what?"

"I'll figure it out."

"Where are you staying?"

"I'll stay at firehouses. I have a bunch of FDNY tee shirts to give away. They'll be glad to see me."

So, he left. Miraculously, he did come back in time for the long drive back to Madrid for the flight home. There were no fistfights with Paul on the way, but it may have come close.

In contrast to 2009, 2010 was an awful year right from the start. The summer was particularly brutal, after Patti underwent a colon resection that removed ten to twelve inches of intestine. According to her doctor, the abdominal surgery had been complicated by her long-term steroid use, a double-edged sword according to him, which had made her insides "like paper."

Rheumatoid arthritis had first struck Patti in her early thirties, less than two years after Matthew was born. I don't have much recollection of the onset, just a vision of her lying on her back in bed crying, wondering what had happened to her formerly athletic self. Fortunately, in short order, thanks to Aunt Agnes who worked as a medical secretary at NYU Medical Center and always knew which doctor you should see for whatever ailed you,

Patti was referred to Dr. Bertrand Agus, who has since passed. He was a wonderfully calm and kind man who helped Patti manage her condition for the next thirty plus years.

Dr. Agus explained to us how the disease would progress, and how ever-strengthening lines of medical defense would have to be thrown at it as the prior ones eventually failed. In our early thirties, we probably listened politely, but didn't really believe him, in any event deciding – like we did with most everything else, like financing our children's college educations – to deal with that later. I remember saying on way more than one occasion, "I guess we'll have to figure that out when the time comes."

The time had apparently already come, unnoticed by us, with respect to the steroids Dr. Agus had been prescribing for years to allow Patti to lead a normal life. My questions to the surgeon as to what her intestines should be like – cardboard, garden hose – all went unanswered. Her recovery was slow and painful.

September 11, 2010 the next shoe dropped. We had a birthday luncheon scheduled for Patti with the family, but Matthew could not come due to a conflict with a 9/11 ceremony he was supposed to attend. At some point in the late afternoon or early evening, I wound up in our upstairs bedroom to change my clothes. Matt burst into the room wearing his dress blue uniform, appearing very agitated and pretty high.

"I have to go away."

"What do you mean, Matt?"

"My friends say I have to go away." They had reported him to the union.

I figured there had been drinking after the 9/11 memorial

service. It was odd for me to even know where he had been on a given day. For a long time, I didn't know much about his whereabouts, and I felt uncomfortable asking what he'd been doing.

We now know that the union representative reported Matt to FDNY's Counseling Services Unit (or "CSU"), which signed him up for a stint at one of the rehabilitation centers the FDNY used. He wasn't happy about it, but he was resigned to going and being compliant.

Matt explained that his friends had told him he was drinking too much and had to do this. It wasn't hard to believe. With all the overtime he had been working, he sometimes spent a couple of days in a row at the firehouse, and then would take off for his Jones Beach job, at least through Labor Day. He would look disheveled when he finally returned home, and hygiene had apparently become an issue with his fellow firefighters.

I probably knew this had been coming. We didn't see that much of each other given his schedule. It was my conscious choice to leave some space to a 30-year-old son occasionally living under the same roof – a situation with which, I assured him, I had no experience whatsoever with my own father. That summer we barely saw each other except for Yankee games every other Friday night, using tickets I split with an old friend. Before driving to the Bronx with Paul, he'd greet me with his customary "Hey DaddyO," drop a large bag of dumplings from Chinatown on the kitchen counter, and pretend everything was fine.

The late afternoon sunlight was still flooding the bedroom as Matt paced about. I told him it would be wise to respect his friends' opinion and, if he needed help, he would be smart to get it now.

The FDNY's Counseling Service Unit was sending a car and an escort to pick him up and take him to a place called Marworth in Scranton, Pennsylvania. Still angry, he went upstairs, and I could hear him banging around, packing up clothes and whatever else he would need.

Patti and I tried to play it very low key, like going off to rehab is something everyone has to do, sooner or later. In a short time, a car showed up with a driver and a young firefighter escort. Matt was quickly on his way to his first twenty-eight-day stint.

I left early the next morning to accompany The Nephew on a Jet Blue flight from J.F.K. to Buffalo to see The Father at the state prison in Gowanda.

If you ever feel the need to stop a clock from moving, try spending an afternoon playing cards at a table, visiting a prisoner you detest. Let me explain why I felt that way. The incident that led to The Father's manslaughter conviction was not the result of poor judgment and simply having "one too many". The level of intoxication that resulted in the high speed crash, against a backdrop of years of physical and emotional abuse, made it look borderline intentional to me. The Father had initially told the cops that he did not even know "that woman," his wife, whom he falsely claimed was driving the car. While The Father ultimately abandoned that story, he perpetuated the myth of "The Accident" with his son, instead of owning up to what he had done and being immediately forgiven by a boy desperate to love his surviving parent. The Nephew did not know any better, at the time, and one of my jobs as Uncle Ed was to hide my true feelings, say nothing about "The Accident," and just make polite small talk about the boy's schooling and activities during these prison visits.

When the guards mercifully called time to leave around 3 p.m., we still had a few hours to kill before the return flight. We detoured to take a peek at Niagara Falls, which neither The Nephew nor I had ever seen. It was as magnificent as I had always heard.

As you might guess, there was an awful lot going on in my world at this time.

*

There were only phone calls for the first days Matt was at Marworth. Then we went out to Scranton for Family Day on September 20, 2010. They were starting early that Monday morning, so Patti and I booked a room in a nearby motel the night before in order to be on time. I remember there was a nice Italian restaurant across the road. We each had a martini, then some red wine, not anticipating the next day's shame arising from the counselor's question as to what alcohol and drugs we had consumed the night before. Apples don't fall far from their trees!

*

Marworth's main building is a big old white mansion, which once belonged to the Scranton family, after whom the City was named. William Scranton had been governor of Pennsylvania and a political rival of Richard Nixon back in 1968, and the family had donated a great deal of money to expand upon the mansion and build a modern alcohol and drug treatment facility.

We spent the day going to educational sessions, at first to some offsite facility with no patients, then later back on the grounds of Marworth. We traveled in a group with parents, girlfriends, siblings, and other loved ones, all of us concerned, nervous, but very hopeful that this would be the first step in the right direction. The instructions were intended to give us all a basic grounding in the causes, nature and likely conditions of substance abuse, which was undoubtedly a "family disease," a fact with which Patti and I were both quite familiar.

In the afternoon, we met jointly with Matt and his counselor. It was good to see Matt, and he was glad to see us. He was clear-eyed and calm. The counselor was a big guy and a bit patronizing. I suspected right away that he had not been a great fit with my son. Nevertheless, everything seemed to be in order, given the circumstances, and we left hoping that Matt was going to be able to overcome his drinking problem. A little more than a week later, we received a letter from Matt that was definitely encouraging:

Dear Mom and Dad,

I hope all is well and that you are doing well. I am making more progress here every day. They are teaching me the skills I need to get better. A big part of my main problem, probably my main problem, is that I have stuffed down so many thoughts and emotions over the years. I have not been able to talk about serious things or events (sometimes mentally traumatic) and they all piled up in my head. I'm feeling much better now though. I'm sure you noticed my communication problem because my voice gets strange and I feel like someone is stabbing me in the throat when I try to talk sometimes. Alcohol certainly does not solve my problems with this though, it makes it worse and I become more isolated. I would rather keep the conversation light or not speak at all rather than discuss anything serious. I know you understand.

My head is much clearer now and I feel relief. I am remembering things that I haven't thought about in years, like my birthday party in the backyard on Wachusett Street. We were balancing eggs on spoons and doing that race across the yard. Then Peter Gillen placed his hot dog order with Mom and I was astonished that my classmate wanted ketchup, mustard, and sauerkraut on his dog (maybe even relish too). You are a great mother and that was a great party.

Being away from the family and out of state on September 11, 2001 was not a healthy experience for me at all. I never dealt with that day in my head properly. I realize that now though. I isolated myself. I isolated myself after that drowning at Zachs Bay in 1997. When I went to the fire at the Deutsche Bank and those two men were killed I didn't speak about it. I shoved it down. Every time I see anything that is traumatic at work I shove it down. This is very unhealthy and drinking copious amounts of alcohol does not make it better. I'm learning to deal with these things though and I realize how dangerous it is to let things pile up.

I love you both dearly and am working hard on getting my head straight. I have great respect for what you have both achieved at such young ages. You've built your own businesses, are both highly educated and have made a great family. I do not want to mess up our family. This experience has humbled me I hope.

Thank you for Everything and Thanks for Visiting,

Matt

I'll be back soon.

P.S. Say hi to the gang and give Portia a treat."

It turned out I was right about something not clicking between Matt and his counselor. When we picked Matt up in Scranton on Sunday, October 10, 2010, we did not know that his entire stint at Marworth had been a charade. Using a classic defendant's maneuver, Matt had pled to the lesser offense. He convinced the counselor and everyone else at Marworth that he had a drinking problem, only that. In fact, his issues ran much deeper. The substance abuse professionals had been fooled and hadn't scratched the surface.

XII.

When Matt hit fourth grade, he faced a dilemma. Did he want to be a choir boy or altar boy? There really was no third option, like none of the above, so he elected joining the St. Agnes Men and Boys Choir since Brian's older brother, Kevin Jr., was a member and Matt always looked up to him.

The choir was really quite professional, and it was a very good experience for him. He was still a relative newbie in the summer of 1990 when the group was booked for a tour of Austria, Germany and Switzerland. Patti's Mom had turned 70 that April, and Patti decided it would be a great birthday treat for her, Lorayne, and Elizabeth to accompany Matthew's choir group to Europe like some other families were doing. That meant I would stay home with Paul and Ann, who had just turned one that April, and try to keep my father-in-law, Frank, from starving in Lorayne's absence. It sounded manageable, especially since my own mother and father were coming up from Florida to help out.

It turned out to be a nightmarish ten days or two weeks, however long it was. The plan had been to send Paul, who was only five years old, to the Bible school run by the local Lutheran Church. After day one, when I arrived home, he became hysterical crying because he hated Bible school so much. Since he seemed crushed by the fact that his mother and older siblings had abandoned him and gone to Europe, I relented and let him stay home and get spoiled each day by Grandma Catherine and Grandpa Don. Paul was okay with that, and the initial crisis was averted.

The next crisis developed within a few days. Baby Ann was starting to get really sick. She was all congested with a runny nose, labored breathing – in short, the full respiratory works, which bordered on croup at night. I called my friends' mother, Dr. Adelaide, made an appointment, and hoped that she could rescue us once again, as she had when Matthew was a baby.

The moment she came into the examining room and looked at Ann, Dr. Adelaide barked, "Is your father up from Florida?"

I responded, "Yes. How did you know?"

She ignored the question and directed, "You tell him to get those damn cigarettes out of the house! If he has to smoke, tell him to go out on the patio or down the block, but nowhere near that baby."

When I got home and broke the news to my father about Dr. Adelaide's pronouncement, he just nodded his head, picked up his pack of cigarettes and lighter, and left the house because no one I ever knew was brave or foolish enough to take on Dr. Adelaide.

Within a few days, with the benefit of the medicine Dr. Adelaide had prescribed, Ann recovered. By the time Patti and the rest had returned from their wonderful trip, Ann seemed fine and I had avoided a huge loss of stature in the parenting department.

*

The biggest difference I noticed between my boyhood and

that of my sons was fighting. Notice I said my sons. My blond hair, blue eyed daughter, Elizabeth, once a total fraidy cat, was not one to be messed with once she approached her teens. She had several memorable school-bus bouts, with both boys and girls, all of which she apparently won.

Maybe it was concern with lawsuits – more likely than increased civility – but my kids didn't grow up in a world that was simply divided between those you could take and those who could take you.

I happened to grow up three doors down from Joey, who was acknowledged as one of the best fighters in our area of Queens. It was like being a sparring partner for Muhammad Ali; you took many a beating but became well-prepared to fight anyone who wasn't as tough as Joey. This was important because you could unexpectedly find yourself following dismissal at St. Anastasia on the fight "card" that unseen juvenile matchmakers put together nearly every afternoon. One day Joey told me I was going to fight Bobby from Overbrook Street on the way home. "Who says? What for?" I protested. Bobby was a grade ahead of me, and I barely knew him, much less had reason to fight him. "It's already on the schedule," Joey assured me, "and you better show up." I dutifully did and fought Bobby, who was already working on cars in his driveway and had some impressive dirt under his fingernails. We mostly wrestled to a boring draw.

Maybe Elizabeth was a feisty throwback to that earlier generation, but Paul only fought under extreme provocation, and Ann just never fought at all. To my knowledge, except for defending Paul and his friends as a big brother must, Matthew only fought someone one time, but the incident is worth recounting.

Matt was in fifth grade and playing baseball in the fall Little League season, having come off a season in the minors where he had led his team in hitting. His manager, Coach Bill, with whom I later coached teenage players for years, was a great guy, and Matthew and all the other kids on the team loved him.

One afternoon, Bill, who worked for the Sanitation Department, rode by St. Agnes hanging off the back of his truck at dismissal time and gave Matt a big hello. One of Matt's classmates, Ryan, had something snarky to say about that, literally trash talking Matt's favorite manager, and Matt must have at least punched him.

I received the obligatory call from Miss Helen that Matt had gotten into a fight defending his manager's honor. This didn't upset me too much, and I don't think I even had to report to school, just agree to instruct him that violence was not the way to resolve such disputes. I dutifully gave that lecture, hoping, however, that Ryan had learned his lesson.

Unfortunately, the matter was not so easily put to rest. Due to a bad twist of fate, Ryan's mother happened to be Paul's kindergarten teacher. Never one to suffer in silence, when he detected a new frostiness in his teacher's attitude toward him following the fight, Paul called it to her attention in words like this: "I know why you don't like me anymore. It's because my brother beat up your kid!"

This time a trip to St. Agnes was definitely necessary. Ryan's mother felt accused of decidedly unchristian behavior and went ballistic. Only a visit to Miss Helen's office was going to calm things down.

I took the punishment for the Byrne family like a man. "No, Miss Helen, we talk about other things at the dinner table than Ryan's mother." "Yes, Miss Helen, even though I happen to think Paul was right, I'll make sure he never brings it up with her again."

Thanks to Miss Helen's skillful diplomacy, everyone backed off: Ryan, Matt, Ryan's mother and Paul. We all managed to survive the balance of the school year.

*

I never played anything but team sports, and I think Matthew tolerated them for my sake and because they were probably the major social outlets for Rockville Centre kids.

Rockville Centre was a particularly basketball-crazed town, which was fine by me. I had coached Elizabeth's teams, then Matthew's when he was old enough to play. He would hustle and play hard, but was far from consumed by the game, as I had been as a kid and teen.

Baseball was far more his thing, both playing and rooting because he was a devoted Yankee fan. As I mentioned, true to his early aspiration, he had led his team in hitting in the minors when he was in fourth grade and, finally recognizing that he did indeed have to play the field, settled on the outfield as his preferred position. Coach Bill had wanted him to "play up" in the National League the next season, when he was eleven, which would have meant competing against 12-year olds, some of whom were as big as me. Matt was still quite little and scrawny and since, I confess, I tended to be protective of him as far as sports were concerned, I kept him down and managed his team, Palmieri Pizza, in the American League, where most 11-year olds and the 12s who were not picked for the National League played.

I figured that, with another year under his belt, Matt would be ready to go it alone next season in the National League while I managed Paul's team during his rookie year in the tee ball league. Another well intentioned plan backfired completely. The coaching staff of the National League team that drafted Matt did not understand that you should treat every player on the team like he's your own kid, not just the one you drive home after the game. Matt had a miserable season, which was mercifully cut short when he broke his thumb hitting at a batting cage, still practicing and trying to stay ready, if he ever got more than one at-bat in a game.

None of the knocks got him down, I incorrectly thought, or drove him away from sports. He continued to play baseball and basketball through high school, but strictly for fun. What he decided to take seriously, not surprisingly, was a sport at which he had an edge over most of his contemporaries: swimming. It became his all year-round activity, no longer just summers at the Rockville Links, but practically every day of the school year as part of a club team, Long Island Express, which worked out at Hofstra University. The kids on the LIE team were from all over, and the friends Matt made broadened his perspective and put him on the birthday, bar/bat mitzvah, and every other kind of party circuit for the next couple of years, as Patti and I chauffeured him all around western Long Island.

*

Matt's years in the choir went by quickly as the group sang at Masses at St. Agnes each Sunday and gave concerts and made special appearances on occasion. In December of 1992, when Matt was twelve, they were booked to sing at the annual Christmas tree lighting ceremony at what was then EAB Plaza – Long Island's answer to the Rockefeller Center Christmas tree lighting in Manhattan.

Just like Rockefeller Center, EAB Plaza had a skating rink, and the big Christmas tree was positioned adjacent to the ice. (Since I did not actually attend the event, my descriptions are somewhat imprecise, recreated from eyewitness accounts.)

The choir's performance went off without a hitch. As the boys watched the rest of the ceremony, however, leaning against the boards of the ice rink, apparently the conversation drifted to how cool it would be for someone to scale the boards and go out on the ice.

We'll never know whether Matt suggested it, or someone dared him to do it, but the deal was cut: for $20 from each of his friends, Matt was to go over the boards and out on the ice to shake hands with Santa Claus, who was skating around and waving to the crowd. And he did.

Needless to say, there was a heap of trouble as a result of Matthew's stunt. The choir director, Mr. Bower, was irate, but not nearly as steamed as Patti was. When I got home from wherever I was, I got an earful.

The appropriate punishment seemed very simple to me. I asked Matt how many of his friends were in on the plan. The number came to approximately five, since some had plainly committed to paying the $20, while others had been a little cagey as to their financial responsibility. So I said, "Okay, you were supposed to make $100 for that stunt. You're going to give Mr. Bower $100 of your own money as a donation toward the choir's next trip. And whatever you collect from your friends, you get to keep as reimbursement."

To my knowledge, none of his friends ever paid off.

Matthew had been known to go for the big laugh before. At the end of fifth grade, he was invited to tag along with Elizabeth for a pool party thrown by one of her eighth grade graduating classmates. Matt wound up pushing the host's mother into the pool. She took it well, but the event was a bit shocking. Hopefully a lesson would be learned for good from the similar EAB incident.

*

Other than his group experience in the choir, Matt's career in the performing arts had peaked with his pre-K performance as Morris the Mouse. Piano lessons had been short lived. Jazz dance class didn't even last that long. He and Paul had wanted to sign up because another neighborhood kid who was a good athlete was learning how to dance. My boys told me they had to have jazz shoes to be any good at it. I said, "Okay, but only if you promise to stick with it." As soon as I bought them the shoes – not inexpensive – they quit. I still complain about it.

So, when seventh grader Matt announced that he was going to participate in the spring talent show at St. Agnes, we were quite surprised.

"That's great. What are you going to do in the talent show, Matt?" I asked.

"I'm going to be Michael Jackson," he replied. I just nodded. This was going to be interesting.

When the big night came, Patti and I, as well as Matt's siblings, didn't know what to expect as we sat in the basement cafeteria of St. Agnes School that doubled on occasion as an auditorium. We watched a bunch of acts displaying talents of varying sorts and abilities, then the kid announcer said: "Next are Matthew and Michael."

Out the two of them came, dancing to Michael Jackson's *Black and White*, wearing, of course, black trousers and white shirts. Michael had on dark glasses, but it was clear he was the backup dancer. Matthew was front stage, with his stovepipe pants hiked up to show off his white socks and black loafers. To complete the look, he had on a single glove and a white plastic fedora with a black band.

Matt moonwalked and, a little bit herky-jerky, did his best impression of MJ's moves, while Michael sashayed behind him throughout the song. By the end, they were winded, but gratified by a resounding reception from the audience.

When the show was over, the father of one of Matt's friends approached me. He was usually a fairly hard-boiled guy, but he was uncharacteristically gushing. "I had no idea Matt had that kind of nerve. My sons would never do something like that." I responded saying something like, "Yeah, the kid is full of surprises."

*

Naturally enough, given his predilection for water sports, during the summer that followed his twelfth birthday, Matt discovered surfing. I think this may have started on weekend visits to the Murtaghs in Long Beach, and it had definitely turned serious by August when we took a trip to North Carolina's Outer Banks. The surfboard was crammed into the minivan with all the other junk, and Matt spent hours on the steeply inclined beach, trying to stand up on at least one wave, while his siblings watched with varying degrees of interest and boredom. Patti and I thought it would be a passing fad; it wasn't. Matt's interest in surfing only deepened over the years, and it became a major influence on his adult life. I was never able to convince myself it was a positive one.

XIII.

The FDNY doesn't give up on its firefighters easily, and its Counseling Service Unit doesn't give up on them ever. When a firefighter returns from rehab, he isn't given some limited number of second or third chances to get it right. My impression was that the counselors of the unit were going to do whatever they could to get you back to full duty, for as long as it took, as many times as necessary. The only one whom it seemed could call this process off was the firefighter, by finally refusing the help that was being offered.

Matt returned from Marworth on Sunday October 10, 2010. Since the next day was Columbus Day, he was to report on Tuesday to the Counseling Service Unit's facility on Lafayette Street, rather than straight back to Engine 9.

Matt was a few weeks into the unit's program when Patti and I attended its Family Day event on October 28, 2010. The invitation had stated: "Studies show that family support and healthy involvement in your loved one's recovery process are essential parts of their success." We were certainly ready to do whatever we could to help.

We met several of the unit's counselors and attended sessions both with and without Matt throughout the day.

The sessions without the FDNY members were primarily educational, explaining seventeen different principles of family recovery from alcoholism. Some of this was familiar stuff, but it took on new meaning when the application of the principles was to your own family.

We were told that alcoholism is a disease, for which no one is to blame, but the disease affects the whole family so that those close to the alcoholic both deeply affect and are in turn affected by its progression. This disease can't be cured, but it can be arrested and its damage healed – only if the alcoholic stops drinking immediately, completely, and permanently, changing his prior attitudes and behaviors and literally transforming his life. Obviously only the alcoholic can make these changes, yet he can't do it without help from others in rebuilding his shattered self-worth.

This last point made the biggest impact on me. "Shattered self-worth" sounded very serious. As a sports coach, I had worked with several kids who had juvenile diabetes. They always seemed to accept without question that they had a condition that made them different from everyone else, and which couldn't be ignored. They knew better than to ingest things they shouldn't. I had the same experience with my grandson, who would politely shake his head and say: "No thanks. Nuts make me really sick." Why is it so hard for so many of us to stay away from something we know does us great harm, even when this fact is proven over and over. The inability to handle sugar or peanuts doesn't shatter a person's sense of self-worth. Why is it different with alcohol? Matt's treatment records reveal that he never accepted alcohol abuse as a disease, rather than a personal failing, and he criticized those who did as just making excuses.

One group session held on that Family Day was attended by both firefighters and their families or significant others.

A young firefighter who had been in Matt's probie class was

there, accompanied by his brother, which I thought was a very considerate thing for the brother to do. The group that stood out, however, were an older firefighter, his wife, and their two daughters. At some point in the session, without much of a prompt from the counselor, the two daughters launched into their father, berating him for all the times his drinking had embarrassed them or otherwise caused the family hardship. The girls' mother really didn't say much at all, basically just nodding in agreement.

This public shaming may have been well deserved, but it looked staged rather than spontaneous, and in any event was definitely uncomfortable to witness. I recall our trip home. We had all driven in together rather than drag Patti up to the LIRR train platform and through the subway. We were stuck in horrific traffic heading to one of the Lower East River crossings, and everyone had a different take on the beatdown the older firefighter had taken. I'm sure that, at some point, I made my standard observation that, unlike his unfortunate comrade, Matt was lucky to be addressing his problem sooner than later.

I have no recollection of how he reacted to that trite comment. I do remember something else he said while we were sitting on Houston Street going nowhere. He told us that, for several months, he had actually dated his probie friend's sister, a high school Latin teacher.

Once again, I took note of Matt's other life, of which we had no knowledge. For some reason, his romance with a classicist struck me as very out of character. This girl must have been really pretty for him to give that mismatch a shot!

*

Matt spent five weeks at Lafayette Street before heading back to Engine 9, nearby in Chinatown. He resumed his irregular work schedule and things settled back into familiar patterns at home.

As recommended by the Counseling Service Unit, Matt attended evening Alcoholics Anonymous meetings at a church in the neighborhood, as well as weekly sessions at a recovery counseling center in Oceanside. He seemed fairly serious about it, and I was feeling encouraged. When I shared with him that I was being proposed as a candidate for a federal judgeship, however, he looked me straight in the eye and said: "Good luck with that!"

I wasn't exactly sure what that comment meant, but it was nothing good. Was he giving me a heads-up on what would come to light on a background check? I didn't press the matter, and just mumbled "Thanks" as I walked away.

*

In March 2011, Patti and I were supposed to go to Puerto Rico – a business trip, but very light duty. The problem was that her mom had been failing, and we were uncertain as to whether we should go or not.

Lorayne had always been an incredibly vibrant and energetic person, into her late eighties. The summer before, however, she had suffered a mild stroke and it had really set her back, way more than it should have.

I suspected that the root cause was her belief that she had brought the stroke on herself. A few years before, my friend, her doctor, had recommended that she take two pills of a certain medicine to ward off a stroke or heart attack. Lorayne had been very obstinate, insisting that she would only take one of the pills, not two. My friend patiently explained to her that she could take that approach, if she wished, but essentially was doubling her risk of an adverse episode.

Lorayne had stood her ground, however, and no doubt later became convinced that her stubbornness had cost her. Once she could no longer drive and be totally independent, it seemed she lost interest in everything that had mattered to her before. There was no real physical reason for it, but Lorayne seemed to have given up on life and was just fading away.

We convinced ourselves, however, that the end was no time soon. Lorayne had two aides in place, so someone was with her all the time. We figured we could safely sneak off to Puerto Rico for a couple of days and return without incident.

We left on Friday morning, March 18, 2011. We had a nice Friday afternoon and evening and all day Saturday in Rio Mar. Then the phone rang before dawn on Sunday morning, and Patti's cousin, who is also my law partner, told us Lorayne was gone.

I got on the phone with the airlines immediately. It had to be some kind of miracle, but we were back in Rockville Centre before 1 p.m. to rendezvous with the rest of the family at the mortuary and view Lorayne's remains. Like her late husband, Frank, she was to be cremated, with a memorial Mass scheduled for Saturday, March 26, at St. Agnes Cathedral.

I had delivered a eulogy for Patti's father, and Patti resolved to do the same for her mother. Our sons, Paul and Matthew, were to do the readings at their grandma's service because the granddaughters all contended Lorayne loved the boys best.

The night before the Mass, we had decided to take the family out to dinner for Paul's birthday, which had been neglected in the week's confusion. Matt and GF were with us, and Matt remained quite shaken up by Lorayne's death. They had been close, and he would often spend the night at Lorayne's place, perhaps not so much to keep her company as to awaken close to the beach if the surf were up. When we left the fish restaurant, Paul's birthday choice, Matt and GF took off for parts unknown, probably her place or Grandma's, as it was known, even though we had bought it from her some years back.

The Mass was scheduled to begin at 10:30 a.m. and all the Byrnes and Murtaghs were dutifully assembled outside St. Agnes by 10:15, except for Matt and GF. When we simply couldn't wait any longer, the procession started without them, down the center aisle of the church to the front pews.

As the Mass began, I was filled with dread. How would Patti react if Matt missed her mother's funeral? I made a hasty contingency plan. If Matt weren't there by the time it was his turn to read, I would just go up on the altar and take his place like I had been supposed to do the reading all along.

I think Paul had finished the first reading and the responsorial psalm was actually underway when Matt and GF finally slid into the front pew from the side aisle. He was dressed in a suit but, oddly, wearing black sneakers. He rose from his seat when he should and unsteadily climbed the few marble steps to the lectern.

Matt was very choked up, from getting "stabbed in the throat" as he described it in his letter from Marworth, but he managed to get the words out. Others may have attributed it to sheer emotion, but I knew he had gotten wasted the night before as well.

With a disaster averted for the moment, I finally leaned back in the pew. At the end of the Mass, using the cane that had become her constant companion, Patti tapped her way up the altar steps and delivered a beautiful eulogy for her Mom.

*

It was about two years later, when many other unpleasant truths were bubbling to the surface, we learned of another one. After the family had gathered at the mortuary for Lorayne's brief viewing, Matthew had raced to Long Beach to grab his beloved grandmother's painkillers before her aides disposed of them. He must have taken some on the spot; he told us he somehow fell off the dock, hit his head and nearly drowned.

*

It has always been amazing to me how, when we want things to be "normal," we all have a huge capacity to pretend they are so, despite overwhelming evidence to the contrary.

I think this fantasy land was where we found ourselves for a long time after Matt returned from Marworth. He was heading to work as scheduled and at least going through the motions of recovery; we were, too, attending a parent support group weekly that we used as an excuse to go out for dinner and drinks when it was done. Everyone seemed to be doing what they were supposed to be doing, yet it all had an insincere quality to it, as though we were all floating on the surface, even though we knew that a deep dive was required.

Lorayne had died in late March, and, after Memorial Day, the Byrnes all agreed that for the summer we would finally move into the beach house we had owned for several years.

The house was filled with bittersweet memories of Lorayne and Frank, but it was a nice change of pace. Although everyone was working, coming home at night to an ocean front community gives you a little taste of vacation every day.

Between working in Chinatown, then at Jones Beach whenever he could, we saw very little of Matthew, who spent whatever free time he had at GF's place, also in the West End of Long Beach. But we did spend at least one nice day together with him that summer. The FDNY was hosting something called the International Firefighters Olympics. I had never heard of it but, much like the regular Olympics, it consisted of competitions in various events at different venues throughout the N.Y.C. Metropolitan area. Matt informed us that he would be entered in the surfing competition held at Rockaway Beach.

We lathered up with sunscreen on a very hot late August day and headed to Beach 90th Street in Rockaway to watch the final day of the competition. There was a decent crowd, with contestant firefighters from as far away as Australia, New Zealand and South America. We met some FDNY members Matt knew from

surfing who had parents along, too, and it was a very festive at-
mosphere, like one of his old high school or college swim meets,
but with the competition dial turned way down. It was a remind-
er of days in the past we had taken for granted.

*

After Labor Day, we returned to Rockville Centre for the
coming winter months, at least officially. Nothing stopped any of
the kids from going back to the Long Beach house, and I know
Matthew frequently did, for romantic or other purposes. This
was far from an ideal situation, but I didn't see how I could defend an unenforceable edict that a 31-year-old live at home with
his parents rather than occupy an otherwise vacant beach house
he could at least keep an eye on.

The Fall back in Rockville Centre was beautiful, and uneventful, as well, until October 28, 2011. That was the day we received
word that Matthew had fallen off the Engine 9 rig. According to
the emergency room report, he was wearing heavy gear and an
oxygen tank when he lost his footing getting out of the truck and
hit his lower back on the engine's step.

I don't recall ever receiving any explanation of what caused
the fall. There was no indication that Matt was doing anything
other than performing his job that day and just had an unfortunate accident. He had hurt his back, not terribly, and had been
taken to Bellevue Hospital.

Matt wound up with painkillers, probably prescribed by a local doctor who actually got in trouble with the law for a number

of misdeeds, along with some anti-herpes drug he was given at the hospital. We didn't know it then but, as often happened back then when opioid scripts were written with little regard to the general consequences, much less the particular susceptibilities of the patient, we were off to the races. Things would deteriorate rapidly for our family.

But life can never be denied. On November 1, 2011, while her uncle was probably starting his search for Oxycontin, Percocet, or other opioids in earnest, our third grandchild was born, a beautiful little girl named Catherine Lorayne after her great grandmothers.

XIV.

As far as we had known at the time, Matt really enjoyed his final year of grammar school at St. Agnes. He was popular with boys and girls and had no problems with the faculty and administration. Matt had done fine academically throughout grammar school. Crunch time would come in the fall, when practically all the eighth graders would sit for the dreaded Co-ops, the entrance exam for the Catholic high schools.

I wasn't too concerned for him because he usually seemed unflappable and had some credentials as a clutch performer. For example, I used to tease him that there was no point in letting him have three strikes in baseball, because he'd always foul at least two pitches off, then finally bear down once the threat of striking out hung over him. Similarly, during his brief stint as a pianist, he had crammed all afternoon the day of the annual recital at his teacher's house, only managing to learn his piece at the last possible moment before playing it that evening without embarrassing himself.

Matthew was never much for studying throughout his academic career, but if he had to take a standardized test, watch out. The Co-ops were no problem, and he was accepted to his first choice high school, Chaminade, run by the Marianist Brothers in Mineola, New York.

If the Jesuits were the Catholic Church's CIA operatives, skilled at covert action and subtle persuasion, the Marianists who ran Chaminade High School were its U.S. Marines. Their philosophy was akin to that of the Corps in processing new recruits: Break the old identity down, then rebuild it to form a Chaminade Man, who would do the right thing at the right time, because it was the right thing to do – regardless of who, if anyone, was watching. Departures from this aspirational conduct gave rise to demerits, assessed in numerical quantities by means of slips of varying color. The word was that if you hit 30 demerits in a single academic year (they rolled back to zero each September), you would be expelled – and even a call from the Pope to give the kid a break would be futile. I warned Matthew when he selected Chaminade that the brothers were very serious, and it was their way or the highway. I also made the comparison to my experience with the Jesuits who never wrote a rule that they didn't leave a way around if they liked you!

The process of indoctrinating the incoming Chaminade freshmen began the week before Labor Day each year at something called 3-C Week. The letters stood for community, confidence and commitment. The students were sorted alphabetically into the homeroom classes that would remain unchanged, except for departures, for the following four years. They attended classes together covering math, study skills, and writing, had field days and other team-building exercises, and received instruction in other nuts and bolts topics that would permit them to be grounded academically and socially after Labor Day. Matthew seemed to buy into the Chaminade system immediately and completely, so his transition to high school was no problem.

*

Naturally enough, Matt went out for the swim team at Chaminade. The fact that the school had its own pool – to which all the other local Catholic high school swim teams had to travel for practice – had been a determining factor in his decision to attend. The freshman season began early in the school year. When it ended, the better freshmen were brought up to the varsity, essentially to ride the bench and watch how things were supposed to be done so they would know what would be expected from them the next year.

The varsity was run by two non-staffers, Head Coach Steve and Assistant Coach Eddie. They were both New York City Firefighters who worked summers as lifeguards at Jones Beach. They obviously made a huge impact on Matt, who ended up modeling his career path after them.

In particular, Matt became Coach Steve's guy. Whatever Coach Steve told him he could do, Matt believed it was so. When he was a junior, Chaminade was swimming for the New York State Championship, and it was going to be a close meet. Matt was one of the team's few distance swimmers, and Coach Steve needed Matt to beat his previous best time in the 500-yard freestyle by something crazy – ten or fifteen seconds.

Coach Steve told Matt: "Nobody's tougher than Matt Byrne. You can do it."

I heard the plan that Sunday morning as we drove to the meet in the Bronx. It was certainly a big ask by the coach, but I kept my skepticism to myself. When the time for the 500 free came, most people left the pool area. (When asked why he swam the 1000 free, one famous distance swimmer reportedly said, "It sure beats watching it!")

I was never any good at splits and all that swimming stuff, but as the race progressed, I could tell that Matt had a steady pace and seemed to be having no trouble maintaining it. He made the time Coach Steve had been looking for, finished second, and Chaminade won the meet.

*

In May 1996, days after he had turned 16, Matt told me he wanted to try out for the Jones Beach Lifeguards that coming Sunday. He wasn't old enough to drive yet, so I agreed to take him to the test, which had a pool part, a run on the beach, and a final ocean swim.

On a gray, cold morning, I dropped him off outside the East Bathhouse pool, parked the car, then returned to watch the try-outs from as inconspicuous a place as possible.

Initially, it certainly didn't look like it was going to be Matt's day. For the most part, the candidates looked like big strapping men, while Matt was still a skinny kid. But size didn't matter. To my surprise, Matt wound up as one of the top finishers in each of the events and got the coveted lifeguarding job for that summer and years to come, beginning with a soft assignment at the calm waters of Zachs Bay, then progressing to more crowded and dangerous beaches until he finally served at Field Four, Jones Beach's Central Mall, where buses dropped off loads of weak swimmers and the action was nonstop.

*

The late 1980s and early 1990s were lean times for the Yanks, and Matt grew up confusing the current crop of players he unduly admired with former Yankee greats. For example, his particular favorite, Jesse Barfeld, had a great outfield arm but, with a .256 lifetime batting average, Jesse was no Reggie Jackson.

Things got much better in the 1995 season, however, when the Yankees won the wild card spot and entered the playoffs. They won the first two games, then lost the next two games to the Mariners. As we sat in our basement watching the final game broadcast from the Kingdome, Matt set me up early in the game using Paul as his witness. This was not an infrequent tactic, although there were variations in the roles played. Matthew was the behind-the-scene mastermind, determining which Byrne child should pose the question to maximize chances of Dad agreeing to something one or more wanted. This time he decided to take the lead himself.

"Dad, if the Yankees get into the World Series, will you get us tickets?"

"Sure," I responded, without giving it much thought. "I'd stand on line to get us tickets, if I had to."

My sons had never had the World Series experience. After a gut-wrenching loss to the Mariners that night, they would have to wait at least another year.

Matt was never one to forget a promise, once he had wangled it out of you. On the Sunday night of Columbus Day weekend, October 13, 1996, the Yankees were playing the wild card Orioles in Baltimore in the fifth game of the American League Championship Series. Matt approached me before the game started.

"Hey, Dad," he opened, "do you remember promising to get us World Series tickets last year if the Yankees got in?"

I played it coy. "I have some faint recollection of that."

"Same deal this year?" he ventured.

"I guess that sounds fair."

Shortly thereafter, Mike, my friend with whom I was coaching Paul's Fall baseball team called. We had become friendly despite playing on opposing teams in Rockville Centre's Over 40 basketball league. I always had to guard Mike, who was built like a comic book superhero, because everyone else refused. I had never minded defending someone much stronger than me, so long as he wasn't faster too. Mike wasn't, but I came home bruised every time.

"What are you guys up to, watching the game?" Mike asked. He was a former FDNY firefighter who had become a fire marshal.

"Actually, Mike, I was thinking about skipping the game and heading to the Stadium to get on line. Series tickets go on sale tomorrow, if the Yanks win tonight, and I'm pretty sure they will."

"That's a great idea," Mike responded. "I'll drive. We can stop at Fort Totten and get my FDNY vest and my gun. We'll be all set."

"You're my dream date for a night in the South Bronx, Mike," I replied. "See you in a bit."

The line of prospective ticket buyers was already wrapping

around the stadium when we arrived in the twilight. We queued up and began the wait before realizing we had goofed. First off, we had neglected to invite the third coach on our kids' team. Worse yet, I learned that there was a four ticket limit per person on the number of tickets you could buy and that would leave me short of both money and a second buyer if I wanted my father and the rest of the family to have a ticket and come to the game.

I called Patti on my clunky cell phone and asked her to scrounge up enough cash for another four tickets. Since Matthew had swim practice the next morning, Columbus Day, a school holiday, I told her to dress 11-year-old Paul warmly, stuff the money in his sock, and I'd have the other coach pick him up and meet us at the line, which they did.

That night was like a Fellini film. A very mixed bag of Yankee fans surrounded the four of us – three straight old guys and a kid – on the ever longer line snaking around the stadium. You needed to bond with your neighbors, however, so they would hold your place on line when, inevitably during the long wait, you needed to get off to use the rest room at one of the nearby all-night joints. So, we became friendly with some of our young line neighbors, most of whom had done plenty of drinking before arriving. I gave most of them nicknames: Thurman, the clean-cut Fordham undergrad wearing a Number 15 Yankee away jersey; Boyfriend and Girlfriend, who spent most of the night either bickering or falling asleep; Barabbas, a born rabble rouser with a stud recently implanted in his nose, the oozing pus from which suggested a significant infection from the body piercing parlor's dirty tools.

At some point, while the game in Baltimore was still under-way, I walked with Paul up 161st Street to fetch pizzas for our new and old friends. The bonding dynamic was complete once we shared them. When we finally heard over the radio that the Yanks had defeated the Orioles, everyone relaxed, secure in the knowledge that we had not wasted the night lining up prematurely.

Sometime after midnight, the Yankee team bus pulled up right in front of our place in line, shuttling the players and coaching staff from the airport to the stadium parking lot after the short charter flight from Baltimore. The crowd went wild as the victors came down the bus steps, and Wade Boggs, who had apparently partied his way back to New York, just kept going right into the throng where he chest bumped young Paul, who beamed in delight. The next day's Newsday showed three adults surrounding Wade, but you couldn't see Paul, still so short he was hidden in the midst of us. Come Tuesday, when he returned to school, Paul's classmates had to take his word for where he had been.

By daybreak, the adventure of the night was over, and it was still hours before the ticket booths would be open. Everyone on line was getting tired and cranky, particularly those who were hung over. At some point, Girlfriend and Boyfriend got into their biggest shouting match yet. When a young NYPD patrolman told them to knock it off and they didn't, he called in his superior, a tough old Irish sergeant, who told the young cop to take them off the line.

This really set Girlfriend off, who redirected her cursing and yelling from Boyfriend to the cops, who soon took them both to a paddy wagon they had kept at the ready on the plaza. Our band of fans was dismayed: the cops had the handcuffs out and, after waiting on line so long, these two idiots weren't going to get tickets.

I told my friends I would be right back and climbed over the blue police barricade that separated us from our captured comrades. I walked very slowly up to the sergeant.

"Excuse me, Sergeant," I said, as respectfully as I could. "Can we talk for a minute?"

"What's up?" he responded curtly.

"We just spent all night with those two knuckleheads. They're not bad kids."

"It doesn't look that way to me."

"Tell you what, Sergeant. I'm a lawyer. Why don't you release them to my custody? If they behave, you won't have to bother processing them. If they start acting up again, you can run them in later. How about giving them another chance? We've all been on this line forever."

"All right," he finally said, eyeballing me suspiciously. "But remember, it's on you to keep them in line."

"For sure, Sergeant. Thanks for giving them a break."

The handcuffs went away. I took Boyfriend by one hand, Girlfriend by the other and led them back to the barricade where their friends helped them under and back in line. Boyfriend had been chastised and was almost silent. Girlfriend needed to be reminded several times whose custody she was in, but she, too, made it the rest of the wait without incident.

When the ticket booths finally opened in the morning, the line started creeping forward ever so slowly as we wound our way clockwise from home plate toward right field. It was a beautiful October day, but the temperature was more like September as the sun rose high in the sky, causing the sweaty, dirty and unshaven fans to start shedding the layers of clothes that had been welcome the night before.

It may have been after 1:30 p.m. when we finally were close to the ticket booths. Word had filtered back: Game One had been sold out, and there were only nosebleed seats left for Game Two.

My friends accosted me. "This was your bright idea, Ed. What are you going to do?"   I didn't hesitate in answering. "You can do what you want. I'm betting the ranch on Game Six." Paul and I approached one window, while our companions went to separate ones.

About twenty-two hours after leaving Rockville Centre, we all had Game Six tickets in hand for seats near the area now called the Judge's Chambers. I took lots of ribbing when the Yankees were crushed by the mighty Braves in the first two games at home. My weak retort was that the Yanks had to lose two for my master plan to work. Starting with Game Three in Atlanta, the series slowly began to turn, and when backup catcher Jim Leyritz, the self-proclaimed "King," led the Game 4 comeback with a pinch-hit homerun, I was certain that the Yankees, underdogs for the first time in my life, would pull the upset off.

Saturday night, October 26, 1996, the entire Byrne family sat in fair territory in the lower right field stands, watching Joe Girardi have the finest game of his playing career, leading the Yanks to a 3-2 win and their first World Championship in 18 seasons.

Our ticket line buddy Thurman had shown up in a full Yankee Number 15 home uniform, including shin guards, chest protector, and catcher's mitt and mask. He was delighted to see his companions from the long night once again. There was no sign of Boyfriend, Girlfriend or Barabbas, but their place was taken by Trumpet Man. Seated a few rows away and dressed in a suit and tie, this guy played beautifully, entertaining the crowd between innings and leading them to cry "Charge!" whenever the Yankees came to bat.

My boys couldn't have had a better night, and both thanked me profusely. Matt's master plan had actually worked to perfection, with all of us witnessing the final game of the World Series, the only one that really matters. As we left the Stadium, my friend Mike said, "That was great. What are we going to bet on next time?"

I responded prophetically: "Don't you understand? We've used up all our good luck for the next 10-20 years with that one."

*

At some point late in Matt's junior year, Elizabeth informed me that he was a "player." After I determined what that meant through outside sources, I figured I better have the talk with him I had postponed so long. In my defense, I don't honestly recall my father ever having much of a talk with me, so avoiding the topic of sex seemed to be a longstanding Byrne family tradition.

I figured a neutral site would be best for this uncomfortable discussion, so I suggested we have breakfast Saturday morning at a local diner.

When, after some preliminary dodging, I finally broached the subject, Matt straightened out of his customary slouch over the table when eating. As his back stiffened, Matt looked at me coolly and assured me, "I know all about that stuff." Within a few minutes, he proved to my satisfaction that he most certainly did. Afraid my lack of comparable expertise might be exposed, I quickly withdrew from the engagement.

*

As I mentioned, the younger lifeguards received the less demanding assignments at Jones Beach. Following his junior year of high school, I believe Matt started the summer at Zachs Bay, but moved on to Field 2, an ocean beach, where he worked under the tutelage of Reggie Jones, the legendary "World's Oldest Lifeguard" who was a regular guest on television talk shows.

Wherever he was, Matt had his first really bad day that summer. The word went out to all the beaches one afternoon that a teenager was missing at Zachs Bay. By the time Matt got there, from the way he later described it, the mission had turned from rescue to recovery.

A line of lifeguards locked arms at one end of the bay, advancing in unison to drag it for the body. As Matt would later describe his feelings, he was terrified that he would be the one to bump into the boy, who was his contemporary, a Mexican native visiting relatives in Corona.

Matt wasn't the lifeguard who found him, but he was there when the kid's lifeless body was pulled out of the calm bay's waters. Matt wasn't at all prepared for the experience. He had lost his beloved Grandpa Murtagh when he was almost fourteen, but Frank had been sick with cancer for a while and had been cremated in Florida. Since there was no wake, Frank's death seemed so remote as to be almost unreal. The drowning at Jones Beach was Matt's first frontal encounter with Death, which would eventually come to follow him around, as his letter from Marworth reminded us.

*

In the fall of 1997, Matt's senior year at Chaminade, all the college applications and requests for recommendations had to be filed quite early. (While the rest of the school labored through three trimesters, the seniors were scaled back to two semesters, then shown the exit door in early May.) One of his friends floated the notion that, since the "senior slump" had begun, their friends should have the "Great CYO Basketball Reunion Tour" for one last season, assembling all the kids who had played together throughout grammar school but had moved on to other sports in high school.

I don't know if I were consulted before being volunteered by Matt. He would have been certain that I would agree. I had been one of the old grammar school coaches, and was a likely candidate to coach once more, because the unorthodox tactics I had used when his friends were boys were even more suitable now that they were young men who wouldn't tolerate having their time wasted.

Even when they were sixth, seventh and eighth graders, I had tried to treat my players as individuals. I was definitely in charge but gave them the option of respectfully recording their dissent. When I gave an order, there were two permissible responses: "Yes, Mr. Byrne," which meant the kid heard what I said, agreed with it, and would do it, or "I hear you, Mr. Byrne," which signified that the player heard what I was telling him to do, disagreed, but would proceed to do it anyway.

I had always figured that if a kid didn't get to play at least a full quarter of a basketball game, he was probably better off doing something else. So, I would devise what I referred to as shifts, like in hockey, only comprised of five players. My view was that some kids played better with certain kids than with others, so that if, as coach, you could figure out the right five to put on the floor together you would get additional "juice." Taking it one step further, I would play two shifts a quarter, and ask the players to give me everything they had for what would be half of a quarter, just four minutes. At that halfway point when everyone was starting to get winded, via clock stoppage for a foul or out of bounds play or by using a timeout, however reluctantly, I would substitute an entire new shift with fresh legs.

Ideally, at the end of three quarters, all my players had played a full quarter. The fourth quarter was then reserved for me. It was the coach's prerogative as to where the playing time went down the stretch, and I would typically allot it based on who had the hot hand or was shutting down the other team's best offensive player that day.

The kids I had play for me all liked the system, which basically had our team trading baskets and trying to keep the score close for the first three quarters. Maybe if my own kid had been a "star," I wouldn't have been inclined to use a format under which the better players had to share some of the additional playing time they would have gotten under a strictly on-the-merits approach. Kids have a very strong sense of fairness, however, and the enthusiasm of getting everyone involved before the pull-out-all-the-stops fourth quarter apparently more than compensated for the slight deprivation of playing time the stars suffered. Moreover, I'll insist to my dying day that the way we distributed the playing time never caused us to lose to another team that we should have beaten.

Now this Senior Blue team was a ragtag bunch, by St. Agnes CYO standards, and the disparities in talent were stark. But I stuck to my system on the theory that a high school senior could have a job, a girlfriend or, God forbid, spend more time studying rather than come to a basketball game where he wouldn't get off the bench. There were only a few practices, and my only demand was that you respect the game and play as hard and as well as you could when you got your chance. The guys enjoyed each other's company, and for the most part complied, but two particular games stand out. (I still have the scorebook, so I'm not making this up.)

On Sunday, January 4, 1998, we played St. William the Abbott at their gym, and they beat St. Agnes by 55 points. Now, having renounced my childhood competitiveness, I'm not a "winning is everything" guy by any means, but losing by 55 points in a 32-minute game is nearly impossible to do. My guys did it, however, and I never saw such a humiliating defeat in any basketball game at any level. To make matters worse, I must have been so upset that I walked out of the gym after this debacle without my mesh net bag of basketballs, maybe hoping never to see them again. When I returned for the balls a short time later, I was told that no one knew where they went. I didn't believe that for a minute, but the game was lost, the balls were gone, and that was that.

I continued to stew for over a month until our rematch with St. William's, scheduled for St. Valentine's Day, on a Saturday night. I was probably working on the perfect shifts to avenge our still stinging loss when the phone calls started rolling in, with only minor variations.

Player: "Mr. Byrne, I can't make it tonight. My girlfriend expects me to take her out."

Me: "It's Saturday night. Take her out later. Let her come watch you play at 7 p.m."

Player: "That's not going to work for her, Mr. Byrne."

And so it went. Counting heads, I was only going to have six players to face the St. William's buzzsaw, and they weren't exactly the six you would pick. But, like life, you never know what's going to happen in basketball. Brant, a little skinny eleven-year-old with quiet spunk when I first met him, had turned into an excellent athlete, especially in lacrosse. He had a monster game against the hated St. William's guys, controlling the offensive and defensive boards and scoring 25. Ricky, a junior who was quick to give me "The Look" and "I hear you, Mr. Byrne" before doing what he was told, poured in 11 jumpers from the outside for another 22. Allie, an incredibly funny kid who had played for me for years, battling diabetes throughout, dropped in another seven. Chris, a kid from a different town who was not well treated by some of the missing players, played a solid game on defense, spelling other guys as necessary. (There was plenty of playing time to go around this night.) Sean, another junior who balked at his assignment of bringing up the ball, never got pressed all game and did just fine. And my own Matt rumbled with the big guys under the basket all night, grabbing a bunch of rebounds and managing two putbacks on the offensive end.

We beat St. William's by 15 in the "St. Valentine's Night Massacre." I confess it was a very satisfying win. Every Valentine's Day, Brant's performance is still fondly recalled in the Byrne household, much like a rare Irish victory on the battlefield. When the other guys apologized for missing the game the next time I saw them, I just said: "That's okay. I hope you had a good time with your girlfriend. We didn't really need you."

I have one more comment on that last season of coaching my son.

My own father had coached my baseball teams when I was a kid, and he was perhaps obsessively impartial. When I was a short seventh grader who couldn't reach second base when throwing from behind the plate, he traded his catcher for post-pubescent eighth grader Wayne Donahue, who was a foot taller and had five o'clock shadow. Even I acknowledged that the old man had made a good deal.

I never would have traded Matt, but neither would I give him any special consideration as my kid, as the foregoing narrative demonstrates. We had some discussions about this family tradition over the years, and I hope I convinced him that, although I treated him just like any other player, he was indeed my favorite, because of his hustle, and always the one I loved the most.

*

I was still working in Garden City when Matt was a senior at Chaminade. They had another successful swim season underway when I walked into a local deli for coffee one weekday morning and ran into a freshman swimmer's father.

"That was really nice of Matt to invite my son to the party he's throwing Saturday," he said.

"Yeah," I responded. "Very nice. Would've been nice for him to tell me about the party, too!"

The poor fellow looked totally abashed from letting the cat out of the bag. I reassured him: no big deal, I'll take care of it, but don't plan on dropping your son off.

That evening at dinner, as soon as I led with "The funniest thing happened today ….," Matt knew that he was busted; somehow, I had found out about the party he was planning while Patti and I were out. I reminded him of Rule Number One ("Never have the party at your house"), which I had often seen violated with terrible results as a kid growing up in Queens. I figured that was the end of the scheme.

Unfortunately, the party plan was not retired, only postponed. I had not realized that our kids actually took notice of Patti's and my schedule, and that they knew we attended a black-tie business event on the first Saturday of every March.

When we got home from the 1998 affair, an amazing sight greeted us. "Aunt" Zelda, the widow who lived next door, apparently had developed a tremendous thirst that night, because her front lawn was littered with beer cans. Our own lawn was spotless; God forbid that these bird brains would clean up more than the host's lawn!

Punishment must be swift and certain—and it was. But I certainly took note of Matt's obstinate determination to break Rule Number One, despite my warnings of the potentially dire consequences, like befell the guy I knew in Queens Village, who actually called the cops on himself when so many drunken kids had showed up at his house it looked like a riot would break out and destroy whatever in the house had not already been trashed. I just filed that information away.

*

Chaminade's prom night came in the late spring, and it was a big deal, as usual for those days. Matt's class slipped under the wire; a few years later, Chaminade and most other Long Island high schools got very hands on with respect to controlling pre- and post-prom activities.

Matt had invited a girl from Wantagh whose prom he had attended. I remember all the boys and their dates gathering on our patio so their parents could take pictures of them in their tuxes and gowns before they piled into limousines, the drivers of which would cheat them before the night was over in another rite of passage.

There had been much arguing about where the boys were going after the prom, who, if anyone, was supervising, and when and how they were eventually getting home.

I'm sure I should have been more adamant in getting proper answers to all these questions, but I honestly don't think I was, and I let things slide after confirming that there had been no violations of Rule Number Two: Never be the one who signs the lease agreement, even for a weekend.

All I remember is the boys showing up late Sunday afternoon, looking sunburnt and wearing nothing but lacrosse shorts. They were a great group of guys, primed to set the world on fire when they arrived at college in the fall.

"What happened to the girls?" I asked Matt.

"Oh, they've been gone for days," he replied. "It's all about the camaraderie."

"I hope you really like camaraderie," I responded. "At this rate, you're going to have plenty of it."

*

Within months of the Chaminade prom, Matt proved to me that he actually took this camaraderie concept seriously. He approached me one Saturday when I was walking down the driveway. "I need to talk to you about something, Dad," he said.

I listened as he repeated the sad story of his classmate, John, whose father had dropped dead on a treadmill when John was a junior at Chaminade. Shortly thereafter, to compound the trage-dy, John's mother's breast cancer was discovered, and she soon died.

According to Matthew, John's uncle had agreed to take John's two younger siblings in to live with his family, but he had no room for John or the old yellow Lab, Domer. The family house had been sold, so John and Domer had no place to live. "Can they come live in the apartment?" Matt asked. "You should really do this, Dad," he added. "He'll remind you of me when I'm away at college."

"Just what I needed," I responded. "I thought we were going to get a break." I paused, then told him I would speak to his mother.

Patti was sympathetic, and willing to accept the new boarders if they observed her three conditions: no shacking up by John with his girlfriend, since she didn't want to have that situation to discuss with our younger children; no parties; and no smoking in the apartment, because she knew John smoked and feared him falling asleep and burning the place down.

When I met with John to let him know he and Domer could move in, I added one condition of my own: he would not have to pay a dime, but he was expected to take Matt's place on the Byrne snow removal team in the wintertime, when cleanup could be a huge project.

Like all agreements made with eighteen year olds, this one was honored in the breach. John's girlfriend was up in the apart-ment with him all the time. Several parties caught the attention of the neighbors. And John continued to smoke constantly, both in and outside his quarters.

I recall doing plenty of yelling over these issues during John and Domer's stay. The dog I actually felt sorry for, because it became scared of coming down from the apartment to use the far backyard. Josephine was a particularly inhospitable hostess. If she caught the aging male outside, the female mastiff would immediately mount Domer and start humping him, causing the poor dog visible shame.

The first year John stayed with us was remarkably snow free, and there were no issues on the shoveling score. Early in the second winter, however, a blizzard hit, and Paul and I were outside struggling to clear the driveway.

More than an hour went by. I knew John was up in the apartment, but he hadn't made an appearance, despite the sound of the snow blower and shovels. As I grew increasingly irritated, I finally stomped up the interior staircase of the garage that led to the apartment and began banging on the door.

"Where the hell are you, John? Did you by chance not notice the foot of snow?"

John came to the door looking cozy in flannel pajamas. "Paul told me last night you wouldn't need me."

Paul was perhaps fourteen at the time. "Who put Paul in charge?" I bellowed. "Get your ass out there and help."

John always maintained a safe distance from me thereafter. He was very conscientious, however, regarding his snow removal duties, and was outside with a shovel or broom as soon as the first flakes fell.

One day I came home from work and learned that John and Domer were gone. "What happened?" I asked Patti.

"I told him a week ago that it was the last time I would tell him to stop smoking in the apartment," Patti explained. "He didn't, so I told him to take the dog and get out."

I just raised my eyebrows, then shook my head. I would have kept yelling at John forever, but I don't think I ever would have thrown him out. John didn't realize who he really had to watch out for.

For days, I kept getting an image of John and Domer being evicted and walking sadly up the driveway for breaking the no-smoking rule. It faded away, as I realized that Patti had been fully justified in giving them the boot for ignoring her reasonable rules. John eventually figured it out and is doing well today. We had a pleasant conversation following Matt's memorial service, and he no longer seems frightened of me, thank God.

XV.

I have not said much about The Nephew. That's not an accident, but an intentional omission. Effectively, for reasons best if not only known by him, he ultimately resigned from our family, so I don't have his blessing for inclusion in the story, which he has no idea has been written. History has its demands, however, and he was part of the story, like it or not, so here we go.

You might think it cruel to refer to someone by his status, The Nephew, instead of his name, and we never did so. He had a name, a formal one his mother preferred to its standard nickname, and we used the version she chose faithfully for the eight years The Nephew lived with us.

As I explained, The Father had killed his son's mother, Patti's goddaughter, while driving drunk. Her wake and funeral had to be comparable to those the Montagues and Capulets must have held: palpable tension and ill-concealed hatred for, in this case, the sole person responsible.

Poorly advised by not one but two bottom-feeder lawyers, The Nephew's father rejected a one-year plea deal and stood trial in Supreme Court, Queens County. Despite head scratching evidentiary rulings in his favor, e.g., erroneously excluding off-the-charts blood alcohol evidence, he was summarily convicted.

The Father handed The Nephew off to a friend when remanded into custody in the courtroom as soon as the jury rendered its verdict, weeks before he was sentenced to 4-12 years on the manslaughter charges.

The Father's Friend was a good guy, although obviously not choosy when it came to companions, who took the child in to live with his wife and two daughters in Nassau County. Caught flatfooted at the end of the trial, it took a while for the maternal relatives to get organized, but a custody battle eventually ensued, initiated by the dead mother's uncle, who was soon pushed aside by her brother, The Real Uncle, a fisherman from Hawaii with several chips on his shoulder.

I was recruited by the family to help The Real Uncle gain custody of The Nephew. Despite an intriguing due process argument I found in a law journal that was based on superior rights of natural family members, it was extremely unlikely that a New York court would grant custody to a man with unpredictable income and no health insurance who would move the kid halfway around the world from where his parent was incarcerated. When The Father's Friend proposed a possible settlement, I told The Real Uncle that he ought to listen.

I did not know that the settlement would entail adding The Nephew to the Byrne family. Patti and I had discussed that possibility, as recently as the weekend before when we were visiting Ann at her college's parents' weekend. With one grandchild already, another on the way, and a multitude of health issues that Patti was already contending with, we decided it just made no sense to backtrack and raise a thirteen-year-old after having done that for four kids of our own.

That discussion made no difference the following day, Monday, October 22, 2007, as I stood in the Family Court and The Nephew's guardian <u>ad</u> <u>litem</u> asked me straight up whether we would take him to resolve the custody dispute. I had a very strange reaction. I don't know whether it was hearing the call, as Catholics would say, or knowing I would be exposed to my own kids as a total phony if I turned the man down, or some combination of the two. It seems we were nobody's first choice, but everyone's second. I looked at the lawyer and told him I needed to make a call before responding.

To her credit, Patti didn't hold me to my promise not to get further involved. I returned and told the guardian yes, we would take the boy home, with Patti and I nominally sharing joint custody with The Real Uncle in Hawaii. By Thanksgiving 2007, The Nephew was in residence.

I would be lying if I pretended this did not necessitate a major adjustment for all concerned. The Nephew was a virtual stranger. As her marriage deteriorated, his mother had withdrawn from family functions, and we simply had not seen her or her son for years. Not surprisingly, he resented being sent by the court to another new neighborhood, to live with people he did not know and leave the Father's Friend's household to attend another new school.

As an only child, over whom his warring parents vied for affection, The Nephew was well used to having his own way. Suddenly he had four siblings, all of whom outranked him on the family totem pole. They all recognized the importance of being welcoming, and they were, but they were also acutely aware of a clash of values and habits with this young newcomer. They refused to let him get away with much, if anything.

This was especially true in the case of Matthew. I previously

described his relationship with The Nephew as somewhat volatile. While there was more than a little hero-worship of his older
cousin by The Nephew, it bought him no slack or relief from
Matthew's rigid expectations. Maybe it was the firehouse training, but instances of laziness, sloppiness, and deceit simply were
not tolerated by my older son.

Given the nature of thirteen year old boys, who are rarely
model family members, Matt's demands inevitably led to clashes.
One recurring one involved dog-walking.

Upon arriving home, Matt would typically ask The Nephew,
"Did you walk the dog?" The answer was always, "She just went
out." Matt would then ignore The Nephew's stock answer and
take Portia out himself. On one occasion, when he returned with
a huge plastic bag of dog poop he had collected from the animal
on its walk, Matt threw it at The Nephew, who was skateboarding
in the driveway, yelling, "Don't you ever lie to me again!"

At the same time, however, Matt sympathized with The
Nephew's struggles and showed genuine fondness for him. He
went out of his way to spend time with him, despite The Nephew's difficult nature and the fact that their interests rarely
aligned. For instance, the beach was strictly off-limits as far as
The Nephew was concerned, but bowling was something Matthew could get him to do so he took him regularly.

As a traumatized child, at least by his mother's death and
quite possibly by more, The Nephew's view of the world was way
darker than anything we had ever experienced. He arrived with
skull decals sewn to his jeans. There was very little humor or
laughter, much less joy. His kneejerk response to everything was

"No" or "I don't want to do that," and family life became a constant struggle to get him to change his mind and give something new a try. This was particularly hard for Patti, who rightly felt betrayed by me, the guy who had broken his promise. She continued to question how this situation had come to pass, since much closer, in degree of relation, and healthier relatives who had been quite vocal during the custody battle quickly faded out of the picture, leaving her to house, feed, and contend with a surly teenager on a daily basis.

My own deal with The Nephew had been a very simple one. I remember picking him up from The Father's Friend's house in Inwood. His dark hair hadn't been washed in some time, and his fingernails were quite long. He stared at me, mistrustfully, when I had made the double-edged promise to treat him just like one of my own children. Unlike my commitment to Patti that we would not take him, I believe my promise to The Nephew was one I fulfilled, even when he did not like it.

To avoid undercutting The Father's role, we agreed he would be my nephew, as far as the rest of the world was concerned, although I was to act toward him just like a parent would in all other ways. I made him do things he didn't want to do, like get on the phone that first Thanksgiving with his estranged grandmother, who understandably had sought to maximize her son-in-law's prison sentence. The Nephew and his grandma later became great friends once again. I similarly made him visit his mother's gravesite occasionally. I don't apologize for any efforts to make him act like a normal, caring person would, even when he objected.

The reason I'm setting this forth is to provide a missing point of the story. For eight years, while my world went from nearly perfect to almost destroyed, I always had some semblance of normalcy because I was responsible for raising The Nephew.

There simply wasn't all that much time to obsess over the problems that beset my "real" family, as The Nephew would call it, as opposed to his "real" family. I got him up every morning, made his lunch, went over his homework each night, at least for his final year of grade school, a practice I assured him would cease once he reached high school. I convinced him, with great effort, to initially attend St. Agnes, where Sr. Kathy and Miss Helen somehow made room for him in the middle of the school year, then go to Chaminade, where he played drums in the Pep Band, studied Latin, and fared well academically if not socially. I chauffeured him around to SAT prep courses, driver's education classes, away football and basketball games, and Communion breakfasts, but most notably, at least once a month in accordance with a court order issued to me, but not my co-guardians, I drove him to visit The Father.

Initially, The Father was sent to Malone, spitting distance from the Canadian border in northeastern New York. Since there was no real airport nearby, you had to go by car, a 7-8-hour ride under the best of conditions, and God knows how long in the winter's sleet, snow, and ice storms. Depending on the weekend, you could either visit on Saturday or Sunday, and I could never decide which was worse. If the visit were Saturday, you had to drive to Malone on Friday night, stay in a cheap motel, sit at the card table most of the following day, then drive back in the dark

Saturday night. If the visit were on Sunday, you could at least drive up in the daylight on Saturday, and only face "white line fever" on Sunday night after a day at the card table. Either way you were burnt come Monday morning.

I have forgotten most of the details of those dreaded drives upstate, but a few stick with me. They would be preceded by trips to different stores to gather various items The Father told The Nephew he either needed or wanted. It was very important to The Nephew that every item on the list be procured and transported north, but it was far from certain that they would all be admitted to the facility. That seemed to depend on which guard in the entrance trailer was checking the "care packages." Individually, the guards could be decent, if approached with respect. If more than one guard were present, however, all compassion went out the window, and a contest to see who could be the bigger bad ass began. I sometimes couldn't believe I was speaking to the same person I had dealt with just a short time before.

After a few years of that grueling drill, as The Father inched toward release, he was transferred to Gowanda Correctional Facility, outside of Buffalo. At that point, I drew the line on driving. Thereafter, until The Nephew stopped talking to or visiting The Father after he turned eighteen and awoke to the fact that the man had been lying to him all along about "The Accident" and the true circumstances of his mother's death, we flew to Buffalo, made the visit, and came back on the same day. Jet Blue and a rental car cost more money, and we encountered plenty of airport delays, but it was a far more civilized way to go.

In hindsight, particularly in view of the unhappy ending of

The Nephew's stay with the Byrnes, I have questioned what that whole exercise was about. Did it do anyone any good, other than keeping me distracted and focused on someone else's wellbeing while my own son was falling apart? Would it have made a difference if I had spent all that travel time with Matthew instead, assuming Matt would have let me? I'll never know and will have to settle for believing that, like plenty of things I did in my youth that didn't turn out well, it seemed like a good idea at the time.

*

When your kid goes away to rehab, you can't help but remember taking him to the doctor's office as a child, or perhaps to a hospital, if something more serious prompted that trip. Most times, thankfully, the medical professionals are able to fix what was wrong and send the child back to his normal activities.

You hope it's going to be the same with rehab, but we're all informed enough to know that the fix is not nearly as certain. Therefore, you walk on eggshells and hold your breath much of the time, hoping that your kid is the rare one who gets it right the first time, and spares himself and his family all the additional heartache that will inevitably follow if he doesn't.

That's where we were in the beginning of 2012, hoping it wouldn't but waiting for the next thing to go wrong in Matt's world. We weren't far into the new year before it did. On January 18, 2012, Matt went back to FDNY's Counseling Services Unit ("CSU") and asked for help. He had relapsed and had an unspecified "incident" at his firehouse over the weekend.

Matt resumed weekly sessions with CSU after admitting he had not followed the treatment protocol. For instance, he had been lax in attending AA meetings and had never found a permanent sponsor, despite being told that this was the level of commitment required to make the program work. The CSU counselor got him to resume attending alumni group sessions, as well as weekly one on one sessions.

We tried to be more encouraged by his self-reporting than disappointed by the relapse. Matt was back at work, and apparently trying to comply with CSU's directives, but we couldn't stop listening for the other shoe to drop. The feeling falls short of dread, or even anxiety, yet uneasiness doesn't do it justice.

Even under such circumstances, gloom is never constant, at least it wasn't for us. In late January, Elizabeth and Manny threw a 6th birthday party for their son, Manuel at F.A.O. Schwartz. I laughed and joined in the fun when the employee dressed like a giant toy soldier escorted the kid and his friends through the crowded store, announcing in a booming voice, "Make way for Manuel, the Birthday Boy!" We also took hope from our discharge from a program at the Oceanside Counseling Center for parents of recovering children. As I mentioned, we had used the weekly Wednesday sessions to launch "date nights," but we were happy to forego them if it meant we were coming out of the woods together with our son. In late March 2012, Patti and I even got to attend my trade association client's convention in St. Thomas for a few days. In April, I returned to Little League as the "Safety Czar" of the Challengers, a new division formed to accommodate disabled players. Catherine's christening took place on May 5, and we threw a birthday party for Matthew on May 20. Maybe things were beginning to look up.

June 3, 2012 was a particularly good day. The Nephew graduated from Chaminade in an all-day affair; Mass in the morning at C.W. Post's Tilles Center followed by the actual ceremony in the afternoon at the same venue. Members of his "real" family joined the Byrnes for a restaurant dinner thereafter. Dressed in a white dinner jacket with black slacks, like the rest of his classmates, The Nephew looked like nothing would stop him when he matriculated at an elite Eastern college in the fall. We were all quite proud of him.

Whatever limited optimism was emerging turned out to be misplaced. Within days of The Nephew's graduation, Matthew reported to CSU that he had relapsed again, and he was back off to rehab, this time to a facility called Mirmont, again in Pennsylvania but in the Philadelphia area.

On Saturday, June 23, 2012, Patti, Elizabeth, Manny and I attended the wedding of Kathy and Big Jim's second oldest daughter, Tara. Matthew had always been close to Tara, and he was supposed to be in attendance too. It was a grand affair in Manhattan, concluding with a throng on stage with the band singing *Pretty Woman* and *My Girl* to the bride. Matthew would have been right there with the rest of us and would have loved it all, but I was glad he was absent. His stay at Mirmont was one of the first times I welcomed Matt's being away at rehab. It gave us a strange sense of relief because, even if things would not get any better, they also were not going to get any worse while he was in treatment.

Patti and I were able to visit Matt at Mirmont on Sunday afternoon, July 1. The trip was much shorter than to Marworth, and family visitations were much less instructional and more an opportunity to simply spend some time with the patient. We did meet Matt's counselor, with the understanding that this visit would be supplemented by periodic conference calls with the counselor and Matt during the balance of the stay.

I can't recall if the disclosure were made face to face or during one of the calls. Somehow the professionals at Mirmont finally got him to confess the full extent of his substance problem, after he became so sick upon his arrival that he had to be transported by ambulance to the local hospital to complete the detox process. Matt admitted to us, at last, that he wasn't just a drinker; he was a drug abuser as well. Unpleasant as that revelation was, it had to be made to avoid repeating his charade at Marworth where he had only acknowledged half of his problem.

On July 9, 2012, Matt was discharged from Mirmont and transported home. The responsibility for getting the patient to and from the rehab facility never fell on the family. FDNY took care of all the arrangements. He resumed sessions as assigned at CSU's Lafayette Street headquarters.

There was trouble almost immediately. A note from one CSU counselor to another dated July 13, 2012 states:

Matt's father called yesterday afternoon, 7/12/2012, stating 'extreme difficulty getting son out of bed', and it was 'not from sleep deprivation'. He states there is evidence his son is still using. He says he does not want to be a snitch, but

will do anything to get his son help. I explained confidenti-
ality to him and that I was not at liberty to converse, but if
he has something to say I will listen."

At a July 20, 2012 counseling session, which took place despite his reporting for duty hours late, Matt reported several
traumatic incidents on the job that he could not get over. One
was the Deutsche Bank fire that I previously mentioned. Another
likely one he had uncharacteristically shared with us was his
team's recovery during the summertime of the badly decom-
posed body of someone who days before had jumped or fallen off
the Manhattan Bridge. The worst one, we subsequently learned,
involved a traffic accident in Chinatown. Two young children
had been hit by a truck and died in Matt's arms. He was subsequently ordered to clean their splatter off the sidewalk and had
come close to refusing.

Matt had also reported two other traumatic incidents from
his youth. The Jones Beach drowning on which he was part of the
recovery team was something from the past we knew. The other
came as a stunning revelation when we finally learned of it.
When he was fourteen years old, Matt had tried to slit his wrists
after his baseball team's season ended with a loss he felt responsible for. I was out of town, and another father had driven Matt
home, berating him and his own son for their poor play. It
couldn't have been too close a suicide attempt, but the fact that
no one ever knew this happened – or how seriously he could take
a ballgame – remains disconcerting and a huge parenting default.

Matt had told the counselor that he hoped these memories

would disappear over time and that he wished he could just "wash his brain." He was to be referred for PTSD counseling and a psychiatric evaluation. Two days later, however, Matt went AWOL, and the fire marshals were dispatched after him. On July 23, he admitted another relapse but insisted he wanted to get back into recovery. Matt was warned that if he relapsed again, he would be sent away once more.

Patti and I returned to CSU on Family Day, July 26, 2012. We didn't know it, but we were pinch hitters. GF had originally been signed up to attend when Matt returned home, but apparently, they broke up again within the week. No one remembers whether that was the time it was for good.

We were now "regulars" at CSU, and practically becoming leaders in the group discussions, proving how, regardless of the circumstances, sufficient repetition will make almost anything seem routine. I remember addressing the "shattered self-worth" issue that bothered me so much in one of the day's group sessions, asking the firefighters, "How bad can you really be? You're firefighters. You certainly didn't choose this job for the money. You wanted to help other people."

I also recall that everyone, firefighters and family members, received an acupuncture treatment that day. The needles in the ear didn't work any miracles, but they weren't half bad. When individual family counseling sessions were offered by CSU at the end of the day, we requested one as soon as it could be scheduled.

On July 30, Matt caused a car accident, failing to yield while driving through Garden City, the latest black mark on a driving record that was strongly suggestive of his substance problem. He had been prescribed Zoloft and Naltrexone while he was in Mirmont, but it became obvious during our conversations that Matt was taking more than prescription medicine. I may have agonized over it a bit – not too long given what was at stake – and I called his counselor on August 1 to let CSU know he was using again. That same day, Matt arrived home to pack a bag, escorted by CSU personnel, and he was headed to Marworth again, his absence bringing an unhappy peace to the Byrne household once more, along with heightened concern over whether this third time would be the charm and the cure would take for good.

We returned to Marworth several weeks later for Family Day on Monday, August 20, 2012. The morning educational sessions were reruns for us, but later we met some of Matt's own counselors, then had lunch with him and another family from Rockville Centre whose father was there as well. We had sat with them on a terrace, enjoying the beautiful summer day, all thankful our loved ones were getting the help needed to move in the right direction.

Shortly thereafter all hell broke loose. Before we could go to the scheduled afternoon family session with his counselors, we were summoned to the director's office, who told us that, although he was supposed to receive another ten days of treatment before discharge, we would have to take Matt home with us immediately. The director, a mental health professional oddly dressed in a bright red tie that a stockbroker would wear, told us that Matt had been insubordinate to a counselor, admittedly not his own, who had caught him chewing tobacco in a lounge area. When he told Matt to get rid of the chew, he had refused. Words had been exchanged, and now Matt had to go.

Matt argued with the director to stay, pointing out that he had been fully engaged in the program, contributing during all the discussions, and pleading that he really needed the treatment if he were to get better. Matt sounded pretty desperate, and I tried to back him up as best I could; it seemed like some sort of final warning might have sufficed, rather than expulsion for a first and relatively minor offense.

It was all to no avail. Patti and I went with Matt to his room where he gathered his belongings. As we walked with him out of the facility, one of the counselors who had worked closely with him, a woman our own age, chased us down. Crying, she confirmed what he had told us regarding his participation in group therapy and assured us that throwing him out had not been a consensus decision, nor even put before the staff at all.

The three-hour ride home seemed like a week. The turn of events had been staggering, with a hopeful visit turned into a crushing setback we had no reason to see coming. As Matt sat in the back seat, all that desperation I had witnessed an hour before was gone. He was singing along to oldies tunes, like he had when he was a child, probably Neil Young's "Old Man" just to annoy me. The gravity of his situation seemed lost on him.

Patti and I made quiet conversation in the front seat, trying to come to grips with the fact that, on his third rehab try, Matt had been thrown out of the program. Nothing comparable to this had ever happened in the kid's life. How much worse could this become before it started getting better?

I remember the same imagery coming to mind repeatedly.

Patti and I were in a small row boat, far out in the ocean. It was starting to get dark, and the seas were swelling as a storm approached. In minutes, it was totally dark, and the boat was being tossed wildly as we clung to its sides. I kept telling myself what I knew to be true: sooner or later, the storm would pass, the swells would subside, and the ocean would get as calm as a lake. The question remained: would the boat still be afloat, and would Patti and I both still be in it?

XVI.

In the spring of 1998, Matt was keeping us in suspense. He had narrowed his college choices down to two schools, Hamilton College and Bowdoin College, the latter being my own alma mater which, no doubt, I shamelessly promoted. Matt had met with coaches at each school and planned to continue swimming in college. When he learned that Bowdoin's team would train in Hawaii over the winter break when the surf was best, while Hamilton was only going to a pool complex in Florida, the decision was made.

In late August, we tackled the job of getting Matt and all his stuff to Maine. Grandma Murtagh had insisted that her late husband, Frank, would not have let Matt go off without a car, so she gave him her old minivan and bought herself a new one. The Byrnes left for drop-off day in two minivans: Matt driving the gift he received from Lorayne, with me riding shotgun, and Patti driving our own larger model, with Ann riding up front.

It was an eventful trip. I had hoped to serve only as a guide, giving Matt a heads-up when necessary to anticipate lane and route changes on his initial trip to Brunswick, Maine. The plan derailed as soon as we reached the Throgs Neck Bridge.

I didn't even see it, but apparently Matt cut someone off as soon as the minivan started up the incline. By the time we reached mid span, there was a Jeep alongside my window, swerving dangerously close, with its driver hanging out his window, outstretching his arm to display a police badge in his wallet. I rolled down the window, and he was screaming at me: "I'm a cop. You pull over as soon as you get off the bridge!"

I had no idea what was going on, but repeated the command across the van to Matt. He started crawling the rest of the way off the bridge, and I pointed to a place where I thought we could safely stop. The cop pulled up behind us and came flying out of the car. I jumped out of my side to intercept him.

The man was apoplectic, shouting that he had just lost a friend last week in a crash after his friend's car had been cut off. He was heading for the driver's side window when I stepped in his way. "He's sorry," I said. "He's just a stupid kid, driving to college for the first time," I blurted as the traffic whizzed by, closer than anyone would like.

It was a fortunate choice of words. Calling him a "stupid kid," instead of mounting any defense, calmed the officer down immediately. He went from angry to looking embarrassed to be standing on the side of the highway shaking with rage. "Don't worry," I assured him. "I'll drive the rest of the way so it doesn't happen again." He returned to his car with a relatively meek instruction to Matt to be more careful in the future.

I had no trouble convincing Matt to give up the wheel. Plainly shaken by the incident, he had already climbed over the console to the passenger side.

A few hours later, we were in Northern Connecticut where we saw the other Byrne minivan, driven by Patti, flying by us in the right-hand lane. She and Ann had left a bit after us, but we were to rendezvous for lunch in Sturbridge, Massachusetts. Right after crossing the Massachusetts border, we saw the flashing lights of a cruiser that had pulled over a minivan. Guess whose? Matt's spirits had returned along the way, so we decided we'd run an integrity test, and make no reference to what we had witnessed and see whether the matter of a speeding ticket came up during lunch. The girls failed the test miserably.

*

Coach Charlie had been running Bowdoin's swim team since I was an undergraduate. He was an amazingly peppy guy, for a man of any age, and Matt had been crazy about him since he had met him the summer before on Long Island where he had a summer gig running the swimming pool at a swanky country club.

Despite having quickly acquired the nickname "Ice Man" on the Bowdoin party circuit, which prompted a few warnings from Coach Charlie that he ought to "clean up his act" before practices and meets, Matt was all in with swimming in his first year. We traveled to a few meets at other New England Small College Athletic Conference ("NESCAC") schools, including a harrowing Friday night drive through an ice storm to Williamstown, where we caught our Neapolitan mastiff, Josephine, whom we had unwisely brought with us at Matt's behest, beginning a rampage after we left her in a motel room she would have torn apart. She eventually lay quietly outside in the minivan, her rolling home away from home, while we ate something quickly in a restaurant about to close.

What I remember most vividly, however, was arriving at the

pool at Williams College again at the end of the season for the
NESCAC Championships. We had no idea that, in addition to
the usual swimming ritual of "shaving down" before a big meet,
Matthew had been "Bic'd." He was as bald as a cue ball, and at
first sight looked like a total stranger who had sadly been receiving chemotherapy. We reflexively wondered if that were the case.
When we saw he was actually very fit and totally engaged – leading the cheers and congregating with both male and female
teammates -- the hairless look quickly grew on us. He looked
very different, but he was still our Matt.

*

Elizabeth had gone to Gettysburg College, a school with Lutheran origins that had always scheduled a long weekend so its
students could return home for Easter. Bowdoin, in contrast,
made no such religious accommodation, so we were in a bit of a
quandary since the family had always been together that holiest
of days.

Patti decided that, to avoid Matt missing any classes, we
should buy him a round trip air ticket from Portland, leaving late
Friday afternoon and returning late Sunday afternoon, April 4,
1999. The flights were in and out of MacArthur Airport, less than
an hour from Rockville Centre on Long Island, so we would have
time for Mass and an early Easter dinner before taking Matt back
to the airport.

Trouble began late Sunday morning when the airlines called
to say the flight would be delayed. There might even have been a

second call, but the delays didn't sound too hideous, so we stuck to the original plan, hung around the house after dinner, then drove Matt out to MacArthur at the rescheduled time.

When we arrived, we were told the flight had not been delayed again, but simply cancelled. There would not be another one until Monday afternoon.

"I guess you're driving him back tonight," Patti said to me.

"I guess I am."

We loaded everyone in the minivan and drove back to Rockville Centre. While Matt said his goodbyes, I grabbed the suit I would need for a meeting in Manhattan the following afternoon. Matt and I switched cars, and we took off.

It was the ride from hell. Before we reached the Bronx, heavy rain had started and never let up. The six to seven-hour trip took closer to ten, and I drove the entire way because, still in his pre-Lasik stage, Matt had left his driving glasses at school. When we finally pulled into town, I drove past the Comfort Inn where I had previously stayed and dropped him at his dorm, figuring I would not likely lose the last vacancy in the inn at that time on Sunday night.

After I said goodbye and headed for the motel, I felt like a balloon losing its helium. I had been squinting at the white line so long I felt like my eyes were bleeding or melting down my face.

I pulled in front of the motel office and ran in with my overnight bag and suit, determined to collapse into bed as quickly as possible. A young woman at the desk greeted me quite cheerily, given the hour, and began the registration process. To the right of the desk stood a young guy in a Domino's pizza uniform, soaking wet but smiling.

When the young woman handed me the room key, the young fellow finally spoke.

"Can I ask you something, Mister?"

"Sure, son." I had no idea what was coming next. No, I did not want any pizza.

"I want to hire you to give me a ride home to Bath. My car won't start. I can pay you ten dollars."

"Why don't you take a cab?" I asked.

"They say it's raining too hard, and they won't come get me."

I was incredulous at this latest turn of events. This had to be some sort of divine Easter joke. But what if it were my own kid stuck like that?

"Okay, kid. I'll give you a ride but I'm not taking your money. Let me put this stuff in the room first. I'll be right back."

When I returned, the bedraggled delivery boy was doing his best to make time with the desk clerk. Then he gave her a big goodbye, and we headed out in the rain.

We made small talk along the ten-mile drive, and he directed me to where he lived on the far side of Bath. He tried to pay me again, but I barked and told him to get out of the car so I could go to sleep back in Brunswick.

The ride back was a little less tense, not because I could see where I was going, but because I don't think I saw another car's headlights the entire way. It's actually a very pretty ride, during the day or on a moonlit night, but I didn't enjoy it at all as I struggled to stay awake.

As I closed the motel room door behind me, I had already de-cided there would be no meeting in Manhattan for me the next afternoon. I also made up my mind that I would urge Matthew to go to Easter services in Brunswick next year, instead of risking another trip home like that. I didn't even worry about his skip-ping Mass. Oddly enough, while he was certainly the greatest sinner of my four children, he was also the one with the strongest religious streak.

*

The summer of 1999 began well for Matt. He had received re-spectable grades for his first year at Bowdoin, which typically signaled that they would only get better as he continued with the academic program. (He told me his secret strategy was to "always sit in the first row".) He returned home to Rockville Centre and resumed his job at Jones Beach as an ocean lifeguard.

I've heard many times the aphorisms that "nothing good happens after midnight" and "your life can change in an instant" and both proved true in the case of my son. He was out on the town in Rockville Centre with friends in early June, certainly drinking but at least not driving. When he and one friend took a cab from the train station late that night, the plot was hatched to bolt the fare. The driver took exception and pursued them in his cab until they had to scale a fence to escape. Unfortunately for Matt, he landed badly and tore up his ACL.

I didn't see him until late the next day. He was sitting in the bathtub on the third floor, soaking a very swollen right knee, on the verge of tears or actually crying. I don't recall giving him any sympathy whatsoever, and probably told him that he had gotten what he deserved before I left the bathroom.

Patti took him to the doctor, and another plan was hatched, almost as stupid as the first. Instead of having the operation to repair the ligament as soon as possible, he would take physical therapy and wear a brace so he could return to Jones Beach for most of the summer. Then, just a few weeks before his return to school, he would have the surgery and begin rehab. Incredibly, in hindsight, he sold us on this course of action, perhaps because we didn't think he'd actually be able to perform his lifeguard duties without having the knee fixed.

Matt surprised us and gutted it out. On August 14, 1999, as soon as he was discharged from the Hospital for Special Surgery in Manhattan, we all took off, including Josephine, for a family vacation on the Outer Banks in North Carolina, again requiring two vehicles to carry all the people and their stuff.

The place we stayed was a marina, and we all went fishing the first day. When we returned, we discovered that Josephine had rampaged once again, chewing all the molding off the inside front door of the condo unit in a vain attempt to make her escape.

The dog-loving North Carolina carpenter on the property wanted $100 to repair the damage, which I considered quite reasonable. Since I only wanted to pay the man once, I stayed back with the dog the next time Patti took the gang fishing.

They returned with at least two coolers full of mackerel, certainly a decent sport fish but not a very good eating one, particularly when it aged. Overly impressed with their catch, the boys insisted we keep eating the mackerel for the next few days until everyone finally admitted they had enough.

When it came time to head home, I took everyone else in my sedan while Patti drove only Matthew in the minivan so he could stretch his leg out. Somewhere during the ten-hour ride, Matthew began to feel ill. When they stopped for gas, Patti checked him. He was feverish. Instead of completing the trip to Rockville Centre, Patti took him straight back to the Hospital for Special Surgery.

Her worst fears were confirmed. The knee incision had become infected and there was a possibility of sepsis. He wound up in the hospital for a week while they straightened him out with antibiotics.

Matt recovered just in time to leave for the start of the fall semester at Bowdoin. I had to drive him up, since he couldn't operate a car himself yet, but we were assured the college would shuttle him back and forth to classes. The possibility of losing a semester's tuition had been very real, since I had not bothered to purchase the insurance all the colleges sell. I never made that mistake again, learning the lesson that things could quite unexpectedly go wrong.

With Matt back at school, I thought we had finally lucked out that summer. Years later, I discovered that we had not been lucky at all. When treating his torn ACL, Matt's physicians had introduced him to opioids. He eventually confessed to us during his rehab stays that he had "really, really liked them" from the very first moment the euphoria kicked in. In retrospect, it certainly

looks like one dumb decision to bolt a cab fare affected the subsequent course of Matt's life.

*

You may be wondering how a family could end up harboring
a Neapolitan mastiff prone to rampaging, our highbrow but accurate description of how Josephine acted when things didn't go
her way, like when everyone else went out for dinner, leaving her
behind to pull open the kitchen drawer holding the garbage pail
and strew its contents around the floor. It's a very good question.
We weren't big pet people and were not very lucky with the ones
we had.

When Beba and Matt were very young, a relative gave us a
parakeet, Little Bird as opposed to the more famous Big Bird.
Whenever Patti went out, the kids would beg me to let Little Bird
out to fly, something it did not do very well. On one occasion, the
bird flew to the top of the kitchen right into the skylight, then lost
altitude, skittering down the wall until it crash-landed behind
Matt's high chair. "He's dead. He's dead," they yelled.

"No, he's just fine," I said hopefully as I picked him up off the
floor. The bird was dazed but conscious and revived once I put it
back in the cage.

A few months later, however, Little Bird wasn't so lucky.
When I came down that morning, I didn't hear any noise in the
cage. When I took the cover off, Little Bird was lying dead at the
bottom of the cage – really dead.

I went upstairs to tell Patti and figure out how we should play it. Her reaction was that I must be wrong; the bird had to be alive. She went downstairs and only after poking the poor bird repeatedly with the eraser end of a pencil did she concur in my judgment. I was directed to bury Little Bird in Hempstead Lake Park before the children woke up.

That park was responsible for our next pet, a white rabbit I found on the side of the road when jogging at dusk and stupidly brought home. "Runaway Bunny" lived with us uneventfully for one year, but in year two it underwent a personality change and began biting me whenever I cleaned its cage. When my suspected Hodgkins disease turned out to be toxoplasmosis contracted from the rabbit, Runaway made her last trip to the veterinarian with Beba and me. My subsequent ban on pets held until young Ann talked us into adopting Miss Piggy, a misnamed guinea pig Beba hated who, shortly before his death, was discovered to be a male.

In the fall of 1998, however, one of Patti's business clients, a dog rescuer, strongly suggested that we "needed" to go to the Town of Hempstead animal shelter to "visit" three dogs scheduled for destruction. Patti told me we would only go look at the dogs. I replied that no one goes looking at dogs without coming home with one.

One of the dogs was a black whippet that looked at death's door. Another was a Rottweiler, caged along with about twelve others of his breed, each looking so innocent that you could almost believe that they had all been framed for the bites with which they were charged.

The final dog was this big female Neapolitan mastiff. She was long and lanky, and her gray fur was dirty and matted, with tremendous folds of wrinkles drooping below her face. The dog in the next cage was going berserk barking at us as we took a look. The Neo just stared at her neighbor silently as if to say: "If you would just calm down, maybe we could all get out of this place."

To my surprise, Patti did leave the shelter after we viewed the three dogs. As we walked to the car, she asked, "So what did you think?"

"The whippet's definitely going to die, and the Rottweiler must be a biter. The only one I thought anything of was the mastiff."

"That's the one I like, too!" she blurted. We walked back into the shelter, and the next day Patti and Ann brought the dog home to join our family. As my consolation prize, I got to name her, and I thought Josephine was a suitable name for a pretty big lady.

Patti had been told at the pound that Josephine had been owned by drug dealers in Roosevelt, a tough area of Nassau County, but after she and her sister had run off a second time no one came to retrieve them from the shelter. Whether that story were true or not, it was evident that Jojo, as she quickly became known, had never lived inside a house. She initially had a look of amazement on her face whenever you opened the dishwasher or, much better yet, the cold place where you keep food. But it was almost like watching a rerun of the beginning of the movie *ET* as the animal began to soak up knowledge. In no time at all, she became a scarily clever beast.

I supposed I was Josephine's primary caregiver, but she was a bit aloof and seemed to take my fulfillment of that role for grant-ed. The entire family agreed that the real object of her affection was Matthew. When anyone else entered the family room, she would just lie on the black leather sectional she had claimed with her endless drool and dander, but if Matt came in she quickly jumped to her feet to greet him. Sounds weird, but it seemed the dog considered herself his girlfriend and, since there was no steady lady at the time vying for his affection, maybe she was.

Certainly, Josephine's love for Matt did not go unrequited. Whenever we would be going to visit him during his four years of college, he would ask in advance, "Is the dog coming?" More times than not, the answer was yes. This led to some memorable incidents.

During Matt's freshman year, Jojo came along for our first Parents' Weekend. We left her in the minivan late on Saturday afternoon, the window sufficiently open for ventilation purposes, while we went to a 5 PM Mass on the outskirts of Brunswick. When the Mass ended, and we were walking to the rear of the large asphalt parking lot, Ann asked, "Isn't that Jojo?" The dog was sitting alongside the car, front paws crossed like a lioness. She had pulled the rubber gasket wrapping the window out with her teeth. We found it inside the van. That must have given her the extra space she needed to climb out the window head first. The scrape on her snout suggested a serious faceplant. In any event, she never tried that Houdini trick again.

Occasionally on these weekend trips to visit Matt, we would drive halfway then stay at a small hotel in Sturbridge, Massachu-setts when one of the other kid's activities precluded an early departure on Friday. One time, when I was booking the reservation, the Indian man who had recently taken over the motel noted that we had stayed there before.

"You are a very good customer," he said.

"I guess we're fairly regular visitors," I replied.

"Do you have a pet?" he asked.

"Yes, a dog. Why?"

"Our new policy allows pets. And I just had one of the large rooms redone. Why don't you take that one and bring your pet?"

"Sure." The reservation was made.

When we arrived at the motel that Friday night, I left everyone in the minivan and entered the office alone. I met the man, as friendly as he had been on the phone, and he proudly escorted me to the refurbished room, which was attached to his own family's quarters.

I complimented him on the accommodations and returned to the office. Paul, Patti and Ann had taken Josephine to relieve herself, so I pulled the van in front of the assigned room and started unloading. As I moved baggage into the room, the owner opened a side door to introduce me to his own family, three cute little kids. Just then Josephine came strutting in, all one-hundred twenty-five pounds of her. The owner's kids took one look at her and started screaming, crying, and crawling away. My new friend yelled inside to his wife, "Hide the children!"

Once he had slammed the door closed and calmed down, I assured the owner that the old beat up room we usually stayed in at the end of the property would be fine, and we retreated quickly with his children still crying inside.

When Matt was entering his senior year at Bowdoin, he became determined to take the dog back to school with him. Patti and I saw nothing but trouble coming from this, but we eventually cut a deal with him: since Parents' Weekend was early in October that year, we agreed he could take Jojo to Bowdoin in late August, but she would return with us after our visit.

This excursion didn't even begin well. The day after Matt left for school, Patti received a call in the late afternoon from a gentleman with a thick Maine accent.

"I found your dog this afternoon walking on the Harpswell Road in Brunswick, Maine," he announced. He had gotten our address and phone number from a tag on Josephine's collar. The man was already planning his appearance on Letterman with the dog with the wrinkles and jowls who had journeyed from Long Island to New England and was disappointed to learn that the nice lady's son was a neighboring student who had managed to lose the dog almost as soon as she arrived in Brunswick.

As a senior, Matt had top choice in housing and lived in one of the fairly swanky town houses adjacent to Bowdoin's soccer field, just off the Harpswell Road. When we arrived at his place for Parents' Weekend, we realized just what a mistake letting him take Josephine had been. She was no longer a family dog, but a college party girl. As we sat in the living room of the town house with the other residents' families after the football game, the dog acted like she barely knew us. At one point, while lying in the middle of the floor, Josephine ripped a giant buffalo fart, then got up and walked out the open sliding door and across the deck to the party next door.

It took several weeks back in Rockville Centre before "College Dog" returned to her normally abnormal self.

*

On June 13, 2001, Patti and I managed to purchase an office building in Rockville Centre, fulfilling a dream to spend every day in even closer proximity. The early intervention agency she ran would occupy one side of the building and my law firm the other. We have a picture taken in the parking lot of the building, after the reconstruction was finished, probably before Matt left on a return trip to Bowdoin. Patti and I are standing proudly with our four children, brown eyed Ann gazing up at her big brother/hero Matt. He's wearing a black jump suit, like a NASCAR outfit, with a Snickers logo on it. No one else would dare wear such a "driving costume" as we called it, but he faithfully donned it whenever he drove from Rockville Centre to Maine or back. The family joke was that he could cut his travel time by an hour or two if he didn't stop in every fast food joint between Long Island and New England, especially Roy Rogers, whose Double R Bar sandwich he could never resist.

September 11th happened soon after Matt returned to school for his senior year, and I've already described the impact upon him we eventually learned that tragic day had, despite Josephine keeping him company at the time. He must have thought that the world had ended here in New York, which it nearly had – Rockville Centre alone lost 48 current or former residents. Matt felt very isolated and untethered. This wasn't just the typical senior angst over "what will I do with my life after I graduate?" Previously, Matt had always seemed a happy-go-lucky college student. He had been particularly generous with his time and willing to accommodate high school kids who were visiting Bowdoin and needed a place to stay overnight. The transition had begun during his junior year.

Coach Charlie had retired, and two young guys had begun coaching Bowdoin's swim team. Matt didn't say much, but it seemed that his enthusiasm for the program was waning. Uncharacteristically, I made a solo trip to Brunswick in late January to size up what was going on. It was going to be a no frills, get there and turn around trip.

I left after work on Friday and drove straight to the Comfort Inn, fortunately avoiding any kids in need of late-night rides.

I had agreed to meet Matt on Saturday morning at the Brunswick Apartments. This was a dumpy garden apartment complex, recently purchased by the college but probably built to handle the housing shortage – even in Maine – following World War II. Matt and his roommate occupied the same space for both sophomore and junior years, and it wasn't getting any better. He showed me a broken pane of glass in the kitchen window where their "pet" squirrel visited every morning for some breakfast. I remembered giving Elizabeth money to fix a broken window at her off-campus hovel in Gettysburg. Maybe I had no safety concerns this time, so I kept my money in my pocket.

When we were alone, Matt said he had something to tell me. That typically wasn't a good thing.

"What's up?" I asked.

"I'm in a relationship. She's the most beautiful and smartest girl on campus," he announced proudly.

"Then what's she doing with you?" I teased.

"You'll see. She'll be at the meet this afternoon."

I did meet her that day. College Girl was very pleasant, attractive and, apparently, a very high-achieving student, but also quite "exclusive" in how she treated him. You could already see the distance that had grown between Matt and his swim teammates with whom he had formerly been quite tight.

There was lots of drama with this couple over the next two years, as they engaged in a rocky romance. I don't remember having too many conversations with my son about it, other than to occasionally point out that all my friends had always been crazy about his mother, and it had never been hard to be and stay in love with Patti without interruptions like the serial breakups and makeups he and College Girl had. To me, none of this looked like very much fun.

Matt did swim through his final year at Bowdoin, but it seemed more out of obligation than enjoyment. The team captains who had been his friends during his first years seemed to disrespect him because he hadn't lived up to his potential. He didn't seem to care what they thought and was far more concerned with his on-again off-again love affair.

*

May 25, 2002 was Matthew's Commencement from Bowdoin College. No wonder the use of that term filled so many graduat-

ing seniors with dread! Their "real" lives were supposed to be beginning, and many had no more clue as to what that meant than
they had on the day they were born. Matt knew he would spend
another summer at Jones Beach. After that, he had no plans
whatsoever, other than the one he was then keeping secret: to
join the FDNY as soon as possible.

Still, even with no current job prospects, graduation was a big
accomplishment and Patti and I both felt it should be properly
recognized as such. We had rounded up all the family, including
Matt's grandmothers, and had left for Maine the day before.

Saturday morning was a gift, a beautiful early summer day,
filled with pomp and circumstance, but also some discord. As an
alumnus, I was invited to march in the academic procession, and
wound up with a seat right in front of the steps of the Walker Art
Building that the graduates crossed to accept their degrees. I remember letting out a hoot with pride when Matthew's name was
called and hearing the same from the rest of the family, seated
many rows behind in the quadrangle.

The preferred seating controversy died down after the ceremony when we roamed around the campus and duplicated photos that had been taken thirty years before when I had graduated,
and Patti and I both looked like teenagers. This time, as we posed
at the same sites, we were surrounded by our four children and
did not look quite so young. Later, there was a celebratory ban-
quet under a giant tent stretched over the soccer field adjacent to
where Matt lived. We met many of his classmates and their families, and even a couple of underclassmen from Chaminade who
were working as waiters. When the party ended, we headed back

to the two cottages we had rented for the weekend at a small re-sort outside of Bath.

Matt made the trip with us but in his own car. Explaining he had to load all the stuff in his room so he could vacate the town-house by noon the next day, he didn't stick around much longer than it took to receive the graduation cards with checks in them from his grandmothers.

As he took off to be with his friends, I had a sense of disap-pointment which I know everyone else shared, especially the grandmas who had come such a long way and hoped to spend time with him. It might have been the first time I experienced it; it would not be the last.

There had been no sign of College Girl all weekend. I now re-alize that perhaps this is the first time that booze and drugs, not even sex, had won out with Matt over family.

XVII.

They say substance abuse is a progressive disease. I certainly believe that statement to be true. By late summer 2012, Matthew was going downhill fast, probably picking up speed, and taking the rest of us along for the ride.

It seems that even CSU did not know what to do with Matt when he unexpectedly returned after being expelled from Marworth. He told them he was embarrassed by what had happened, but felt well, happy to be home, and ready to move forward. He was warned by CSU that he must remain compliant with the treatment plan, or he would be referred to an unspecified higher level of care.

Patti and I had been booked to leave on a short cruise to Bermuda with a client group on Sunday, August 25. I was scheduled to deliver three lectures on legal topics while on board. We were to return on Thursday, August 30, the same day Matt had been scheduled to return from Marworth, so the trip had looked doable, right until he was thrown out of the facility. I couldn't get out of the speaking engagement, so we decided that Patti would stay home and keep an eye on things, which would hopefully remain calm.

They did not.

On Wednesday, August 29, 2012, it was Patti's turn to snitch Matt out to CSU. She called and left a vague message that he didn't seem well. Matt did report to CSU that morning but seemed sedated to them when he was escorted to Inter-Care, a detox services provider, where he suddenly became angry and agitated.

The cruise ship arrived back in Bayonne at 7 a.m. the following morning, August 30, and I headed for my office from there. Matt had reported to CSU and admitted to his counselor that he had taken Xanax the night before. They must have let him stay and participate in a group therapy session, but he had stormed out after a confrontation. Matt had called someone out as a "pretender" in response to some comment regarding his shabby condition or strung out state.

I received a call from CSU that Matt was "in the wind" and probably headed home. For the first time, the counselor hinted that I should be concerned about him doing something drastic. If possible, I was to try to get him to Long Island Jewish where the emergency room included a psychiatric unit. I changed directions, and I raced to beat Matt home.

I lost. When I pulled up Harvard Avenue, I could see that the front door was wide open. I turned the corner, went down the driveway and saw that the back door was left the same way.

I didn't know what to do. I stood on the front steps, trying to decide whether to get back in the car and canvass the neighborhood, or stay put for a while in the hope that he would return. As I tried to decide, I spotted him walking down Dorchester Road, heading toward me, Portia leading him toward the house as he held on to her choke collar leash. The dog had that look on her face she always got when she sensed something was wrong.

"Hey, DaddyO, what's happening?" he called out as he crossed Harvard Avenue, drenched in midday sunlight.

As soon as I saw his face, I could tell he was flying. "Sounds like you are. I heard you had a rough morning."

There was no sense playing games. I had cut right to the chase.

"Why? Did they call you? I had a little problem with someone there. He's a phony, acts like he's not using when I know he is. I had to get outta there."

"They say you need help, Matt. They suggested I take you over to Long Island Jewish. There's people there who can help. You ready to come with me?"

He said he needed to use the bathroom, but then would go. As I waited for him downstairs, I thought about how, so far, all his resistance and argumentative behavior never took place in front of me. I hoped it would stay like that.

We drove the twenty minutes to LIJ, keeping the conversation light. We parked in a large garage and entered the ER's reception area in the early afternoon. After some confusion while his insurance coverage was verified – he had no cards or wallet – the questions began as to why he was there. I suggested they call CSU to get the lowdown, and they did so.

Eventually they took him through a heavy metal door. Later, I was able to see him from outside. He had a hospital gown on and was plainly in a lockdown observation area.

I waited for hours before a young psychiatric resident came out to see me. She told me Matt was calm and didn't seem to pose any threat to himself. She mentioned that the facility was already very crowded.

I told her about the repeated relapses, and how he seemed to be losing any ability to abstain, even for a short period of time. With Labor Day weekend imminent, I was fearful of what could happen. She promised to report this to her supervising psychiatrist.

Soon after, one of the CSU counselors arrived at the LIJ Emergency Room. I was very impressed. He didn't live that far from the hospital, but he had gone out of his way, with no obligation to do so. He stayed with me for another couple of hours until the young doctor told me that she was sorry, Matt was being released because they had patients in greater need of a bed. The counselor told Matt he would see him the next morning at CSU, and he would resume sessions once again, which he did that Friday.

CSU was closed Saturday September 1 through Monday September 3 for Labor Day weekend. On Wednesday, September 5, 2012, Matt showed up at CSU appearing to be under the influence of some sort of mood or mind-altering drug. He was booked for one of the psychologists the next day.

It is doubtful whether that session took place. After arriving in the morning, he began threatening to resign from the FDNY and making statements suggesting potential violence. The counselors' judgment was that Matt needed in-patient treatment once again. Reluctantly, he agreed to be transported to Holliswood Hospital.

The call we received announcing this decision was quite upsetting. Hidden in a wealthy residential area in Jamaica Estates, Queens, Holliswood was not just another rehab facility, but a full-fledged psychiatric hospital. The CSU counselor tried to downplay the significance of this latest admission, but it wasn't lost on Patti and me. Matt wasn't just dealing with a substance problem, however unsuccessfully, but mental illness as well.

We were able to visit Matt the first night he spent at Holliswood. It was a foreboding looking structure in the dark, and the first-floor reception area was dimly lit. There were two separate entrances off the waiting room, locked off and served by different elevators. The one to the right was for the general populace where Matt was originally placed. Within a few days, however, as promised because he was with the FDNY, Matt was transferred to the Veterans Unit, and thereafter we entered to the left.

This was the PTSD clinic, housing mostly current or former military members, plus a few police officers or firefighters like Matt. They were mostly young, Iraq or Afghanistan vets, who were polite but troubled. Matt seemed to fit right in.

Patti and I, one or the other or both, visited him every day. If we couldn't go together at night, one of us would get there during the afternoon visiting hours. After the initial shock of having your son admitted to a mental institution subsided, we decided it wasn't such a bad place. All the staff members were unfailingly pleasant, and the counselors seemed very engaged. The only flaw seemed to be a shortage of actual psychiatrists. Whether it was true or not, Matt told us there was only one doctor who supposedly owned the place and worked seven days a week until all hours, but even so it was very difficult to see him.

Matt seemed content to be there, but he was obviously heavily medicated. There were two places you could visit on his floor. One was a television room, where some of his fellow patients seemed to spend all their time. The other was a lounge area with tables where food was allowed; there was much more activity there, with patients moving in and out. We would usually arrive at the lounge with some sort of take-out, always a favorite of Matt's, but shortly after eating – not nearly as much as he used to – he would announce that he was tired and heading back to his room to lie down. That would be the end of the visit, unless one of the other patients with whom he was friendly wanted to chat, a not infrequent occurrence because some of the vets were from Texas or the West Coast and never had any visitors. One guy caught me one evening when we were leaving and told me how much he liked the shirt I was wearing, a giveaway at a golf outing. I told him I thought I could get him one and asked him his size. When I showed up with the shirt a few nights later, you would think he had won the lottery.

Matt stayed in Holliswood for the full twenty-eight days his insurer allowed. His primary counselor, an attractive young woman whom Matt plainly liked, explored his PTSD issues, which dated back to the Jones Beach drowning that took place when he was a teenager. He was supposedly responding well to the Seroquel and Wellbutrin he had been prescribed, and apparently doing much better than at the time of his admission.

Initially, Matt had not authorized Holliswood personnel to speak with his family. This was the first time he had exhibited any resistance to our involvement in his treatment. When he told Patti and me he had not given his consent, I was surprised but I just let it go. Matt must have changed his mind as he moved closer toward discharge, however, because I had conversations with both his Holliswood and CSU counselors about continuing his treatment at the Caron Foundation. (He had never revoked CSU's permission to talk to us.) Caron, reputed to be a top-flight recovery facility, does not accept any insurance plans. I told them that finances would not be an obstacle because we would do whatever was necessary to help him.

I never found out why the Caron idea died. I can only assume Matt killed it by refusing to go in-patient again, which certainly was his right, but I regret not pursuing it further. When he was discharged from Holliswood, he simply resumed sessions at CSU.

Once again, Matt's initial compliance with the program deteriorated rapidly. He was supposed to continue his medications and see a licensed clinical social worker on Long Island on a weekly basis, in addition to attending AA meetings. The plan was for him to continue at CSU for four weeks, then return to his firehouse on light duty. By October 18, the recalcitrance that had first surfaced at Holliswood returned. Matt admitted he had stopped attending the AA meetings, and he had only seen the social worker once. He was referred to another psychiatrist for an evaluation and medication management, but never scheduled the appointment. Matt was repeatedly warned by his CSU counselor that a support network is an essential need during the recovery process. His counselor was rightfully losing her patience, "Client understands what steps he needs to take to maintain abstinence but appears resistant."

*

On October 28, 2012, all the news stations were reporting that a big hurricane was heading toward New York. I can't say that I took this very seriously; I really had more pressing things on my mind. Besides, in late August of 2011, Hurricane Irene had received a similar buildup by the media, but the storm had turned out to be a non-event in Long Beach.

Nevertheless, that Sunday afternoon I followed Patti's instructions to drive from Rockville Centre and take the necessary precautions. What she essentially meant was moving the furniture around in the Long Beach Florida room, located on the first floor in the rear of the house closest to Reynolds Channel. I was to place everything I could on the side of the room furthest from the back door, the most likely point for seawater to enter.

In hindsight, this effort was exactly like rearranging the deck chairs on the Titanic. Two days later, Superstorm Sandy hit while we were safely in Rockville Centre, although in blackout conditions. More than four and one-half feet of water entered the Long Beach house. It was days later before we were able to venture down there to see what was left. Before crossing the Long Beach bridge, we had to prove we were owners at a checkpoint set up to dissuade looters. The barrier island looked like a combat zone. When we reached the West End and entered the house, the water had mostly receded, but the Florida room remained full of ocean grass and smelled like the bottom of the channel.

Lorayne and Frank's beloved home, the site of so many fond memories, was totally devastated, the four feet high white stucco border wall collapsed around it, the basement filled like a swimming pool with seawater, furniture soaked and strewn around like a cyclone had entered the house, not just a hurricane. Patti was crying gently as we surveyed the ruins. I started cataloguing the ways in which it could have been worse.

The prior spring, I had contemplated replacing the dock before concluding that other improvements should be made first. Good call! An old dock went out to sea in the storm surge instead of a new one.

Paul had gotten the boat out of Long Beach in advance and to the Oceanside marina where it survived the storm, lashed to a floating dock. Owners who had decided to have their boats hauled found them destroyed, blocks away where they washed up on Austin Boulevard in Island Park, like poorly parked cars blocking the major thoroughfare.

Most important, my otherwise futile trip to the Florida room before the storm had not been totally in vain. While there, I spotted a cardboard box with the entire collection of Byrne home videos. I had been sorting it over the summer, planning to have the films transferred to disks for each one of the four children so the family history would be preserved. When we had returned to Rockville Centre in September, I had carelessly left it behind. I picked up the box when I was leaving and put it in the trunk of my car.

The house could always be replaced. The memories of the life the Byrne family once shared were irreplaceable. As I stared at the wreckage, I realized I was looking at some visual metaphor of what was happening in our world. Both the government and speculators were already offering decent money for the sale of waterfront properties, so we could simply take it, fold, and walk away. Or could we withstand this latest disaster, this time natural, and find the strength to regroup and rebuild?

I found a notation indicating that the planning took nearly a year, but on September 14, 2013, Patti and I were sitting with Paul, our architect, and Maurice, the contractor who would re-build the house, elevated on pilings, with an elevator. There were simply too many good memories set on this small bayfront parcel to let it go. I'm very glad we didn't.

*

On November 16, 2012, Matt was officially discharged from CSU following a session with his counselor. He agreed to contin-ue with his treatment plan, including follow up visits with the FDNY psychiatrist for medication management, weekly sessions with the LCSW, and "alumni" meetings at CSU for twelve weeks. He returned to duty at the firehouse on Sunday, November 18, 2012.

CSU's records suggest that, over the next two months, Matt played cat and mouse with his counselor, at first feigning compli-ance and finally dropping the pretense altogether. He confessed that he didn't take his medication regularly, but only sporadically because of side effects on libido and sexual performance. He was informed how brain chemistry is impacted by on/off use of med-ication and warned that, if he remained noncompliant with CSU's recommendations, his case would be closed.

CSU sent a letter to that effect on January 9, 2013. On Janu-ary 18, 2013, Matt showed up at CSU, without an appointment, to discuss the letter he had received. He told his counselor that he had no interest in continuing with CSU's program.

That was probably Matt's most self-destructive act to date.

*

If there's any part of this long, sad story that is hazy in my mind, it's the beginning of 2013 when Matt decided he was done with treatment, counseling, rehab and, quite frankly, abstinence, and capable of going it alone. Maybe the inevitability of what was going to happen next was so obvious that I closed my eyes and simply didn't want to watch. All I recall are snippets of individual days, and an overall sense of disbelief: I could not understand how FDNY could let someone so obviously impaired report for work and remain on the job for an entire shift. When I did see him, not often, I begged him to quit before he hurt himself, or worse yet, someone else. "Everyone tells me I have the best job in the world," he would respond. "It's not the best job in the world for you if it's making you crazy," I would reply, with no effect.

I'll give you some examples of what was going on. One morning, probably because his car was banged up again, Matt asked if he could have a ride to the train station. "Sure thing, Matt." On the five-minute ride there, he asked if we could stop at the deli to pick up the sandwich he had somehow already ordered.

"Sure thing, Matt. I always buy coffee and a newspaper for your Mother there myself."

We pulled up in front of the deli where, wearing his dress uniform for some official occasion, he staggered out of the car and into the store. I had not even noticed the state he was in before we left home. Maybe he had taken something right before.

As he clung to the counter in the deli, trying to steady himself, Mickey, the counterman with whom I was friendly, came around from the grill with Matt's sandwich in a wrapper. Mick said hello but couldn't hide his shock at what he saw. "Is he going to be okay," he asked.

I could only shrug my shoulders as I paid Mickey for the sandwich, as well as the coffee and paper. As I left the store, Matt was still climbing clumsily up the stairs to the train platform, leaving me wondering how he could ever get through the day.

During the summertime, Matt was again unwisely trying to juggle both jobs, firefighter and lifeguard. He began falling apart.

August 1, 2013, while skateboarding with The Nephew, Matt sprained his ankle. He went back on disability again after another trip to the emergency room.

On August 16, 2013, when his FDNY shift finished, Matt was supposed to join Big Jim and me at a golf outing held as a memorial for his grammar school classmate who had died in a car crash. Matt had been involved in the fund-raising effort, donating some surfboards as auction items. It had been raining heavily all day but, unbelievably, they let us out on the golf course. My cell phone never stopped ringing the entire time we played in the downpour, between Patti, who said the fire marshals had come to the house because Matthew had gone missing, and Matt himself, with some incoherent story about car trouble on the Belt Parkway which ended with assurances that he was on his way to the golf course, fairly far out on Long Island. He never showed up.

After being among the missing for several days, Matt would arrive home unannounced. At this point, you never knew if you were going to get Dr. Jekyll or Mr. Hyde. I confronted him about this several times. "You remember Matt Byrne? I still really like him. But that other guy? I really can't stand him at all. He's scary."

Matt was bound to crash and burn, and he did. At a car fire on the Manhattan Bridge, he mouthed off to some lieutenant who wrote him up for insubordination. Coincidentally or not, he was called for a tox screen which, not surprisingly, he failed. Facing disciplinary charges for violating FDNY's "zero tolerance" drug policy, he wound up back at CSU intake on October 25, 2013. He checked the boxes for anxiety, depression, psychiatric illness, stress, trauma, and grief/bereavement, also acknowledging "job jeopardy."

Even I couldn't ignore where this was soon headed. On October 28, 2013, Matt gave his general power of attorney to Patti and me, at my suggestion and with no objection. The following day he was transported back to Mirmont. As his CSU counselor described it, "He went out like a rock star," flying high. Upon arrival in Pennsylvania, he refused to enter the facility, and instead walked to a nearby bar. Mirmont counselors eventually convinced him to return with them, but only after he had finished his beer and burger.

The preceding months of dealing with Matt's madness had left us all exhausted. At this point, another rehab stint at Mirmont did not just provide welcome relief. It was an absolute godsend. By letter dated October 31, 2013, Matt received notice from

FDNY that he had been suspended from duty as a Firefighter 1st Grade for violations of A.U.C. 202, FDNY's "Substance Policy: Drugs/Alcohol."

I considered that letter a godsend too. At least my son wouldn't get himself or someone else hurt or killed on the job.

XVIII.

For a phrase so clinically precise, "drug addict" carries an amazing number of connotations. Literally, it only refers to a person who is physiologically or psychologically dependent on medication, a relatively straightforward factual determination. How then does the term conjure up such a variety of negative images of who a drug addict is and how he or she acts? Why is it that we resist, despite all evidence to the contrary, applying that label to our own kid instead of simply acknowledging that he is indeed hooked on drugs?

There is now no doubt in my mind that Matt was a drug addict. When he finally left the local bar in Lima, Pennsylvania, and was escorted to Mirmont, a picture was taken as he was admitted to the facility for the second time. It shows a disheveled, wild-eyed young man, wearing his baseball hat backwards and a stoned expression with a hint of paranoia. Matt must have looked much the same when he had left home, yet somehow, I hadn't been ready then to pronounce this scathing judgment upon my son. However we would have described his current condition, Patti and I had clung to the hope that this time, in contrast to the others, the light would go on and "the cure" would take hold.

As soon as Matthew arrived, even though it was after 9 p.m., the people at Mirmont began processing him, even completing an initial history and assessment. He reported a host of problems, affecting all aspects of his life: failing a drug test on the job; abusing opiates; spending all his money; short temper; social withdrawal; even hallucinations: hearing or seeing things every day when using cocaine or when not being able to sleep, a more severe problem of late. He had fallen again off the fire truck about a week before, but had not reported the injury, which aggravated his already chronic back pain.

At Mirmont, Matt acknowledged past thoughts or plans of suicide, "a couple of times," by throwing himself out a window or slicing his wrists vertically. He admitted he had used a razor on a prior occasion as a teen, presumably after the lost ballgame, and more recently woke up to a butcher knife next to his wrist. He also said he felt "diseased," and had thoughts of cutting himself open and washing out his organs. He reported his stay in Holliswood, accurately describing it as a psychiatric hospital, and noted prior diagnoses of PTSD and manic-depressive disorder. Still, he was assessed as "low risk, no follow up needed at this time," apparently because his affirmative answers to suicidality, plan and intent were all "past" and not "current". In response to questions about protective factors, like spirituality or a sense of obligation to others, and the things you value most in life, he had referred to our dog, Portia, for whom he felt responsible. As Matt often commanded, if it somehow did not happen, "My dog eats at 6 p.m.!"

Matt recounted his alcohol and drug usage, beginning in his teens, which included passing experimentation with methamphetamine, LSD, and K2, and present use of marijuana, Percocet, Klonopin, and four bags of cocaine per week.

While ingesting those drugs before his admission, Matt had been neglecting what he was supposed to be taking: Seroquel for bipolar disorder and depression, and Wellbutrin for his tobacco chewing habit and depression. Mirmont's staff began a detox regimen of Phenobarbital, Thiamine and Folate. The following day, he was put on Suboxone to address the opioid addiction. By the fifth day, the detox was discontinued, and Matt was able to begin the actual rehabilitation program.

For reasons that will become apparent, I'll refer to the woman to whom Matt was assigned as the Benign Counselor. She was very professional, also very upbeat, and they hit it off right away. This had not happened during Matt's prior rehab stints. The counselors he encountered, for the most part, had traveled the same road as him, but he was unimpressed with their war stories and warnings of what they could spare him from.

Matt opened up to the Benign Counselor right away. He told her that he and his younger brother had battled over his drug use, and that when he threatened violence against various persons during a group session at FDNY's CSU, he wound up at Holliswood. He had stopped taking the Seroquel and Wellbutrin he had been prescribed there, and reverted to illegal drug usage, which only fed his paranoia.

Matt confessed that he had joined FDNY to potentially die saving someone heroically, and he had thoughts of hurting himself on a regular basis, mostly by cutting. He described the thoughts as a movie reel he could not stop yet insisted that he would never act on those thoughts because he considered suicide a cowardly act and did not want to hurt his family or his dog. He also made clear that he did not believe that Twelve-Step programs work, and doubted that addiction was a disease, as opposed to a character flaw. The Benign Counselor described his prognosis as guarded.

In daily sessions, however, Matt and his counselor delved deeper into his issues. He recognized his selfish behavior during active addiction, such as planning to buy holiday gifts for family members, then instead spending the money on drugs and alcohol and not even showing up for the gathering. He told her about his habit of feeling intense emotion and swallowing it without expressing it. Despite his discomfort in expressing his feelings to his peers, Matt was speaking up more often in group sessions, and the Benign Counselor upgraded his prognosis to fair.

Sunday, November 9, 2013 was visiting day at Mirmont. The Benign Counselor was so accommodating that, although family sessions were normally scheduled only on weekdays, she offered to hold one with Matt, Patti and I after the visit to save us a separate trip.

The twenty-eight day stay insurers allow you for rehab goes very fast; shortly after you start the program, you need to start talking about what's going to happen when you are finished and discharged. The Benign Counselor made it very clear from the outset that Matt would need quite extended care and would be recommended for transfer to Ambrosia Treatment Center in Florida, if FDNY's CSU approved and the insurer would cover it. We were totally impressed with her approach, and Matt seemed on board. Although tempered by all the previous failures, I looked at Patti and could tell we were both thinking the same thing: maybe this was the person who could save Matt from himself.

It was a lively session, with the Benign Counselor noting that both father and son used humor and sarcasm to communicate. She was referring to the banter that had begun many years ago when Matt Byrne Raconteur rode in the back of my car to nursery school. She challenged Matt's resistance to Twelve-Step involvement, and our own negative experiences with Al-Anon, which she was certain would provide positive support despite the additional stress of getting there at the end of the day.

Matt continued to progress at Mirmont as the days until discharge counted down. He was part of a VIPER group of police officers, firefighters, and other first responders that addressed PTSD and other issues common to their occupations by use of EMDR (eye movement desensitization and reprocessing) techniques.

One of the traumatic events he relived dated back to his teens: the recovery effort at Jones Beach for the drowning victim's body. The other was the deaths of the two young children in Chinatown after they had been hit by a truck. Matt told the therapist that when he arrived at the scene, blood was everywhere, and the kids were covered with it. He didn't know what to do and felt helpless, so he held them, lying to the one who asked if he would be okay. By the end of the session, he realized he had done the best he could, and that the last thing the child heard was his kind words, which helped the boy not be scared. Matt was able to work through his doubts about doing the right thing, and his anger at his fellow fire fighters who had just stood back, remaining uninvolved.

On November 13, 2013 Matt reported to the psychiatrist that

the "never ending reel" in his head had stopped, as had the recurring violent thoughts of self-harm, which supposedly had been only "past," not "current." He was prescribed Luvox for depression and Risperdal for bipolar disorder, the diagnosis he had picked up during his several facility stays, even though none of us recalled anything resembling a manic, as opposed to a straight depressed state.

Matt's fog was really lifting. He told his group that the last time he was in rehab, if there were a rule he did not agree with he would not follow it, just as he would break the rules of society and on his job. Now he was following the rules, listening to staff, and feeling good about it because "life is harder when breaking rules." The Benign Counselor was impressed and wrote that Matt "is assessed to be in preparation stage of change … able to relate with peers … focused on acceptance and humility … gaining insight into importance of changing attitudes and behaviors in early recovery … a positive participant in group session." Once again, she deemed his prognosis "fair."

The following week in a group session, Matt tried to convince a peer who was considering leaving treatment to stay. He described the significant change he had observed in this fellow, and his own feeling of happiness to be in treatment and sober. He also addressed his feelings of helplessness, as a first responder, when he couldn't help others. The Benign Counselor tried to help Matt challenge these perceptions, instilled by training, of his role as rescuer.

By November 21, 2013, the plans for Matt to transition the next week to Ambrosia were in motion, thanks to the Benign

Counselor who worked the phones with the insurer and her counterparts elsewhere to make it happen. Matt was excited about the move, conceding his need for continuing care and avoiding the temptations at home, and admitting to the Benign Counselor that he had stolen his mother's pain medications in the past.

November 25, 2013 was Matt's last full day at Mirmont. He was seen by the psychiatrist, reporting good results from the Luvox and Risperdal. He told the doctor he was feeling more "chipper," yet denied the "manic" diagnosis. That afternoon, Matt informed his group that he was preparing for discharge. He shared how, when he had returned from treatment in the past, he had been ridiculed and, in response, lashed out at coworkers. He asked for suggestions from his peers as to how best to handle returning to work and feeling labeled an outcast because of addiction. Matt further told the group that this stay at Mirmont had been a very positive experience for him, and that he felt excited to move on to the next phase of treatment. The next day, two days before Thanksgiving, the Mirmont staff transported him to Philadelphia International Airport for a flight to Palm Beach, where he was met by Ambrosia staff who drove him to Singer Island, Florida. This was all arranged by the Benign Counselor, who cared for him so much and coordinated everything with the FDNY, the insurer, and Ambrosia.

*

Matt's concern when leaving Mirmont that he would be

shunned or mocked on his return to work was misplaced. The reality was that he would never report to duty at a FDNY firehouse again.

Having failed his drug screen, FDNY's zero tolerance policy meant that Matt would eventually be fired. He could drag the ordeal out, exhausting all the due process the Department offered, but he knew he would ultimately be discharged. More important, it became clear, during our telephone calls and face to face visits while he was at Mirmont, that he knew he should be off the job, and it was time to start something new.

Like any other client, Matt authorized me to cut the deal on his behalf. With the good offices of the supervisor at CSU, who served as the intermediary with the FDNY's disciplinary people, and with input from Matt's union representative and the union's attorney, the bargain was eventually struck: CSU would get Matt the treatment he needed to come out of his freefall, first at Mirmont, then at Ambrosia. Matt's December 2, 2013 appearance date to respond to the disciplinary charges before the Bureau of Investigation and Trials ("BITS") would be adjourned. Then, after finishing the Florida program, he would return to New York and retire from the FDNY and get on with the rest of his life.

That was the positive context of his trip to Ambrosia. He wasn't entering the program as the strung out, crushed man he had been the night he finally walked into Mirmont. Instead, he was on an upswing, although still needing to get stronger and figure out what would come next for him.

When Matt arrived at Ambrosia on November 26, 2013, he lucked out again on assignment of counselors. His was a bright young man who had overcome a major problem and turned his own life around in remarkably short order. He was insightful, but not preachy, and Matt connected with him immediately.

Due to confidentiality restrictions, and despite the resulting frustrations, family members of the addict remain very uninformed by the program's staff – at Ambrosia or elsewhere – as to the course of treatment. The knowledge I now have was gleaned long after the fact from medical records, obtained in anticipation of a battle with the insurer over lifetime limits on coverage, a fight that was eventually preempted by Matt's death.

After struggling with the addiction itself, dealing with medical insurers is the biggest challenge facing the loved one's family. You should assume that the patient has no capacity for handling the myriad of confusing explanations of benefits, checks, and denials that arrive in the mail on practically a daily basis. Someone else must take on this project, and it is a nightmare within the bigger nightmare of having your child in rehab once again.

I am not going to bore you with all the painful details of the coverage fights you should expect if you ever find yourself in this position, particularly when there have been multiple admissions, and the "lifetime" benefits are close to exhaustion. I will note, however, that once again the Benign Counselor came to the rescue. Even though she was affiliated with an entirely different program, she managed to get a $4,500 out-of-pocket payment reversed. She was some dedicated professional!

The "game plan" was for Matt to complete Ambrosia's inpatient program on Monday, January 6, 2014, fly to New York that evening, wrap matters up with the FDNY on Tuesday and

Wednesday, if needed, and return to Florida to a second Ambrosia Intensive Out-Patient Program on January 9, during which he would reside in a sober house. Everything seemed to be going according to plan. Matt called regularly and sounded hopeful on the phone.

Saturday and Sunday, December 21-22, 2013, was Family Weekend at Ambrosia, so we flew down to Florida on Friday and planned to return Sunday afternoon. The place on Singer Island was nice, Matt looked better than he had in months, and his friends all seemed very positive about beating their mutual problems – which they had no shame in discussing. Matt's particular friend, whom I'll call Tommy, was a fanatic Boston sports fan, who was riding obnoxiously high on both Red Sox and Patriots championships. Tommy had received a terminal cancer diagnosis and was trying to make things right with his family while he still could. Matt told us how he worried about Tommy's survival, and Patti and I both felt for our son, who was already foreseeing the loss of his friend, all of us then unaware that Tommy would still be fighting for his life after Matt had taken his.

We had a family session with Matt's counselor and discussed his future plans. Matt took him through his imminent FDNY resignation and return to the Ambrosia outpatient program, held at a different facility. Matt then disclosed his intention to leave Florida and travel to New York to "help out" after my hip replacement on March 7. The counselor, normally very low key, was adamant that this trip home was a very bad idea. Matt was unswayed and further informed the counselor that, after I was up and around following the surgery, he would make his annual surfing pilgrimage to Hawaii – another very bad idea, according to the counselor. This was all news to Patti and me, and we simply remained silent and did not react at that time.

The following morning, we went to a presentation at the other Ambrosia facility, several miles away in Palm Beach Gardens. The speaker was a dynamic former client, who first told his story, then worked the room, quizzing clients and their family members alike. He put each person on the spot, pressing for candid answers.

When he reached Matt, our son told the group he was losing his job as a firefighter because of his drug use, and that he now felt a sense of relief. The speaker contradicted him forcefully, telling him that "You will grieve your loss of identity as a firefighter. That's who you are. You don't know who you are without it." Matt didn't have much to say the rest of the visit, and Patti and I had plenty to think and talk about on the flight back. The Byrne family Christmas would take place without our son for the first time since he was born.

Matt wrapped up the first stage of the Ambrosia program in early January, 2014, and was preparing for his flight back to New York on January 6 when a blizzard dumped more than a foot of snow on New York City, closing all the airports. I was a bit panicked, because I couldn't reach anyone at the FDNY to tell them he wouldn't be able to show up on the scheduled resignation date.

When I finally made contact the following day, I initially took some flak. Without explanation, however, the Department's attitude then softened. I was told that it would be alright if Matt completed the second stage of the Ambrosia program before returning to New York. His date to report to FDNY Headquarters to resign/retire was rescheduled to February 21, 2014.

*

I would say the balance of Matt's stay in Florida was uneventful, other than the debate that ensued when he disclosed his future plans to his counselor and us. Patti and I were convinced that his counselor was right. A prolonged stay at home, followed by a trip to Hawaii, seemed like a recipe for disaster. The Hawaii excursion particularly irked me. I felt it signaled a lack of maturity for someone whose chosen career was over and, in my view, needed to redirect himself as soon as possible. It seemed like there would be way too much down time before his next certain steady employment – lifeguarding for the summer at Jones Beach – would begin.

Matt's days were spent again in group and individual therapy sessions at Ambrosia's Palm Beach Gardens facility, together with Twelve-Step meetings and periodic meetings with a psychiatrist for medication monitoring and follow-up. At night, he would return to the sober house, which apparently duplicated the random drug screening performed by Ambrosia, and offered nightly programs on topics like community and spirituality, as well as individual counseling sessions. As far as we knew, the drug screens were all negative and he was complying with whatever he was asked to do.

Matt called one night, all excited and anxious to speak to us.

As part of the program, Ambrosia had been encouraging the clients to secure some part-time employment. He told us that, on his very first try, he had landed a job in a restaurant, probably based on his experience as a waiter over one winter he spent in Hawaii before joining the FDNY.

"That's great, Matt," I told him. "You're on your way back now."

The next time he called, as fathers tend to do, I asked him how the job was going.

"Oh, that's over," Matt responded.

"What happened?"

"I got in an argument with some jerk the day after I started. I quit. I didn't need that job anyway."

As I hung up the phone, I tried to convince myself that this wasn't the end of the world, which it wasn't. At the same time, it wasn't a very good sign for what lay ahead.

On Wednesday, February 19, 2014, Matt flew out of West Palm Beach for JFK. I had prayed it would not snow again and it didn't. He had a day to spare before his resignation at FDNY Headquarters at Metrotech in Brooklyn.

*

That evening, I picked Matt up at JFK from his Jet Blue flight out of Palm Beach. Thursday was our bad weather hedge day, which thankfully proved unnecessary. Friday morning, we took off early for Metrotech. I would usually travel to Downtown Brooklyn by the Long Island Rail Road, and I have no idea why we drove. Maybe we were looking for the privacy that the car provides.

Considerable preparation went into Matt's retirement. I had discussed it with him since he was suspended in late October. He said he had no desire to be placed in a "rubber room" for months like a friend of his charged with a similar drug offense who intended to squeeze every last paycheck out of the FDNY. Although his union representative had encouraged him to "fight it," Matt felt that getting out was the honorable thing to do. I fully agreed.

Since Matt wasn't going to contest the separation, the union rep and lawyer both backed off, and I wound up acting as counsel to my son, probably a terrible conflict of interest since I wanted him off the job so badly for so many reasons.

On January 8, 2014, when Matt became stuck in Florida, I had gone in to Metrotech so at least someone appeared on his behalf. I met with the retirement person and the BITS Deputy Director to compile a "to do" list of everything needed to finalize his retirement when he appeared in person. They needed all his firefighting gear and equipment back, and a friend from his firehouse was kind enough to gather it, turn it in to the Quartermaster, and get me the receipt. They needed documentation showing where he had been since December, and his Ambrosia counselor had obtained the necessary letters from both facilities. Matt also needed to turn in his badge and FDNY identification card. The latter was a problem. While the badge was found in his room at home, the ID card was nowhere to be found. A police report had to be filed with the Rockville Centre Police Department, which would only categorize it as "lost" since its whereabouts, and those of Matt's N.Y.S. driver's license which he thought had also been in his car, could not be confirmed during his last few months in rehab.

The police report was accepted in lieu of the FDNY identification card, but this caused one final complication: a $30.00 fee was due for the lost card, and the FDNY does not accept cash. Ever so close to the finish line, we had to leave Headquarters and find the Chase Bank branch on the other side of Metrotech. This is when two peculiar things occurred.

We entered the bank and walked up some steps to the tellers. There was no line, and I did not have to wait to explain what I needed. The teller verified my account at Chase in Rockville Centre, took my cash, and issued a $30.00 money order payable to the FDNY.

As we started to leave the branch, we ran into my friend and neighbor from Rockville Centre, Mike, the former firefighter I had waited on line with for World Series tickets. Mike had always been friendly with Matt and supportive of his FDNY career. He was immediately aware that something was up. First came the small talk. Mike's son, Paul's age and former teammate, had recently taken a job with Chase and Mike was meeting him for lunch. While we spoke, Matt announced he would wait outside. The conversation turned serious.

"Why are you both down here?" Mike asked.

"Matt's putting in his papers. He got in way over his head, Mike. He's got to get out."

Mike should never play poker; the look on his face was pure

sorrow. "I'm sorry, Ed. That's rough."

"Yeah, I know. He made a big mistake. But it's what comes next that counts, right?" Mike agreed and promised to stay in touch.

It was turning even colder when I caught up with Matt outside. Breaths visible, we walked as quickly as I could, my cranky hip dragging, across the Metrotech campus to the FDNY building. We had been given a deadline to return by – or else come back the next day – and it was drawing near. We hustled through security for a second time and jumped on the elevator.

As we exited, the Chief of the Department was waiting for a down elevator, wearing a black leather FDNY bomber jacket. This handsome gray-haired guy had been a fine basketball player I knew from my Queens playground days. I had seen him more recently at events honoring Harry Ford and his lost comrades.

"Hi, Ed. What have you been up to?" he asked, glancing over at Matt.

"Oh, still practicing law – until I get it right." I didn't want to get into specifics, whether out of deference to Matt's feelings or my own.

He laughed at the joke as a bell rang, then got on the elevator with a "Take care." Matt and I returned to the Badge Desk, turned over the money order, and completed the retirement process.

"Are you starving like I am?" I asked when we reached the campus level.

"Yeah. There's a Five Guys on the other side of the quad," Matt replied.

He was clearly relieved that the day was over. He had been spared the ordeal of a BITS appearance; he only had a brief hallway exchange with its Assistant Commissioner who wished him good luck and left it at that.

Starting in Five Guys, and all the way home, I continued the pep talks I'm sure I had already been delivering. "You have to look at this as an opportunity." "Not many people get a chance to reboot their entire life." "Why don't you try to remember something you always wanted to be and figure out what you would need to do to make that happen. You realize you could go back to school?" I wasn't sure that I was getting through, but I believed it all was true and I wasn't going to stop until I convinced him as well.

*

I don't believe that all addictions are created equal. Why should that be? Isn't it more likely that the degree of compulsion a person feels to abuse substances varies with the individual? I never heard that topic addressed in any of the family support groups we attended. Nor did anyone ever break the bad news that some of your kids might have a compulsion to use that's so strong it's virtually irresistible, and any attempt to recover is probably doomed to failure. For whatever reason, I kept remembering what a bad reaction Matt had to Dramamine as a little boy, when he had to be given it to avoid throwing up on a plane. He would be conked out for the entire flight, then start thrashing violently when we would have to wake him after landing.

Matt was actually serious about trying to help out when I had my hip replaced on Friday, March 7, 2014. He visited me a couple of times in the hospital over the weekend, then again the following week when I was relocated to a physical rehabilitation facility in Glen Cove. I had made sure to get rid of the huge blister pack of Percocet I had been given in the hospital before leaving for rehab, to avoid the pills somehow going missing.

Matt was definitely still in "early recovery," as the professionals called it, always with a preoccupied look on his face. He would arrive alone, never empty handed, but would fidget in an easy chair and couldn't sit still for long. After some brief conversation, typically about his plans to "get back in the game," he would say that he'd better get going and take off.

My impression was that he wasn't using but was very wistful, like a guy who had broken up with the love of his life but is hoping they get back together again. I was also concerned about his prolonged down time, alone at home and sleeping excessively, which I did not know whether to blame on the prescription drugs he was taking or something else.

With an anterior hip replacement, I was out of the rehab facility by Saturday, March 15, and back to work by St. Patrick's Day. The Nephew was on Spring break from college and kept Matt company the last few days he was home. On Thursday, March 20, despite lingering misgivings, I drove Matt to JFK for his flight to Hawaii.

Matt remained in Hawaii for over a month. We'll never know what happened on that trip, but it was nothing good. On April 17, 2014, while surfing in Kahuku, Hawaii, he wound up in an emergency room after suffering a laceration.

That doesn't sound like much and, when he returned home six days later, all you would notice was a blackened left eye. But apparently this latest accident was another near death experience, this time when sober. Matt was held under the surf, smashed against coral in the cove and, unlike the time he had drugged himself and fallen off the Long Beach dock, he became truly afraid of drowning.

I don't think Matt ever got on a surfboard again. He had once told me that surfing was the most important thing in his life, and the fact that he had surfed throughout the four winters he had spent in Maine made me take him seriously. Just like his separation from the FDNY, this new fear of a sport he had loved so much was another great loss of identity.

*

Matt returned to New York on April 23, 2014, two days before our grandson Manuel's First Communion. We had heard about the surfing accident already, but at that time Matt downplayed how serious it had been, and how much it had affected him.

The Mass was held in Manhattan at St. Thomas More Church, where Jackie Onassis used to attend services. Manuel and his second grade classmates from St. David's School were all dressed alike in blue blazers and slacks. After the ceremony, we walked back to Elizabeth's nearby apartment for a family party.

It was nice to see everyone. Manny's parents were up from

Puerto Rico, and my own mother was in attendance for her great grandson's big day. The only ones missing were Paul, who couldn't skip work on a weekday, and "Titi" Ann, who was still in Los Angeles for a few more weeks until she completed her City Year commitment. There were "catching up" conversations, particularly with the Villars, and plenty of photos, including a great shot of Manuel proudly grinning alongside his Uncle Matt, who still had a shiner visible under his left eye.

When the cake came out after dinner, however, things turned sour. I'm sure he only meant to fool around, but when Matt lifted Manuel and turned him upside down over the cake, the boy's hair did hit the frosting. Manuel started crying, Beba and Matt started yelling at each other and, as best I can recollect, the party was pretty much ruined.

That day is emblematic of our lives at the time. How can a First Holy Communion party end up rancorous? I really don't know, but I saw it happen and I know who the catalyst was. It was probably a quiet ride home, with everyone pretending they had not seen what we had all just witnessed.

*

That Sunday, April 27, 2014, Matt decided to accompany me on a trip to Princeton University where a client's son on the Cornell baseball team was playing a doubleheader.

It was lunchtime when we arrived, and we decided to stop in town to eat before heading to the field. We found a pub that was just opening, so we placed orders with the waitress, who warned that the food would take a while. Matt was restless while we waited. He asked me for juke box money, and the next thing I knew he had the box blaring oldies in the empty dining room.

It was hard to speak over the noise, yet I was able to tell Matt that my client, who understood his situation, was willing to offer him a job in September, after he worked the summer at Jones Beach to "ramp back up" and get accustomed to a regular work schedule. Matt was very pleased, and immediately adopted the plan, despite recognizing that full-time, steady employment meant this would be his final summer at Jones Beach.

When we left the pub, Matt insisted that he needed tobacco, which he had been chewing incessantly since his return from Hawaii. It wasn't that easy to find near the Princeton campus, but we eventually did succeed in a gas station.

As we drove to the field, I thought about how much had happened in the twelve years since he walked on a college campus like the students and athletes we saw along the way. It may be hard to believe, but I didn't let the many missteps disturb me. My attitude has always been that we are where we are, and the only question should be where do we go from here.

When we arrived at the field, we joined my client and his family and caught most of the first game, which Princeton won. It was a sunny, early spring day that was perfect to watch a ballgame, just as we had done together many times before. We didn't stick around for the nightcap, which I found out the next day was won by Cornell. Matt was talkative the whole way home, and excited about his future prospects.

*

I'm no doctor, and I don't understand the physiological or psychological effects of drug abuse. It was obvious to anyone, though, that Matt had damaged himself cognitively by his use of opioids and other drugs. He wasn't recognizable as the graduate of a top ranked liberal arts college who could have chosen so many different paths in 2002, nor even the opinionated FDNY probie who would listen to right wing talk radio instead of music after the end of a shift, a habit that I warned could drive you nuts. (How anomalous is the image of a politically conservative drug addict?) What was not clear was whether his labored and interrupted thinking was a reversible condition. If Matt quit using, could he regain his mental capacity and return to his old self, a guy who once could recognize Bob Dylan forcing a rhyme in *Positively 4th Street* when a master thief appeared for no plausible purpose.

My son now had a plan to reclaim his life. The trick was to move forward, without slipping backward to where he had been. The first step was for him to get through the next few weeks of additional downtime in late April and early May 2014, until he could resume lifeguarding and re-enter the workforce.

We thought he had caught a break. Matt had almost fifteen years of service in the New York State Park system, so he was sent out to work as soon as the beaches opened for swimming in May. Since lifeguarding is a job that no one retires from voluntarily, many other guards had much more seniority and could claim the "preseason" spots open at nearby Jones Beach. Matt was sent to Robert Moses State Park, a beautiful ocean beach, but located on the western end of Fire Island in Suffolk County. That was fine by me, longer drive or not. Matt would be going out to work immediately, then would be transferred back to Jones Beach when the summer season began for real.

Matt had only been going back and forth to Robert Moses a few days when the next calamity struck. On Wednesday, May 28, 2014, he did not show up for dinner. We eventually received a phone call from the Park police. When turning to leave the Robert Moses parking lot at the end of the day, Matt had gone past the concrete edge, hit the soft sandy shoulder, and rolled the black Dodge Journey he had purchased when he joined the FDNY. The officers said he seemed okay yet had been transported by ambulance to Good Samaritan Hospital in West Islip to be checked out.

I found my way to this latest place I had heard of but never been before, arriving at dusk. After I had been told by the cops on the phone that he was all right, the only emotion I remember feeling was anger. I don't know whether I had reached the breaking point with all my kid's screw-ups but, on that particular night, I was simply pissed at him and, even though he looked beat up and pathetic lying on a narrow bed in the E.R., I didn't have any sympathy for his latest predicament. I was probably just reacting to the deep disappointment that another mishap provoked. My face must have said it all: "Can't you do anything right anymore?"

We barely spoke in the emergency room, as we waited for him to be discharged. They had run multiple CT scans and other tests, including a drug screen, and concluded that there was no need for Matt to be admitted. Then I heard the motherly emergency room doctor say to him before we left, "This didn't have to happen …." My blood just started boiling again at this assignment of fault. I left him to go fetch the car for a silent ride home.

The following day my anger had already subsided, and I awoke in full mop-up mode. I reported the accident to the insurance company and drove out to the collision shop in West Islip where Matt's car had been towed. A sympathetic employee, who was having a similar heartache with one of his own kids, walked me to the back of the lot where Matt's car had been dumped. The air bags had deployed during the rollover, and the guy told me the smashed-up car was a total loss, posing a new problem of how Matt was supposed to get back and forth to work from then on.

That wasn't a problem for long. The police report apparently recorded the time of the accident as slightly before 6 p.m., when Matt's shift was supposed to end. The beach had been empty, and he and the other guards had knocked off early, signing themselves out since the timekeeper had already left for the day. Since Matt had been written up for missing a "sit" in late August, 2013, the prior season, he was suspended from duty immediately and termination was recommended by the Robert Moses supervisor on June 6, 2014.

The matter dragged on for several weeks, while the lifeguards' union debated what position to take. Ultimately, their lawyer told me that, while Matt had been a high performing lifeguard in terms of saves, the union would not support him due to the prior written warning. Another "deal" was cut on July 9, 2014. Matt resigned his position on the understanding that, if he straightened himself out, he could reapply without being barred from rehire.

Matt was now in deep trouble: no job, no car, and a gaping hole in the employment recovery plan. His inability to keep the lifeguarding job for more than a few days made the thought of him coming to work for my client after Labor Day in the high-pressure construction field look like a total pipe dream. The medications he was taking were making him groggy, and he was still having residual pain from the car crash. He spent most of the day moping around the house.

We tried to keep him as occupied as we could, given that everyone else was working and running around attending to their own affairs. We had a nice night when Bernie Williams and his band played at Molloy College. Matt got to meet his Yankee hero at a reception after the concert, and asked Bernie why the band hadn't played *Disco Inferno*, Bernie's old "walk-up" song when he came to bat. I brought him down to the Challenger game each Saturday, since he had enjoyed working with those kids in the past. Matt had shown up with a giant box of tacos the season before and became the players' hero for life.

While Matt remained unduly disturbed that the Catholic Church had seen fit to change all the prayers he had learned in his youth, shifting instead to a more literal translation of the old Latin versions, he would occasionally volunteer to accompany me to Mass. Even that could become an adventure in Matt's fragile state.

One Sunday morning, he came with me to the Queen of

Peace Residence where my mother lives. Before the Mass started, one little nun approached him where he sat at the end of our pew. "Carry the Cross?," she asked. He looked at me for guidance. I shrugged my shoulders and said, "Up to you." He stood up and accompanied her to the back of the chapel.

When the music started, Matt led the procession down the aisle. Upon reaching the altar, he turned left, eventually circling up a side aisle to the rear of the chapel where I could hear the nun yelling at him: "You walk too fast!" I guess no good deed does go unpunished, even in church.

On July 18, 2014, after he had received his insurance check for the value of the wrecked Journey, Patti and I took him to the car dealer we were friendly with to buy a used 2012 Ford Escape. Perhaps it was a gesture, to show we had not written him off and were sure he would get back into the workforce. As he signed the financing papers, spitting tobacco into an empty Poland Spring bottle while our saleswoman watched, this latest gamble had the look of a very long shot, but we felt it had to be taken.

Monday, July 21, 2014, we were all headed in different directions. I was headed to a charity golf outing in Port Washington. Patti was taking Matt for an MRI in Plainview since he was still experiencing back pain.

It was getting late in the day, and our foursome's final tee shot was supposed to go over a pond and up a hill to the green – not an easy one for me. I'm not sure I ever took it. The cell phone was ringing in my pocket. Patti was on the line, and Matthew was with her.

She began telling me that they had gotten home, but Matt

wanted to go out again, supposedly to an Alcoholics Anonymous meeting. He planned to take the Ford, which had just sat in the driveway for the couple of days since he'd gotten it.

Patti put him on the phone, as I requested. His speech was off, but he kept insisting "I have to go to a meeting". I tried to talk him out of it, saying, "You sound tired. Go to a meeting tomorrow." The most I got out of him was "I'll think about it".

When I arrived home, Matt and the car were gone. Patti said he had stuck with the AA story and took off right after dinner. The evening wore on, like so many others, with no word where he was. We must have given up around 10 p.m. and gone to bed.

I couldn't have been asleep for more than a few minutes when the phone on the nightstand rang.

"Dad?"

"Matt, is that you?" The voice on the other end was very slurred.

"I got jammed up, Dad."

"What's that mean?"

"I got arrested."

"Where are you?" I asked, already getting out of bed. "I'll come down."

It took a while to extract enough information to figure out where he was: a N.Y.S. Police outpost on the Southern State Parkway, several miles west of Rockville Centre.

When I arrived, it was locked up tight. You pressed a bell to get into an interior waiting room. Then after a long wait, and a conversation with an intercom, I was finally buzzed into the office.

The reason for the delay became apparent: Officer V., who made the arrest, was a one-man show; there was no one else in the place. He determined that Matt was my son, then told me how he wound up there. There had been a chase, I later learned on the Northern Parkway not the Southern, after Officer V. had tried to pull Matt over for driving erratically. When he finally slowed, Matt had run the Escape into the side of an abutment. The fun wasn't over yet; Matt was still yelling and struggling inside the car when Officer V. and another trooper who assisted finally managed to handcuff him.

I didn't play lawyer at all. I told him my son was in bad shape: ex-FDNY; ex-Jones Beach; multiple rehabs; and a psychiatric hospitalization with a dual diagnosis. Officer V. listened carefully, before telling me to stay put while he went to another room.

After a few minutes, he came back. He told me he was going to let me take Matt home, rather than keep him there overnight. "He seems like a good kid. But you really need to get him some help!" I assured Officer V. that was what we were trying to do.

The officer then took me to where he had Matt locked up. He was sitting on a long bench which had multiple metal rings implanted in it, so that it would accommodate several prisoners. He was lucky, the only prisoner chained to the bench that night. Matt had only one flip flop on, and his feet were cut and bleeding. When he tried to speak to me, his mouth could barely move and he was essentially incoherent. Officer V., an extremely decent guy, handed me Matt's tickets – driving while intoxicated, reckless driving, leaving the scene of a property damage accident, and resisting arrest – then led us out of the building, holding the doors and wishing us good luck.

Cicadas were going crazy as I had Matt lean on me. I dragged him to my car in the small parking lot adjacent to the parkway where traffic still whizzed by despite the late hour. I almost dropped him when I opened the passenger side door, but I pushed him in and managed to get his seatbelt fastened. We headed west to the next exit, then crossed the parkway and turned back toward Rockville Centre, where the trip from the car to Matt's third-floor bedroom, witnessed with great concern by Portia, was at least as difficult.

*

We did not know at the time that Matthew's spree on July 21, 2014 was intended to take his life. He had purchased a quart of vodka, collected a variety of pills, and hoped to die quietly in his car after finishing them off. When he realized his plan wasn't working, he revised it to include a high-speed car crash. Officer V. had intervened before its execution, so Matt's list of recent failures now included an inability to kill himself.

The next morning, I went to work, figuring there was no point in trying to rouse Matt and start picking up the pieces until at least early afternoon.

I went home to get him then. He could still barely speak, but he got up and accompanied me to another collision yard, this time in Hicksville, where Officer V. had told me the Ford had been towed. Matt was swaying at the counter while we talked to the manager, Bob, collecting glances from several ladies at their desks who looked concerned that he could simply collapse. Bob took us out to a back lot to view the vehicle Matt had for four days and only driven once. Given what it had been through, it didn't look too bad. I made arrangements for my collision guys to have it towed to their shop, then we left.

When we arrived home, we entered the side door where Portia again greeted us in the kitchen. I asked Matt whether he wanted to eat. He shook his head wordlessly, proceeding through the dining room and climbing the stairs to the third-floor room under his own power this time.

He truly looked broken. There was no sign of "Bad Matt," the guy who would forget he left his car in a bank's parking lot in Freeport after using the ATM to get money to buy drugs from the dealer down the block. That sometimes arrogant, sometimes frightening guy was gone for good, replaced by a new version who just seemed totally beaten.

No one saw him the rest of the day and he just kept sleeping into the night. I told Patti my concerns. I called our therapist friend Leslie and booked an appointment for Matt at 9 a.m. the following morning. I warned Patti that, unless Leslie saw some reason to talk me out of it, I was taking him back to Long Island Jewish because he looked like he had a complete breakdown.

The next day's session with Leslie was painful to watch. She would question him, and Matt would try to respond, but his words came out in super slow motion, his lips quivering when he tried to form them. When the conversation finally ended, with Matt's voice hoarse and dry, Leslie told me on the side that I should definitely take him to the hospital.

I had packed a bag with Matt's things that morning and placed it on the back seat of the car. I had tried not to sandbag him, and warned him that, depending on what Leslie had to say, I would be taking him to LIJ. He offered no resistance at all and, when we left Leslie's house, I told him that would be our destination because he needed help.

It was a beautiful summer day, and some views were spectacular as we left Rockaway over the Cross Bay Bridge and drove through the Gateway National Park preserve. I followed Cross Bay Boulevard to the Belt Parkway, wrapped around to the Cross Island Parkway, then exited at Union Turnpike about a mile west of the hospital.

Maybe I was stalling, but I asked Matt whether he wanted to eat. He shook his head yes, and I pulled over when I saw a pizzeria which had its own parking lot in the back.

When we entered, I sat my son at a table by the window. "Do you want two slices?" I asked.

Again, he nodded.

"And a Coke?"

It looked like an affirmative response, and I placed the order.

The conversation that followed was extremely one-sided. I told Matt I was proud that he was willing to go for help, and that everything else was secondary and could be handled one step at a time. When the pizza was ready, I got up to fetch the tray. I can't remember a two-slice lunch ever taking so long. My son, who once could practically inhale a pizza slice, ate one slice at a painfully slow pace. He just rolled up the other in the paper plate, leaving it on the tray, which I eventually picked up, emptied in a garbage pail, and returned to the counter.

As we started up in the parking lot, the car's phone rang. It was actually Officer V., responding to a message I had left. Matt's phone was missing, and I had the nerve to ask the trooper whether he recalled seeing it anywhere. He had not and wished us luck in finding it in the car.

I thanked Officer V. again for his kindness, then drove the final few blocks to the LIJ Emergency Room.

Unlike two years before, when Matt had been turned away by LIJ's Emergency Room as no danger to himself or anyone else, this time he was readily admitted on July 23, 2014 and transferred to Zucker Hillside Hospital, LIJ's psychiatric facility.

That evening, as scheduled, all the Byrnes except Matt showed up for the annual barbecue dinner at the Queen of Peace Residence where by mother lives. Life goes on, with you or without you, and we ate hot dogs and hamburgers, with Mister Softee ice cream for dessert, hoping that somehow, against the odds, everything would end up fine.

*

I refuse to say a bad thing about Zucker, other than you don't want a loved one to have to spend time there or anywhere like it. That will probably happen, however, if your kid, like Matt, doesn't take the initial wakeup calls they receive seriously. The FDNY sent him to places that resembled country clubs. Even Holliswood, at least in the veterans' wing, wasn't bad enough to convince Matt that, no matter what, he would never come back.

Matt did not seem to realize that there was an urgency to getting this right, and, that each relapse made it less likely that he could eventually recover for good.

It's not about the building; Zucker's facilities were relatively new and well maintained. It's not about the staff; the doctors were dedicated professionals, and we already knew several of the caring attendants who had formerly worked at Holliswood and found jobs at Zucker when Holliswood closed. It is all about the clientele, and that can be a very mixed bag. Matt's first roommate was just a young man who had hit some hard times in his personal life. He helped Matt adjust to the place over the first few days, and we were sorry to see him go. Not everyone housed at Zucker was nearly such good company. They ran the gamut, from effectively catatonic to potentially violent.

Patti and I came to visit Matt at least once, and sometimes twice a day, always bringing him food, which was allowed during visits. During the week, only one-hour visits were available, either 1:30 – 2:30 p.m., or 7-8 p.m., and we juggled our work schedules to make sure each slot was covered. Weekends were easier, with two-hour visiting periods, either 2-4 p.m. or 6-8 p.m., so we weren't so restricted.

My mother even insisted on coming to visit. Matt had missed her 90th birthday party on July 27, and she wanted to tell him she loved him and that everything would turn out all right. She's an unflappable old woman, and just wheeled into the facility on her rollator, catching curious looks from both the staff and the other "poor souls," as she called them.

Each visit, we would first have to go through security, plenty of it, to reach a long counter which you passed to enter the general population. Patients were always milling around down the hallway from their bedrooms, checking out the arriving visitors. The more enterprising ones would start asking you for food, money or whatever. One obviously pregnant young lady found out I was a lawyer and began calling my office regarding her problem with her landlord. We'd try to keep moving through the crowd to a table at the back of the day room, think *One Flew Over the Cuckoo's Nest,* or in the adjacent solarium which had a nice view of an outdoor garden during daylight hours.

Our visits with Matt were essentially extended, tag-team pep talks, with Patti and I reassuring him that, despite all the setbacks, better days lay ahead. The doctors had changed his medications to Efflexor and Neurontin, but he remained seriously depressed by his circumstances. One early afternoon visit, holding his head in his hands Matt asked me:

"Dad, do you think I'm going to be an institutional guy?"

I paused before responding. "I really don't think so Matt. The fact that you asked that question convinces me that you're not going to end up like that. You'll be able to get out of here and stay out of here."

Another visit with both Patti and I was even more heartbreaking. As soon as were seated alone at one of the tables, Matt's hazel eyes filled with tears, and he began to cry.

"What's the matter, Matt?" Patti asked.

"I had a problem with Johnny Rocket."

"Johnny Rocket" was the nickname I had hung on one of his particularly aggressive fellow patients. He looked like a villain

from a Batman comic: hair bleached an unnatural shade of or-
ange, with a very strange gait which suggested he'd been hit by a
truck, but somehow reassembled by someone who hadn't followed the instructions.

"What happened?" I demanded.

"He came into my room the other night," Matt sobbed.
"Then he crawled into bed right next to me." Matt couldn't continue.

"Do you want me to talk to someone right now, or wait for
the doctor?" I asked.

When he nodded, I left the table. I had seen one of the former
Holliswood attendants on the way in. I managed to track him
down on the other side of the floor and explained what had happened.

"No way that's right! Not going to happen on my watch!" He
was true to his word. There was no visit from Johnny Rocket that
night, and the following day Matt's doctor called to inform me
that the offender had been relocated.

Ever so slightly, Matt's condition seemed to be improving after the Johnny Rocket incident. He seemed more alert and more
communicative. Like every similar facility, however, your length
of stay at Zucker was primarily dictated by your insurance coverage. In Matt's case, the insurer decided that 13 days of in-patient
care would be his lucky number so, on August 4, 2014, ready or
not, out he went from Zucker with a referral to LIJ's substance
abuse program, Project Outreach, and continued psychiatric care
on an outpatient basis.

*

On Tuesday, August 5, 2014, I accompanied Matt to his intake session at Project Outreach. We had been through similar drills enough times before to know what to expect. He would have lengthy group sessions several times a week in the middle of the day, and also individual sessions with a young female psychiatrist to whom he had been assigned.

I recall having reservations about the program right from the intake. We sat in the waiting room with a mother, father and their son. The kid looked about 16 years old and wore an oversized baseball hat sideways and flashy hip hop shirt, shorts and sneakers. I feared that the boy would be assigned to the same group as Matt, who had been accustomed to peer sessions with soldiers at Holliswood and other first responders at Mirmont. Prejudiced and haughty or not, I did not see how much meaningful dialogue would ever take place between my son and this kid, who inhabited different worlds. The only positive I saw from Matt's quick discharge from Zucker was that he would not miss his August 8 court date, as we had feared. He was to be arraigned on the various charges at 9 a.m. at First District Court, in Hempstead, Nassau County. It would be a busy day because, at 2 p.m., he had an appointment at the Nassau Day Training Center, housed in the same building as Project Outreach, to start receiving career counseling.

We had retained a criminal defense lawyer, used in the past by some of our firm's clients, to represent Matt on the tickets, the issuance of which had triggered multiple solicitation mailings from local attorneys. I had a couple of advance conversations with the lawyer, a very professional guy who even corrected a somewhat snarky comment I made in his client's presence by reminding me that my son "feels bad enough already."

The lawyer felt everything would go smoothly, given Matt's history and especially the Zucker psychiatrist's view that he had been misdiagnosed with bipolar disorder by some doctor during his multiple rehab stints, and was being mismedicated at the time of his arrest. The doctor had provided a letter to the court stating that he had ordered that the Risperidone and Fluvoxamine Maleate Matt had been taking for bipolar disorder be discontinued and had substituted Efflexor and Neurontin instead to treat what he considered classic depression.

The evening before the court appearance, the lawyer said he would meet Matt in court a half hour early to go over the case.

Things went south the next morning, even before Matt's case was called. His lawyer's counterpart, a rookie prosecutor, had given him a heads-up as an alumnus of the district attorney's office: the young female judge would not release any drunk driving defendant on his own recognizance. I was told to leave the courthouse and return with $1,000 cash for bail as soon as possible.

I did so and managed to get back before the case was reached on the calendar. Matt's lawyer made a fine presentation, his client blushing as his downward spiral was described to the judge, but she remained on a mission and insistent on making her point. After Matt's not guilty plea was entered, his license was suspended. The judge then set $1,000 as cash bail in lieu of $2,500 bond, ordering the defendant handcuffed by the court officers. Looking otherwise very respectable in a pressed gray suit, white shirt, tie and dress shoes, Matt stood stoically until the officers escorted him out of the courtroom and down the hallway to a holding cell. It was all a show, since Matt was released in under five minutes, but if the desired effect was to shame the defendant, the tactic worked like a charm. He looked despondent when they let him go.

The day continued the way it started. The afternoon meeting at the Nassau Day Training Center was very perfunctory. The evaluation he was promised was never scheduled, despite my numerous follow-up phone calls, and Matt's desperately needed career counseling never started.

Still, we were establishing a new routine of daily activities, and kept in what looked like forward motion, even though we had no idea where this was going. Depending on our schedules, Patti and I would take turns picking Matt up and driving him to West Hempstead, then giving him a lift home when Project Outreach ended for the day. Matt was also supposed to attend AA meetings and, perhaps for the first time, he faithfully did. Although there was a morning meeting in Rockville Centre, he preferred the "Early Riser" meeting in Long Beach, where he quickly integrated into the group. While I mentally questioned the longer trip – which made it harder to arrive on time since he still struggled to get out of bed in the morning – I kept my mouth shut. I was happy he was going to any meeting, near or far. I would walk the boardwalk for the hour, then get coffee before meeting him at the car for the return trip.

Matt was talking again, and there were lots of conversations during all these car rides. He probably thought I was annoyingly positive about the future, which I was whether I was driving him to an Early Risers or an AA meeting at night, or a Project Outreach session in between. On occasion, he would come with me late in the day to the Links. I would try to talk him into swimming laps with me, as we had done in the past there in the summer or at Hofstra's Swim Center during the rest of the year. Matt would politely decline; he had no interest in going in the water. He was content to wait for me at one of the tables, usually chatting with the pool director, Jim, who had been a few years ahead of Matt at Chaminade. They never swam together but had always been friendly and Jim's obvious concern for Matt was a gift he sorely needed.

We eventually talked about the night of the arrest, not as a criminal episode but, as he disclosed at Zucker, an attempt to kill himself. Matt assured me repeatedly that option was "off the table," and ultimately convinced me he was telling the truth. Not only did I want to believe him, I suppose I found the contrary concept that someone would want to end his chance for a comeback far less believable. I took him at his word, and recall being surprised when we met with Matt and his psychiatrist, that she asked Patti and I whether we kept any guns in the house. "No!", we had responded, emphatically, really missing the broader significance of the question and failing to recognize that our son had already explored that solution to his dilemma.

Months later, way too late to do any good, I learned some significant gender related facts about suicide. On a percentage basis, females try to take their lives far more often than men, but men are far more often successful. And if a man fails at his first suicide attempt, he's virtually certain to succeed on the second, which almost invariably follows.

I think someone probably should have mentioned that factoid to us. What If ….? After The Event, I kept imagining Matt making a half-hearted apology for what he had done: "Sorry about killing myself, DaddyO. But you really should have known better than to believe what I told you."

He would have been right.

*

As of Monday, August 11, 2014, we all seemed to be getting by, personally and professionally, operating under these "new normal" conditions. Patti took Matt to an orthopedist in Glen Cove because he was still experiencing back pain from one of his car crashes or a combination thereof. Later that afternoon, they learned that Robin Williams had taken his life. Matt couldn't stop talking about Williams's death or quizzing her for details of how the actor had done "it."

When I learned of the star's suicide, I sensed it was a very bad day, but still did not hear the alarms sounding. I should have realized how Matt must have interpreted that event. "If Robin Williams couldn't face living, with all he had going for him, what chance have I?"

*

For late August, it was a very busy time. I had meetings and a hearing in Manhattan the first three days of the week of August 11, then headed upstate on Thursday to deliver lectures at the Sagamore through early Sunday. As had become a new habit, Patti skipped the trip, staying home to "supervise" and drive Matt to the Project Outreach psychiatrist on Friday.

The next week was not much better, schedule-wise. I had to get The Nephew to the eye doctor on Monday. Patti and I had tickets for "Newsies" on Broadway Tuesday night. They had been purchased well before, and we almost decided to pass on the play until we concluded we could use a light night out. Meetings on Wednesday and Thursday were followed by a rendezvous Friday with the architect in Jamaica to select tiles for the Long Beach house. After Sandy, we had to level its remnants by December 31, 2012 or be taxed throughout 2013 like everything was fine. We made that deadline, but the lot was just rubble for a long time. Finally, things were looking up on that front. Construction was underway, and we hoped to occupy a brand new structure by the following summer of 2015.

Saturday, August 23, 2014 was move-in day at The Nephew's college in Pennsylvania. Since he had wrecked the new car his trustee had bought him during his freshman year, I was no longer able to wave bye-bye as he drove off with his stuff. Instead, I loaded up my car, drove the couple of hours to the school, helped him unpack and schlepp it all up the dormitory stairs, then headed back to New York. The hot and fairly grueling day was completed by a stop at a birthday party held for my aunt in Brooklyn.

When I finally arrived home, I had the encounter with Matt I described in Chapter I, when he left the family room to go upstairs for the night, but then returned.

I didn't know it was to say goodbye. I failed to convince Matt to come fishing with Paul and me in the morning, and I never spoke to my older son again.

XIX.

Suicide may be an ironic act. In order to take your own, you must have experienced life intensely – at least its depths, but probably its heights as well – much more so than the average person. Let's face it: most people don't take life seriously enough to end it. They're not terribly judgmental, at least when it comes to themselves and, even if things aren't exactly going their way, they are satisfied to go on living. It's those who feel most strongly about life who are likely to deprive themselves of it.

Leslie the therapist had dropped everything once more to meet with us the evening of Monday, August 25, 2014. We certainly needed it, in the wake of The Event.

Patti was devastated. Paul, who had gone to work, was full of rage. But Ann was easily the biggest concern. A recent college grad, she had just returned from her year stint with a volunteer program in Los Angeles, City Year, which serves inner city teenagers.

Ann and I had battled before she left; not over what she was doing, but where. Things had been deteriorating rapidly with Matthew. I felt helpless and wished selfishly I could have one more sane hand on deck. Besides, there are plenty of poor kids in the New York area who needed help.

Ann didn't see things that way and took off for Los Angeles. When she returned on July 1, 2014, I think she was shocked at how bad things had become in her absence. The Event on August 24 soon followed.

Since that Sunday, Ann had mostly been in her room, day and night, talking to her friends from City Year who were either still in Los Angeles or had relocated.

I didn't know how we could bring her back. The problem was that we didn't have much time to do so. Ann is an artist and had been admitted to Columbia University's Teachers College master's program in art and art teaching, with classes to begin on September 2, just nine days after she had found her brother hanging and tried unsuccessfully to bring him back to life.

I feared that she wouldn't be able to start the Columbia program on time. That would certainly be understandable but, after weeks had passed and things had settled down as they inevitably do, no matter the tragedy, Ann would have missed out on a great opportunity. Worse yet, she would have nothing to do but dwell on what had happened. Rightly or wrongly, it was critical to me that she be able to start classes the day after Labor Day, as scheduled.

If suicide is perhaps an ironic act, it's certainly a thoughtlessly cruel one too. We'll never know what dark thoughts were in Matt's mind when he took that last walk to the far backyard. Maybe he was just looking for respite, not finality, and overlooked the fact that you can't interrupt life without ending it. What I am sure of is that in carrying out his impulsively impatient act, there was no actual intent to inflict pain on others, although that was the inevitable result, which even he could have envisioned if he had only bothered to consider the consequences. I didn't want Ann's education to be additional collateral damage from Matt's decision.

Her psyche already was. Ann had always worshipped her older brother, all through the good years. We have a picture of them that tells the whole story. Taken after a snowstorm, a perhaps fourteen-year-old Matthew in a ski jacket smiles at the camera while his five year old sister, still in a snowsuit, is just glowing from being out together with her hero.

When Ann returned from Los Angeles, following Matt's release from the Zucker psych ward, the two siblings spent much time hanging out together, watching television at Matt's insistence – any show would do: "Come on, Ann. Let's watch something" – or taking the sun on the patio together when the weather cooperated.

Ann had been unaware of the battle over painkillers that was raging that Sunday between Patti and Matt. After going through the motions of their recent routine, he tricked her into thinking he was through with sunbathing and was instead going back inside to bed, as he often did in his depressed and heavily medicated state. She believed him and fell asleep in the lounge chair as he finally put the plan he had prepared into motion.

The What If Game was really torturing Ann. There were so many different variations that could be played, which would have led to her catching him looking for the rope in the garage, walking to the backyard, anything but finding him hanging in the backyard when it was too late to save him, despite the CPR she administered.

It certainly was not her fault. It may not have been anyone's, even Matt's. I am now thoroughly convinced that, Robin Williams or not, The Event was destined to happen, if not that Sunday when people were around who would question forever what they might have done to stop him, then some other day when eventually he would be left alone, and the people who had not been home would ask the same questions about what they might have done to avoid the horrific outcome.

As I mentioned, Paul was also with Patti, Ann and I for that Monday evening meeting with Leslie. He was still so upset and filled with anger at his brother, he didn't have much to say.

It was understandable. Paul probably had the closest relationship with Matthew of any of us, and it was very painful for him when, bit by bit, Matthew set out to destroy it before ending it altogether. The two brothers had been engaged in a huge war over how life should be lived, and Matthew bailed in the middle of it, leaving Paul trying to reconcile his hurt with his ire.

It took Paul the longest time to learn to forgive his brother, whom he loved so much.

A cousin of mine recently informed me that our common grandfather had suffered bouts of melancholy, as it was once known, the likely cause of his extended periods of unemployment during the Great Depression. I had never been told that and had unintentionally but incorrectly answered many doctors' questions about mental illness in my family by only identifying my own father, not his father as well.

This disclosure made me wonder whether the timeless free will debate will ultimately be resolved by chemists and geneticists, not philosophers, when they discover our actions too are controlled by our DNA, not our conscious decisions. No one doubts that depression is a family tradition. What little research I have checked indicates that more than half the risk for opioid abuse is also genetic, and when those marked people begin to use, they will quickly develop limited ability to resist. On our family tree, it looks like at least one leaf got the full package: a strong predilection toward getting high, as well as a tendency for depression when he came down.

Until the science of addiction and its connection to mental illness is fully understood I think the medical community should at least come up with a less innocuous name for depression which, like its polite predecessor "melancholy," doesn't do it justice. You don't say a tire has "low pressure" if it's "flat" or "shredded." This sneaky disease can be every bit as fatal as cancer. It should have a name just as scary, even if it doesn't have the decency to kill you by itself, but rather recruits you to do the dirty work.

XX.

There is no doubt that my own perception of the world went off kilter on the day of The Event. The best analogy I can draw is to a scene in an action or war movie where, following a sonic boom or other explosion, the characters lose their hearing for a while. They stumble around, disoriented, trying to reintegrate themselves into the silent movie they've been watching. In my case, there was no loud noise nor hearing loss, but maybe an inability to listen, and certainly no capacity to concentrate.

The haze began lifting gradually after a day, because my diary shows I actually did a couple of hours of legal work on Tuesday, August 26, 2014. Maybe that means I'm an inhuman robot, or a raging workaholic. More likely, it was just another retreat to my safe place. Practicing law had been by refuge during the recent years of turmoil with Matt, since it kept me focused on problems other than my own that I actually had a chance of solving.

Midday on Tuesday, I picked up Patti and visited the funeral "home," a phrase, like all its fellow euphemisms such as funeral "parlor," had always made me snicker. I'm sure I brought a check for the services that would be rendered to Matt, and I brought along the newspaper death notice I had prepared which, as Matthew would have wanted, listed both Paul and The Nephew as the brothers he left behind. Our real mission, however, was to select a prayer card. Patti wanted to have enough of them made so that everyone attending Matt's memorial Mass could leave with one. I had decided, unilaterally, but without objection from the family, to skip having a wake. Nothing other than convention forced us to, and it seemed an ideal time to finally refuse to do something you didn't feel like doing. I figured that if someone wanted to pay respect to Matt, they could just sit through his Mass. So we had hundreds of prayer cards made, with his picture on the front, same smiling movie star-like image as on the cover of this book, and the following prayer Patti had selected on the back.

> "Grieve not ... nor speak of me with tears,
> but laugh and talk of me as though I were beside you.
> I loved you so ... 'twas Heaven here with you."

I didn't debate the prayer selection at all; if Matt's mother had decided to put an off color joke on the rear of the laminated prayer card, I don't think I would have voiced an objection. But, in my anger with Matt for what he had done to himself – and the rest of us a result – I initially thought this particular saying an odd choice when the deceased had taken his own life. If it were such Heaven for Matt to be here with us all, why had he decided to leave and plunge us all into Hell?

As I reflected on it later, however, I realized that, as usual, Patti had been right. My problem was that, from the time he was old enough to understand, Matt – like all our other children – had been drilled that the one thing you must never do is give up. Yet he had quit on life, in this irreversible way. I resented the fact that Matt had rejected this all-important lesson, but I began to realize I had no idea how unbearable his life had become to him.

How much I knew about Matt's life had always been shrinking the older he got. I knew everything about him, when he was a baby, then less and less as he progressed through school. I barely knew anything about his world at all when he was with the FDNY and kept his thoughts and experiences a total secret. Finally, in his last few weeks when he became like a child again, I learned a lot more about him, like I used to, but plainly not enough. Maybe you can get victimized by a prior successful life when everything turns against you. Whatever the reason, even in his very diminished state, Matt kept hiding the darkest secret of all.

I started to understand. His act wasn't a rejection of his family, whom he actually would have said, however inconsistent with what he did, were Heaven to be with. It was borne of frustration, perhaps self-loathing, and an inability to tolerate for one second longer the disparity between whom he had been and thought he should be and the person he had become.

Understanding, however limited, is a first step toward forgiveness.

*

Our next stop that Tuesday was to St. Agnes, to meet with the grief minister, a gentleman I knew from morning Mass, which I had developed the habit of attending.

Patti and I went through a book of readings and hymns suitable for a service like Matt's and made our choices. When I told the counselor that I would like to speak at the end of the service, he resisted, saying that was not something the parish permitted the bereaved to do.

I suppose I was adamant; I certainly had seen it done and had even spoken myself twenty years before following the death of my father-in-law, Frank. I wasn't going to be denied what I felt was an essential step if we were going to pass The Test. "Don't worry," I assured him. "It'll be short and appropriate," nothing like the "open mike" nights I had occasionally seen at memorial services held at other denominations.

The grief minister and I didn't reach impasse. He actually would be out of town on Thursday, to be replaced by a woman whose son swam with Matt at Chaminade. So the eulogy issue was cordially deferred for discussion with the Monsignor when we met with him the following evening.

XXI.

I believe I spent all day Wednesday, August 27, 2017, writing and revising Matt's eulogy. I realize how obsessive that sounds, particularly when I was determined to keep my remarks very short, but it's the truth. I needed to get it right if we were to pass The Test, and I think I kept at it until I was to meet the rest of the family at 5 p.m. at St. Agnes Rectory. This was to be an all hands on deck meeting, with Patti, Elizabeth, Paul, and Ann in attendance.

As I walked around the corner from my office, which is on the next street from the Cathedral, I thought about how fortunate we were that Matt's service would be handled personally by our Monsignor, who ignored his title and went by the simpler "Father Bill".

I had been told that he had returned early from vacation on the East End of Long Island to say Matt's Mass. This was typical of the man, who is as holy and unassuming a priest as I have ever met.

Let me explain how I know this to be true. Some years before, I heard from a law school friend of mine who had suffered enough undeserved personal difficulties to fill another book. He had sacrificed his own life to become caretaker for his mother who, following an operation, had landed in a rehabilitation center in Glen Cove.

My friend wanted to arrange for a priest to visit his mother in the rehab facility. Since he lived in Brooklyn, and I was his "Long

Island Guy," he called me for advice.

I must have been busy and was less sympathetic or helpful than usual. "I don't know any priests up there," I explained to my friend. "I'll give you the number of my pastor, Father Bill. Maybe he has a friend up there from seminary or someplace." I should have offered at least to serve as intermediary, but I didn't, and that was the end of my involvement.

Much later I learned not only did Father Bill respond to my friend's call, but he went himself to Glen Cove to visit the mother. That's quite a hike from Rockville Centre, and I don't know another priest who'd be willing to make the trip for a perfect stranger. As a result, Father Bill became my friend's go-to "Long Island Priest," eventually saying his Mom's requiem Mass and remaining close with him thereafter.

So, I knew the Byrne family was in very good hands with Father Bill.

The purpose of the meeting that afternoon was to finalize arrangements for Matt's memorial Mass the following day. That included giving Father Bill some idea of who Matt had been and what had happened to him. Essentially, we were feeding the priest the material he needed to prepare the homily he would deliver the next morning.

Of course, there were plenty of tears as Father Bill spoke to each of us in turn, gathering our memories of a son and brother. We each told him funny stories about "Good Matt" from long ago, and even that summer, when on an "up" day he had buried himself on the beach and placed a towel covered with potato chips over his head. Matt didn't quite succeed in his old lifeguard game but came very close to capturing a seagull or two as we had all laughed.

"Bad Matt" had already been totally forgotten by his family, like he had never even existed. Suicide is funny like that. It generally reduces the list of grievances against the deceased to one big item. Everything else is immediately erased, but you still have a major issue with this person for killing someone you loved. In my case there was still a second issue: his disregard of the impact on his mother and sister from his choice of time and place.

Several years later, Ann remarked that Father Bill had seemed somewhat shocked by the amount of laughter. I told her I had not noticed. I was probably too accustomed to the use of humor as a defensive tactic – what the Benign Counselor noted the year before. The grimmer the situation, the more the Byrnes instinctively poke fun at it. We still do.

XXII.

Thursday, August 28, 2014, was another beautiful day, keeping intact the stretch of spectacular weather that had persisted since The Event. I was up early and out with Portia, on her usual patrol of Harvard Avenue, certain this would be the final day of The Test.

Elizabeth, my son-in-law Manny Villar, and their three children would pick up my Mom and meet us at the Cathedral. I pushed to make sure the rest of us were up, dressed, and down there as much in advance as possible. There was lots to do. I would have to get Matt's ashes into the Cathedral. They had been placed in a simple redwood box with a carved Celtic cross and had to be positioned on a table set at the foot of the altar, along with the largest version of his college graduation photo we had, borrowed from the living room wall. I also had a box of prayer cards that Patti wanted distributed in each aisle, and a stack of directions to the Rockville Links, where lunch would be served after the Mass was over.

Our family may not be habitually late, but we are very rarely early. By the time everyone was out in the driveway, loading into my car, it was later than I had hoped. I checked my dark suit jacket pocket one last time for the one page, single spaced eulogy Father Bill had agreed I could deliver at the conclusion of the service. Then I jumped in the driver's seat, and we took off.

It was only a five minute drive from our house to St. Agnes Cathedral, so I still had enough time, I hoped. Besides, for once I felt entitled to pull right into the no parking zone reserved in front of the church for hearses and limousines, since there would be none.

When I arrived at the space, passing cars parked everywhere on Quealy Place, to my surprise it wasn't wide open. There was some sort of Winnebago type vehicle pulled in front of the church. There was still room to squeeze in behind it, and I did so, noticing assorted hunting and fishing decals all over the back of the camper unit. "WTF?" I had muttered mentally as we all hastened out of the car before I realized who had parked there: Dillon, my old high school friend and ballplaying buddy, who had recently retired and was touring around the country as he pleased. I grabbed the ashes and the picture, assigned the prayer cards and directions to Ann and Paul, and rushed off toward the church, leaving Patti and the kids behind.

I think that's when the dream sequence I'd been living for four days became totally surreal. The Cathedral was already packed, and there were many more people still milling outside. Some faces I knew well, others I hadn't seen in years, and others I didn't know at all since they were friends or co-workers of Matt's I had never met, or friends of Patti, Elizabeth, Paul or Ann who had come to give their support. No one said anything to me as I walked by. They just had that look on their faces that was becoming too familiar to me: "That's his father."

I snuck down the side aisle with the ashes and photo for the table, then I retreated the way I had come to the rear of the cathedral where our family was assembling. When I got there, I checked to make sure the directions to the Links had been distributed on both sides of the main aisle. That's when I saw Mike, leaning against the back wall next to a stoop, crying so hard his whole body was shaking.

Mike had been in on the 1996 World Series ticket escapade and was also the FDNY veteran I had met in Metrotech back in February when I had to go to the Chase branch in Brooklyn for the money order needed to complete Matt's separation. Mike was with NYC's Office of Emergency Services on 9/11 and had wrecked his health by staying down on "The Pile" for months after the attacks. Mike is still a big guy, built like "The Hulk" with massive chest, arms, and legs. I approached him, getting my arms around him as best I could, feeling the sweat that had drenched his dark suit. "It's going to be alright, Michael," I managed to whisper before releasing him and moving out to the vestibule.

We had declined FDNY's offer of a ceremonial funeral. While being a firefighter arguably killed him, Matt had really quit although officially retired, so pomp and circumstance seemed quite hypocritical. Instead, we hired a single bagpiper, a firefighter himself, whose pipes' plaintive sounds filled the nearby streets in Rockville Centre until Father Bill met us in the back of the church and the procession began, our three grandchildren clinging to their fair haired mother and Manny, lined up directly behind Patti and me.

I practically held Patti up as we marched into the entrance hymn she had selected, *Here I am, Lord.* The first row, never a place where I wanted to sit, was reserved for us, just as it had been eleven years before when Elizabeth and Manny married, and thirty four years earlier when Uncle Tom baptized Matthew.

I sat there uncomfortably through what seemed like the longest service ever, because the final part of The Test was still to come.

When I thought to ask Father Bill for the notes of his homily, a few days after Matt's memorial, they had already disappeared. I recall he spoke beautifully, using the simplest of metaphors: water, the common theme in Matt's life, from his Baptism, through his lifeguarding, through his time as an FDNY "nozzle man" -- like designated hitter when he was a kid, the only role on the firefighting team he really wanted to play.

When Communion came, the heartbreaking *Be Not Afraid* played. Hundreds of people followed us to receive the host. As I knelt at the end of the first row, I remember Big Jim placing his hand on my shoulder as he passed by. It was all he needed to do.

Finally, the four-day wait ended. Father Bill called me up to the pulpit to deliver the remarks I had so carefully prepared.

As I approached, I heard the sound of my leather heels clicking on the marble floor in an otherwise silent Cathedral. I really did not know how I was going to get through this remembrance of Matt.

Until that day, it's probably fair to say that I never really believed in the Holy Spirit. At best, he was the Mystery Man of the Trinity. There's a historical Jesus who everyone knows was real, whether they believe He's divine or actually rose from the dead. God Almighty is a concept most people can appreciate as well, if they take the time to watch a National Geographic show or visit the planetarium to appreciate the complexity of our world and vastness of our universe. But the Holy Spirit, the artist formerly known as the Holy Ghost? Who's He?

Well, according to Catholic doctrine, the Spirit is the guy Jesus left behind to take care of us in his stead. For those of us who weren't lucky enough to meet Jesus, the Spirit may be the most important of the three Persons, since it's supposed to be Him that actually helps us get through the struggles of life, by giving us a boost over a wall we couldn't otherwise have climbed.

I am convinced I experienced such a boost that Thursday morning. When I reached the pulpit, a strange calm came over me, and I was able to address the huge, watchful crowd without hesitation. What I had to say, with the thank yous and housekeeping details redacted, is set forth below. The surge I felt – you can call it adrenalin if you don't like my explanation – let me keep my emotions in check until the very last comment:

"This is going to be a bit difficult, but we'll get through it together.

"People get real worried when they see me step before a microphone. Half of you are afraid I'll grab it and start belting out old rock and roll songs. The other half are afraid I'll start arguing or begin a long lecture on some boring legal topic. Let me assure you that none of that will happen today. Msgr. Mulligan instructed me long ago: 'Be brief. Be very brief.' See – only one page.

....

"Matt was one of the good guys. He was a good son; a good brother; and a good friend. He was a good man who made some bad mistakes, and he paid dearly for each and every one of them. He wasn't able to overcome a series of setbacks that had brought him very low. He was sick of doctors and taking medicine, sick of not being himself, sick of wondering whether his wicked sense of humor would ever come back or whether it was gone forever. So he surrendered to a mental illness so monstrous that it could take your life on a beautiful late summer day, right in the middle of a ballgame the Yankees were winning. That's not exactly the time to call it quits. But that disease is so insidious it steals the one thing we all need to survive: hope – the belief that as bad as today may have been, tomorrow might be better.

"Over the past few weeks, we got to spend a lot of time together and I had quoted him everyone from Teddy Roosevelt to Tug McGraw in daily, sometimes hourly pep talks because he literally had lost everything except his family. But as much as I begged him to 'stay with it' and 'hang in there,' and told him that it was 'all about the comeback,' and things really would get better, I couldn't convince him. Matt could no longer hear, or no longer believe, that 'all things are possible with God,' and he left us all behind filled with anger, sorrow, and love. The anger has gone away, the sorrow will fade, but the love will endure. And eventually, I hope, we will come to remember only the good times, not the bad ones, and we will forget these last horrible days.

"So, while what Matt did may have made perfect sense to him on Sunday, I like to think his brother Paul is right and that if he saw all the people here today who loved him, it might have changed his mind and kept him from breaking his Mom's heart. She loved him at least as much as any mother ever loved her child. We all love you, Matt, and always will. I'm proud to have been your father, and all is forgiven already – because we never could stay mad at you for very long. I only have one regret, and it relates to something I neglected to tell you long ago, when you were a little boy: I should have warned you, Matthew, this world was never meant for one as beautiful as you. Rest in peace at last, son."

It was all true, except the part about all is forgiven already. For me, that had not happened yet.

The recessional hymn was *On Eagle's Wings* and the somberly dressed Byrnes and Villars struggled through tears past the filled pews and made it out into the bright late morning sunshine. In front of the Cathedral's steps, Patti and I covered what turned into two separate receiving lines for the best part of an hour, when she finally started yelling that she couldn't stand with her cane any longer.

The crowd that returned to the Links was smaller but still impressive. There were quite a few FDNY firefighters in uniform whom I suppose had trained or worked with Matt, and many Jones Beach lifeguards we had met over the years. There were also a representative sampling of Matt's fellow drinkers and drug abusers together with, I more than suspect, a former supplier or two, who kept the bar busy until closing time. I kept my resentment for some of these individuals in check. They certainly facilitated Matt's demise but were not responsible for it.

I couldn't help remembering all the prior events at the Links, almost all of them happy. Saturday swim meets. Birthday and Easter dinners. Elizabeth's wedding reception, when the entire kitchen staff joined us on the stage to sing *Guantanamera, Pretty*

Woman, and *My Girl*. Lorayne's 80th birthday celebration, when the Able-Ride bus carrying one disabled guest ran into the overhang at the club's front entrance. My own mother's recent 90th birthday party. This occasion was nothing like them, but it was a really big party, however subdued, and Matthew would have been impressed.

When it was all over, we headed for home, exhausted in every way imaginable. I just kept thinking how avoidable all this somehow should have been. What If Matt Byrne, like Tom Sawyer, could have attended his own funeral? It never would have happened.

Later, as I walked Portia down Harvard Avenue in the twilight, I reflected on the day's events. I was convinced that the Byrnes had passed The Test, but it had not made any difference at all. Nothing had gone back to normal. It all had really happened. Our Matthew was gone, and we had to give up the faint hope of his returning.

The following evening, Ann and I had a huge blowout. She really had not slept since The Event and had talked on her cell through every night with her friends in Los Angeles and elsewhere. I was afraid she would have a breakdown, and demanded she hand over the phone.

She became hysterical, and all the emotion poured out. When she cursed Robin Williams, whom she thought had become Matt's role model when he had taken his life less than two weeks before, I lost it too and started screaming back at her.

I will always regret that night.

*

The next night, Ann told me that she had gotten a call from two old friends of Matt's who wanted to know whether they could stop by. This threesome had gone through grammar school and high school together, and Patti and I were of the opinion that, putting it mildly, they had never been "good for each other". Nevertheless, I told Ann, "Fine," and we awaited their Friday night visit.

Sure enough, fairly close to the time they said they would arrive, the doorbell rang. I answered it, greeting them on the front stoop, then let them in, even though it was apparent they were stoned out of their shoes.

What followed was the most unusual hour long visit I have ever endured. One young man could barely speak, and the other not at all. They literally spent the entire time giving us meaningfully sad and soundless looks.

As you might imagine, this became tiresome rather quickly. I had a very strong impulse to just throw them out of the house, which I successfully resisted. Somehow, they had wordlessly convinced me that their grief was as genuine as their intoxication.

XXIII.

I have good news and bad news for you, if you ever must go through an ordeal like the death of a child from a socially unacceptable cause, e.g., suicide or overdose. I'll give my bulletins to you in reverse order.

The bad news is that some people think tragedy and sorrow are contagious, so they shun you and keep their distance for fear of catching it. Some of these people you considered friends, and you thought they would be there for you when you needed them. It's very disappointing to learn how badly you misjudged some people and gave them credit for compassion they either didn't have or, for some reason, were incapable of showing.

The good news, however, is that those fair weather friends will be replaced, one by one, by people you didn't realize cared for you. It's almost like some cosmic balance must be kept, so that unexpected people step forward, and you end up with the same number of people you thought might help you get by, although the group is differently comprised.

For us, the absence of certain deserters was conspicuous and painful, even though their replacements quickly surfaced. Ultimately, the Byrnes had no reason to complain about the support we received from our friends and community; it was tremendous. Suicide is not what Father Bill calls a "casserole" disease or death. Yet we had a parade of neighbors ringing our doorbell with food for at least a month, while others contributed to a well-funded charge account at a local eatery. Going hungry was one thing our family did not have to worry about.

One unforeseen group came to the rescue immediately after Matt's funeral, before the letdown following that day's activities could fully set in. His former supervisors at Jones Beach called and invited us to attend a memorial "Paddle Out" service they would be holding at 8 a.m. on Labor Day morning. That meant cutting our weekend visit with Beba and her family in the Hamptons short, but I eagerly accepted.

Since he was sixteen, Jones Beach had been Matt's magical place. The lifeguards there were the real "Boys and Girls of Summer," manipulating their lives and careers so they could somehow keep working on the beach, even if it meant a hectic schedule, like Matt's had been. They all considered it worth the effort.

I remember how happy he would be when he came home for dinner after working a shift at Jones Beach. Tanned and relaxed, he would tell us the latest jokes stolen from the "Bucket and Buoy," the lifeguard union's newsletter, and fill us in on the latest misadventures of what I would call the lifeguards' "groupies". These were patrons who tried to hang with the lifeguards, like "Marty from Merrick," legendary for the "Marty Parties" he threw on Long Island in the summer and in "Boca" during the winter. Matt would do his Marty impression, tease Ann and The Nephew, and entertain us all with stupid antics. A favorite was his mockery of the family rule that no one eat until everyone had a plate. In Matt's mind, the rule was only violated if someone used utensils. So, if his arrived first when the plates were being passed out, he would put his arms behind his back, then stick his face into his plate and scarf a few bites, pretending no one was watching.

Loving the Jones Beach job as much as he did, losing it had to be a crushing blow. I only sensed relief, not regret, when he left the FDNY. In contrast, having to leave Jones Beach because of the incident at Robert Moses had to be like getting thrown out of the Garden of Eden: the biggest screw-up of all time. In hindsight, it really was the beginning of the end for Matt, for I suspect he began keeping score of the things he had lived for that were gone.

Speaking for himself and the others, one of the Jones Beach supervisors started crying when he told me they had known Matt had been having trouble but had no idea how serious it had gotten. Now, he was gone before anyone could do anything to help him.

Matt's Jones Beach colleagues couldn't have been nicer to Patti and me at the Paddle Out. They sent a dune buggy up to the parking lot to fetch her and take her down to the ocean's edge. There we met all the friends he had made over many seasons in this other, happier world, each of them holding a surfboard and a bouquet of flowers. They entered the water soon after so that this ceremony they performed whenever any lifeguard died could be completed before the patrons arrived.

Patti and I stood on the beach, holding hands, unable to see what was going on even though the waves were calm. All we could tell was that the guards were floating on their surfboards, hands joined in a big circle. Then, suddenly, there was a lot of yelling and splashing. Then it was over, and the group paddled back to shore.

We spoke some more with the "bosses," lieutenants and captains in the Corps under whom Matt had worked. They had a number of gifts for Patti, all with the Jones Beach logo – a beach hat and baseball cap, rash guards, seemingly anything sold at the gift shop – and gave her a plaque commemorating Matt's years of service. As the time approached 9 a.m., the gathering broke up and the lifeguards headed for their posts. We were very grateful to have been included, and drove home remembering all the times Matt had invited us down for the "Lifeguard Races" held each summer, when the Jones guards would compete against lifeguards from Robert Moses, Long Beach, Rockaway, Town of Hempstead and other rivals, and we would cheer our son on when he was entered in one event or another.

A day or two later, we received an even greater gift from the Jones Beach Lifeguard Corps. A young man named Cary Epstein had filmed the Paddle Out, start to finish, and set it to a soundtrack of Israel Kamakawiwo'ole's version of *Somewhere Over the Rainbow* and *What A Wonderful World*. It's still on YouTube if you search "Matt Byrne Paddle Out". The short film is painful, but it is a priceless memory for us.

XXIV.

Tuesday, September 2, 2014, was a regular workday and posed a new question. How are you supposed to go on living when your heart has been ripped out of your chest? I don't pretend to have a universal answer, but I do know that routine may be your strongest ally. In the wake of a life changing event, the best thing you can probably do is, as advised in many old songs, "keep on keeping on".

So, I got up early, took care of Portia, and resumed going about my business in a world that was now quiet and no longer crazy, as it had been sporadically for years. I had many new assignments to complete. We had received a flood of Mass and sympathy cards, and each had to be acknowledged. In addition, Matt's estate affairs had to be handled, and I was determined to put that job behind me as quickly as possible.

I think I was fortunate. I was able to consciously postpone grieving, knowing I would have to deal with it later. I chose to get lost in my work and everything else that had to be done. Ann was still very fragile but had been able to begin her program at Columbia, a very good thing in my mind. Beba and Paul seemed to be handling everything in stride.

Patti was the one who was struggling. During Matthew's descent, she began losing ground to the health issues she'd been battling for years. She found it harder and harder to get out of bed each morning, get dressed, and drive to her job as director of the early intervention agency she had founded to service disabled infants. It had gotten so difficult that "Bad Matt" had begun mocking her and calling her "Half Day Pat". After he was gone, she was lucky if she reached the busy office by mid-afternoon to catch up on what had been going on that day.

I honestly believe that the better a person is, and the happier the life she or he has lived, the harder it is for them to deal with tragedy. Maybe people who have had their hearts broken before become emotionally calloused and don't succumb as easily the next time. I know a brother and sister who had horrible child-hoods, followed by a series of misfortunes throughout their lives that is hard to believe. It made them almost impervious to heart-ache, or at least unwilling to give in to it. Patti had not had any-thing resembling that kind of sorrowful life, and I began to won-der when she might recover, or whether she could survive Matt's death at all.

*

There is an old English common law doctrine called "abate-ment". If a criminal defendant dies while his case is still pending, even on appeal after conviction, the slate is wiped clean and the charges against him are dropped *ab initio*, as though they had never happened, because the defendant's death, however it oc-curred, deprived him of his right to defend against them.

On September 9, 2014, the four charges against Matthew were officially abated in the District Court. In October, we re-ceived a Nassau County check in his name for $970.00, the return of the bail money that had been so important to the judge, less some sort of fee.

I had considered writing the judge to advise her what Matthew had done some two weeks after appearing in her court to let her know that the message she sent may have been more effective than she intended. I decided to let it go.

*

In late September, I took Patti with me on a business trip to Chicago, a beautiful city we both had always loved, even before we had pushed six month old Ann in an umbrella stroller into one of its fancy restaurants in late 1989.

The trip was not a disaster, but it could have been. Patti couldn't get up in the morning, and I was spending far too much time in the hotel room waiting for her, brooding over everything that had gone wrong and wondering how it had happened to us.

I never looked it up to verify the point, but I am under the impression that half of the couples that lose a child break up, whether soon after the event or some time thereafter. If this misfortune happens to you, I think it's impossible not to wonder which half of the sample you and your spouse will end up in.

As I sat in an easy chair, watching Patti sleep, I had one issue that kept nagging me, a very sinister "What If?" I started asking: "What if she hadn't needed those painkillers?" That immediately seemed totally unfair, since it wasn't her fault that she had contracted rheumatoid arthritis. So the question was quickly and cleverly rephrased: "What if she kept better track of her meds, so our son never got access to them and could never steal them?"

I wrestled with the refined question for the full time we were in Chicago, finally realizing it wasn't any fairer than the first. Patti had kept the bulk of the opioids she was prescribed in a combination safe kept in the basement of our office building. She only put in the pill vial she carried in her pocketbook the dosage she was prescribed for the day. You can be quite vigilant, but sometimes you are going to go into another room without your pocketbook or otherwise let your guard down. Matt had become an accomplished and patient thief and, the moment any lapse occurred, he was ready to pounce and grab what he wanted.

The last night of our stay we ate in the same place we had gone with Ann more than twenty years before. By the time we returned to New York, I had ended this version of the "What If Game" forever. Even if Patti had left her painkillers in plain sight on the kitchen counter, it wouldn't be her fault if Matt took them. If you resisted the understandable urge to blame someone else for what happened to him – the Sacklers, New York State Parks, the doctors, the judge – the only person you could legitimately blame for Matt's drug addiction and demise was him.

I realized it would be better not to blame anyone at all than place the responsibility where it belonged.

*

I mentioned the number of Mass cards we received following Matt's death. Many of them were from neighbors, who had booked the services at St. Agnes. I made up my mind that I would do my best to attend them all. I entered each date and time in my calendar, and tried to schedule meetings, conference calls, and all my other professional obligations around them.

Someone actually asked me how I could still believe in a God who would let my son take his life. Now there's an interesting, if not novel question. Let me defend myself, because any time I've faced that kind of question in my life it has felt like some sort of an attack.

That was particularly so when I was in a nonsectarian college yet chose to take religion courses. My friends couldn't understand why, and I couldn't explain. If not yet a "fallen away" Catholic, I was close, but I began experiencing this "pull," perhaps due to the man who taught the courses whom I'll just call "The Professor".

The Professor was my freshman year advisor and was the first faculty member I met. His office was at the end of a winding staircase that led to the top floor of the oldest building on campus, built around 1800. The room was so littered with books, papers and folders piled on his desk, chairs, windowsills, and wherever, that it looked like a Hollywood set. The Professor, a large, suspender-wearing man who took his suit jacket off at every opportunity, had scheduled a meeting of his group of freshman advisees; there were no "freshwomen" in the school then. He took great pains that afternoon to introduce us to each other, and query us individually about our goals for the next four years in a soft spoken manner. I left that meeting with a few new friends, including him.

I saw another side of The Professor when I took his class the following year. In weekly conferences, where we met in small groups to discuss the book that had to be read that week, The Professor was much the same guy I had met in his office, but no longer toning down his brilliance. It seemed as though there was no topic he had not studied, and no book worth reading that he hadn't read.

It was in the lecture hall that I saw a totally different character. I had heard that, in addition to teaching full time, The Professor was a Congregational minister. When the large class had settled in, he hung his jacket on the back of the desk chair, then just let it rip. I had never seen someone master the spoken word like that, before or since, as his voice would thunder at times, then drop to a whisper you had to strain to hear. The Professor would squeeze his eyes shut at times, making you think he had in fact made contact with, as he would call it, "the ineffable". I don't think I had a classroom hour pass as quickly or enjoyably as when I watched one of The Professor's lectures.

During one conference, whatever the book we were discussing, I got into a heated argument with a visiting student from another college, a hippy looking guy wearing gauzy pants and sandals, not an overalled and booted freak like the rest of us Polar Bears. I think I was hungover during the early morning class, and I confess I went after him hard following one too many snide comments about the shallow beliefs and practices of Sunday Christian churchgoers. I didn't exactly tell him he was full of it, but I asked him whether he had ever been to church and intimated that he didn't know what he was talking about – certainly a breach of academic etiquette. I must have come on strong, because at some point my ponytailed target sought The Professor's intervention, which only made me press harder for the facts on which his pontifications were based.

Fortunately, the class period was ending and The Professor, wearing a slightly bemused grin, was able to separate the verbal combatants, but not without letting the class hear him tell me to report to his office that afternoon.

After letting me know that the morning's class was as much fun as he'd had in years of teaching, The Professor and I had a very interesting session, not as teacher and student, but more like priest and penitent. (I once told him I was always on the verge of calling him "Father" rather than Professor.) His comments and questions were those of a believer. Something very unusual did in fact happen two thousand years ago, according to The Professor. Did I really think this Jesus happened along out of nowhere to say the things he did? Is it reasonable to believe that an uneducated carpenter could be the greatest teacher and clearest thinker of all time? The Professor left me a simplified version of the Pascalian wager: if it is just as reasonable to believe as disbelieve, there is no reason to apologize for your belief. His parting comment made reference to the Roman Catholic birthmark he thought I bore, which I would never be able to erase.

I continued to wrestle with the question of belief in Christ on my own. I added my personal favorite to The Professor's list of unlikelihoods: how likely was it that the bunch of loser followers Jesus had assembled, scared out of their wits after he was killed, could rally and then set the world on fire without even a newspaper much less internet to spread their good news? To me, that was the most unlikely thing of all. I decided that, if a man as brilliant as The Professor were humble enough to acknowledge that some things are beyond understanding, I would do so too and hopefully become as comfortable with belief as he seemed to be.

I didn't realize until many years later, when quizzed by my children regarding the practice of the Catholic faith, that I still hadn't grasped the full implications of the decision The Professor had guided me in making. I told them that it is not possible to be both candid and casual about your religious beliefs and status as a Catholic, who is someone who believes that Jesus was God incarnate, who died for our sins and rose from the dead. If you actually believe that short proposition is true, it must necessarily dictate your entire view of the world and your place in it, because it is so remarkable it changes everything!

I don't ask how a good God could let my son take his life. I don't share the arrogance of modern humanity, who think that the ancient mysteries of life and death can be either understood – or ignored – without even turning off our laptops and smartphones. I don't pretend to have any insight into the big picture of what is going on in the world that we all seem to share, but I do sense it is very sacred, despite all the outward profanity.

I didn't make all the Masses said at St. Agnes for Matt, but I came close – even though each time I stood after the Gospel while they read out his name, I felt a knife run somewhere through my heart. Now the Masses for Matt are long over, except for one I schedule each year at St. Agnes on the anniversary of his death. I still attend Mass there almost every day, despite the latest disclosures of clerical misconduct, even more shameful for the Church hierarchy that covered up the atrocities than the conflicted souls who committed them. The clergy has been periodically screwing up Jesus's message for thousands of years, and no doubt they will continue to do so again in new and imaginative ways. That still doesn't make the message wrong, and something to be discarded. It just means we need new messengers who will deliver it correctly.

I don't underestimate this churchgoing habit's effect on my ability to carry on. I have become acutely aware, however, that when the name of the person for whom the Mass is offered is read aloud, there's probably someone in St. Agnes Cathedral feeling that same sharp pain, no matter how long ago the loss took place.

*

By October 2014, we were trying to resume some semblance of a social life. The weekend of October 11, we flew down to Virginia where one of Kathy's and Big Jim's kids was getting married. On October 25, I attended my 45th high school reunion. It was a typically raucous affair, which the girls declined to attend, and I felt as though I was pushing myself to have a good time – like I always had in the past – just so I wouldn't ruin the evening for the other guys, some of whom are like brothers to me.

It wasn't until late October that I received in the mail the "Report of Autopsy" from Nassau County's Office of the Medical Examiner, "Case No.: 14-3702-Byrne, Matthew E.". The cover page concluded very concisely: "Cause of Death: Asphyxia, Due to: Hanging. Manner of Death: Suicide". I will skip the details, other than to say my impression was that Matt had not yet done irreparable harm to his body before ending his life.

After reading the report, I kept it in my office, determined never to show it to Patti. Several weeks later, however, she surprised me by asking whether the coroner's report had ever arrived. I didn't lie; I told her it had but advised against her reading it.

She was insistent, so I made her a copy. She wanted to know if there were opioids in Matt's system when he died. There were, but she was unable to determine whether he had gotten the drugs on his own or stolen them from her.

As Hillary Clinton erupted at the Benghazi hearing: "What difference at this point does it make?"

XXV.

I'm not sure how you end up on this particular solicitation list but somehow, whether through the police, hospital or otherwise, the word gets out that you and your family have become suicide "survivors," and you begin to hear from support groups.

At the risk of being labeled a nitpicker, since I know what is meant, I'll give you my reaction to this oxymoron. There obviously is no survivor of a suicide. There may be victims, but these do not include the deceased, who achieved the relief he was looking for. Matt's family members certainly all felt like victims, the ones left behind to struggle with the whys and "What Ifs". Whether we were more properly called victims or survivors, we certainly needed help.

So, Patti and I decided to attend an event sponsored by one of the support groups on a Saturday in November 2014, purposely scheduled to prepare attendees for the upcoming holiday season, always the toughest for those who have lost a loved one. I didn't know what to expect and tried to synthesize all my thoughts about Matt's suicide together in anticipation of what we might encounter.

This was not easy because, some two to three months after The Event, I was still in denial or at least some lesser stage of disbelief like, "I can't believe that all happened to us". We were getting a crash course in a topic with which we were totally unfamiliar, except for old preconceptions.

I recalled thinking as a kid that taking one's own life was

something only Japanese people did, because they take their honor so seriously. I had heard about the *harakiri* practiced by failed Japanese commanders during World War II. After Matt's death, so many mourners had said they "had no words" but then stated that what he had done "made no sense". I always remained politely silent, but I could not have disagreed more. While madness typically doesn't make much sense, Matt's actions were as logical as those of the Japanese commanders who preferred to end life rather than endure a shame they felt they had no hope of overcoming.

The only other suicide I was familiar with growing up was that of Judas Iscariot, and you certainly didn't learn much about it in Catholic school beyond the fact that it happened and was a terrible sin for which he could never be forgiven. I really didn't understand this because hanging himself seemed as sincere an apology as anyone could make for selling Jesus out. Was it all Judas's fault when somebody had to betray Christ to set the plan for mankind's salvation in motion? How could Judas be entitled to no sympathy whatsoever when perhaps he was only trying to raise some money for Jesus and his followers, and maybe thought the Jews and Romans would give the troublemaker a good beating and let it go at that?

So plainly I had much to learn about suicide when Patti and I attended the survivors' event, which was held in a hotel in the middle of Long Island. I have a very clear recollection of that day.

We first learned that there is no single stereotype that fits all the people who take their lives or those who mourn them. The audience was a very mixed population by any measure. The first people Patti and I met were three adult sisters who attended the program every year. Maybe twenty years earlier, when he was perhaps in his sixties, their father had simply gone to the garage and taken his life without warning. The sisters' grief still seemed as fresh as our own, and hearing their stories left me unconvinced that we would ever be able to outlast or outrun Matt's death.

After some films with various prevention messages, and lunch at large tables which did not impede discussions of everyone's shared experience, the attendees were broken into smaller groups based upon relationship with the deceased. Patti went off with a group of mothers who had lost a child, and I immediately worried about her being on her own. I went off with a bunch of other fathers. There were groups of spouses, siblings, seemingly any relationship you could imagine.

Each group was moderated by a veteran survivor, in my case a husband and wife team who had made helping others their mission since their only child's death. They asked each of us individually how long it had been since the loss of your child before you were asked to speak.

As they went around the room, I thought I could see a correlation between how long a person had been dealing with the suicide and how well he handled it. My loss was the most recent of the people in the group, and I don't think I was handling it very well when asked to recount what had happened. When I made reference to Robin Williams's suicide two weeks before Matt's own, the husband moderator immediately stopped me.

"You know," he began, "the research shows that there is no

such thing as a copycat suicide."

"Really?" I replied. "It certainly looked that way to me."

I've since been told that well-intentioned gentleman was wrong. I can't say I independently checked the point out further, certain as I was of the impression the celebrity's death had made on Matt's choice. Besides, something else happened during the session which caused me much greater concern.

The final father to speak had lost his only child three years before, a son who sounded like he had been close in age to Matt. The man seemed still deeply depressed, which was totally understandable and made me wonder how much my thinking was affected by the fact that I had three other children plus The Nephew that I needed to go on living for.

The Grieving Father told us how good his late son's friends had been. They would come to visit him, in groups or singly, and tried to keep him up to date on happenings in their lives. In other words, they were trying to keep the bond of friendship with his son alive by a continued connection to him.

They sounded like a wonderfully thoughtful group of young men to me. I don't think I am overstating it when I say I was horrified to hear him say how he resented them. The Grieving Father was painfully honest as he explained why: every life event and accomplishment of one of his son's friends was something his boy would never experience. The unfortunate man was both saddened and jealous that the friends were still alive when his son was not.

I reflected on a similar visit I recently had from Allie. He called out of the blue when he and his wife and two little kids were in Rockville Centre visiting his parents from Notre Dame, where he was studying for his MBA. He had been Matt's friend and classmate at Chaminade, but he had also played on my basketball teams for several seasons and was plainly one of my favorites, not just for his wit but for the grace with which he handled his childhood diabetes. If he would start to fade in the middle of one of his shifts, he would just run past the bench and yell, "I'm getting pretty low out here, E.B.," his signal for me to take him out of the game.

"I need to come see you, E.B.," he said over the phone in late October 2014.

"Sure, Allie," I replied. "That would be nice." We agreed he'd come to my office at 3:30 p.m. on Halloween afternoon, while his wife and parents took his kids trick-or-treating.

I probably hadn't seen Allie since 1998, when he and Matt graduated from Chaminade. So much had happened in between that I feared long awkward gaps in the conversation.

So I talked Allie into getting into my car, and we drove to the construction site in Long Beach. The new house was not only framed out, but enclosed for the winter, with staircases and floors in place. We yakked during the car ride down, then inspected the construction to date, climbing up and down the stairs to check the several bayfront views. We talked all the way back to Rockville Centre about Allie's young family, his studies, and his future career plans – although we did touch on some old stories, like the time he came to practice with a large poster on which he had drawn an in-bounds play designed to get the ball to him and no one else! Coming when it did, I think that visit by Allie was one of the most thoughtful things anyone ever did for me. It was also a prime example of the kindness that can come to you from an unexpected source following a tragedy.

At the end of the support group session, I collected an exhausted Patti and we headed home. She told me she had mostly cried when she had been with the other mothers. I told her about The Grieving Father who spoke, and I vowed that, no matter what, I would never be that guy.

Patti and Ann have gone to some support group meetings since. I don't recall ever going back myself, probably for fear of encountering The Grieving Father or someone like him. That was probably not a good decision.

XXVI.

Do you think it's possible that, from watching what her son endured and standing at the foot of His cross, Mary the Mother of God contracted PTSD? After Jesus instructed John to take care of her as he would his own mother, we never read much in the Gospels about Mary again. I think she was in the upper room with the apostles on Pentecost, but there are no more accounts of what she had to say, like her typical motherly dialogue with her Son at the wedding feast at Cana. Did she ever recover from Good Friday?

I wrote at the start of the book that I was fortunate enough to marry the best person I ever met. I didn't explain why she earned that title.

Patti is literally my secret angel. Her unwed mother was an Irish teen straight off the boat, and Frank and Lorayne, who had longed for a child, adopted Patti weeks after her birth from the New York Foundling Hospital. They all hit the jackpot, both the proud parents and the beautiful blonde baby girl.

Three years later, Patti's brother Frank was born with cerebral palsy. Like so many children affected by an illness or medical condition of their own or a sibling, Patti set out to help others facing similar problems. She took special education courses at both Marymount College in Tarrytown, New York, a fine, all-women liberal arts college which, to its everlasting shame, Fordham University acquired and then closed, and Columbia University's Teachers College, where she earned her Master of Arts degree. After a short stint teaching "normal" kids when we were

269

first married, and her hectic years of commuting to the League School in Brooklyn to work with older "involved" kids, she began her life's work of evaluating and providing special educational services to infants who had been diagnosed with delays and disabilities. She became known as the "Baby Lady" to parents, which wasn't surprising given her almost magical way with infants, all of whom brought a special glow to her face, not just her own.

Shortly after Paul was born in 1985, she took a job in Rockville Centre at the fledgling Long Island Infant Developmental Program ("LIIDP"). The format for delivery of remedial services, intended to catch at-risk babies up with their peers and eventually reduce expenditures on special services for school age children, was in transition. Instead of being authorized by Family Courts throughout New York State, the program would henceforth be administered by the various county Departments of Health and implemented by private agencies. Patti walked in at the birth of a whole new industry.

In addition to her office duties at LIIDP, Patti spent much of her day in the field, "shaking toys" as we jokingly referred to her professional activities. The families loved her, and she soon developed an expertise in "evaluation," the process by which the infants' delays were measured to determine whether they qualified for services in one or several disciplines that would be delivered in the child's home or other "natural environment" by therapists licensed in the various fields, such as special education, speech therapy, physical or occupational therapy, etc.

Patti had ten productive years in at LIIDP when her boss announced he was retiring, moving to Arizona, and selling the business to one of her co-workers, since he didn't think Patti had the money to buy it, an assessment with which I did not disagree since our four kids would hopefully one day head off to college. Patti couldn't see herself working under her former co-equal and began weighing her options.

I encouraged her to start her own agency. She was extremely organized and, if she operated out of our spacious basement, she could not only minimize the business's overhead but be something of a "stay-at-home" Mom. Her Dad, who always had a conservative mindset forged in his Depression-era youth, thought Patti was crazy to give up a steady paycheck. To her credit, though, she authorized me to form Early Intervention Professionals, Inc. ("EIP") in early January 1995.

We thus had the getaway car ready, although it had not been thrown into gear, when Patti informed me that one of her co-workers wanted to ride off from LIIDP too. I had my doubts, particularly when told that it would be a 50-50 arrangement despite my advising Patti to retain the majority interest in the startup. After we met with her co-worker and her husband at a diner in Baldwin, I asked Patti again: "Are you sure about this?"

"Don't worry," she assured me. "I can handle her."

She couldn't. By living upstairs from the office, Patti essentially spent most of her waking time on EIP, while her partner devoted much of hers to cases she had insisted on retaining "privately". Since there was no staff nor money for an accountant, I was pressed into service as bookkeeper, tracking the billings to Nassau's Department of Health and calculating the "split" of the fee collected by EIP with the therapist who had rendered the service.

Remarkably, from such humble beginnings, the business took off because Patti and her partner were acknowledged as top providers in the field. Soon the Department of Health referred as many cases to EIP as it could handle. Just as quickly, the working relationship between the two women hit the rocks. As we reviewed the partner's perceived offenses, serious or trivial, each night after dinner, it became clear this arrangement could not be salvaged.

Dividing the thriving business was as bitter a battle as a contested divorce, and it took a tremendous, unseen toll on both of them. Her co-owner's marriage broke up. Both her and Patti's health became compromised permanently, in my view, by living with this stress from personal and legal skirmishes for over a year.

Finally, after I almost attacked her lawyer brother when he told me to "shut-up" at a settlement conference, I realized I was too protective of my wife to serve effectively as her lawyer. I had heard about "white rage," but now I had experienced it firsthand in the brother's office, yelling out loud and shaking as months of emotion came bursting out, while he watched with fear of the angry genie he had uncorked. My lawyer friend, now a federal judge, came to the rescue and in no time worked out a truce agreement between the disputants, who went their separate ways as competitors. Patti had to discontinue use of the perfect name of the company she founded, but that was the only tangible cost of her mistake. On July 30, 1997, Infant & Toddler Interventionists, Inc. ("ITI") was formed.

Patti picked up right where she left off, but this time flying solo. She recruited the best therapists, took on the hardest cases, and achieved some nearly miraculous results for many families who needed help. The money wasn't bad either, and I always tell my children that it was their mother who financed their college educations, while I kept them fed, clothed, and housed.

By 2000, ITI had grown so much that it was going to have to leave its basement headquarters, one way or another. I started dreaming about buying a building, in our home-town, where we could operate our businesses side by side, and maybe even have lunch together once in a while. I found a suitable building and, after a protracted negotiation with its owner, formed an LLC, bought the property and converted it from industrial to office use. We threw an open house for our respective clients in June of 2002 to celebrate what we had made happen.

From the time she first had employees, Patti was singularly focused on their welfare. If a clerical staff member showed aptitude or initiative, she would try to bring the person along, and several moved on to positions of greater responsibility in the organization. She served as a mentor to them and all the professionals, whether they functioned as employees or independent contractors. Patti was never too busy to talk about anything with them, and I would often see familiar faces sitting across from her desk discussing a child's needs or the therapist's own problems.

The same held true as to compensation. I don't recall a single instance where she put her interests before those of her workers. "Let's do the right thing" was the woman's mantra when it came to year-end bonuses, employer 401(k) contributions, and other benefits.

I would have to say, however, that the party was winding

down for ITI by 2010, just when all our other troubles were ramping up. New regulations imposed by the Department of Health were creating additional compliance costs. Therapists were demanding an ever greater percentage split of the fees collected. ITI's margins began shrinking dramatically. Instead of cutting staff or reducing their compensation, while she hoped for a bounce back, Patti first discontinued paying rent, then shrank her own salary to a level barely sufficient to pay for the expensive radio frequency ablation treatments she was receiving so she could even make it to work. Soon she eliminated her salary altogether, then began tapping into the company's line of credit so she could keep paying the salaries and bonuses her employees had received when things were rosy.

Added to the personal difficulties, the business stress was wearing her down. I warned her that you couldn't be an absentee boss, but she could not respond. She was spending less and less time in the office, and it seemed to me that she was losing control of the operation.

Not surprisingly, Matthew's death was a pivotal point in Patti's professional career. Up until then, she had the desire to fight all her physical ailments each weekday and carry on. After The Event, she looked shell-shocked and gave the impression that everything seemed pointless to her.

After several months of going through the motions as best she could, while the financial condition of ITI worsened, I convinced Patti that she had to make a change. The best solution seemed to be to sell the company to a competitor who would want her to stay on in a supporting role. Patti finally agreed this was the way to go.

I'm going to spare readers the details of the dissolution of ITI, although Shakespeare fans might enjoy this tale of betrayal. In my opinion, employees whose careers Patti had nurtured, and whom she had kept employed when reason dictated letting them go, subverted each of her attempts to sell the business and walk away debt free. She received only a pittance from a competing agency which was interested in acquiring her roster of therapists, because these same employees with short memories actively discouraged ITI's therapists from making the transition. What Patti had done to deserve the punishment they delivered so coldly remains a mystery to me. What is clear is that, less than a year after The Event, any sense of empathy for her was gone and these individuals felt free to attack, knowing full well she would be incapable of defending herself. They were correct. She was no longer the person who had fought her original business partner to a draw. I couldn't realistically suggest that she should pursue the legal recourse she could have had. She just didn't have anything left, and closing down the company she had built and was so proud of was added to Patti's list of losses.

Patti only managed to work for the acquiring agency briefly during the fall of 2015. I had urged her to get a driver, but she had insisted on driving herself. She was exhausted by the time she got to its headquarters in Melville and was found sleeping at her desk on occasion. After a minor rear end accident on the LIE, in which a young woman in the second car forward claimed to have been hurt, Patti gave her notice, recognizing that physically she couldn't make the trip and do the job.

We took the financial hit from shutting down ITI, taking care to ensure that every child's therapeutic needs were satisfied and every creditor was paid in full. We once again moved on, disillusioned but with heads held high despite this most recent defeat.

*

In early 2015, change was not just necessary on the business front. The house on Harvard Avenue was extremely vertical, and it seemed that it was more of a struggle each night for Patti to mount its grand staircase with her cane. The house in Long Beach was supposed to be ready for occupancy in the Spring. No one had ever said it out loud, but I'm sure everyone else felt as I did. The recent bad memories outweighed the good ones, and the sooner we left our home for a fresh start in a new house in Long Beach the better. We gave the listing to a realtor friend whose son I had coached on February 1, 2015. Her boss came to inspect the house on Sunday afternoon, February 15, 2015, to set the price and agree on the commission rate.

Patti hadn't been feeling well and was upstairs sleeping. I went to wake her up, then rejoined the office manager, who was fashionably decked out but gave the impression she had just come from her workout at the gym.

I was on the verge of going back upstairs to get her, when Patti finally appeared on the landing and walked slowly down the rest of the way. She turned into the living room and sat herself next to the realtor lady on the couch. Patti did not seem to know who the lady was or what she was doing there, although we had discussed her scheduled visit earlier. After a few minutes, I suggested that she let me take her back upstairs, which I did.

When I returned, the woman – who had already indicated she was familiar with our recent family history – said something I don't think I'll ever forget: "You certainly have your hands full, don't you?"

I just stared at her. "I guess you could say that," I responded, teeth clenched.

Two days later Patti was admitted to Winthrop Hospital in Mineola. She was extremely ill and became severely disoriented, perhaps delirious over her first few days in the hospital, so much so I didn't think she was going to make it back out. The doctors thought she had C. Diff, which probably would have killed her, but after almost two weeks in the hospital – mostly in isolation – they released her with a diagnosis of gastroenteritis.

The Harvard Avenue house may have been overpriced – the taxes were definitely too high – and the local ladies working for this real estate agency made no progress toward selling it. I couldn't shake the suspicion, however, that they were too familiar with what had happened in the hidden back yard, and that gossip was hindering the sale. As soon as the exclusive period was up, I gave the listing to an out of town realtor that was going to open an office in Rockville Centre. We hoped for a fresh start.

*

The construction on the Long Beach house was going well, but it was a year behind schedule as of Memorial Day 2015. I was starting to worry about missing another summer at the beach, so I gave the builder notice that "ready or not, here we come". I let him know that we would start moving in on the 4th of July weekend, after which they would just have to work around us. The threat seemed to work, and the builders were nearly done by that long weekend.

New construction is not something I would ever undertake again, but the house came out great and the elevator – once the initial glitches were resolved – was a blessing for Patti given the height of the structure. You quickly forget the many battles and aggravation along the way if, at the end of the process, you are satisfied with the finished product. We were all very happy with our new home.

Not surprisingly, the decor includes several paintings by Ann and many nautical touches, including large wood carvings of various species of fish which Paul purchased and hung on different walls.

I told him I need one more to hang right over the front door: a bluefish. The fish tastes terrible, but its fighting spirit is something to behold. A bluefish is Nature's eternal optimist. Even after he's been hooked and dragged into the boat, he's just waiting for the fisherman to open the livewell for a moment so he can bite him on the hand and do a backflip into the ocean. Mr. Bluefish truly doesn't know how to give up.

If I ever get my wooden bluefish, I'm going to have "Resurgence" carved into his side. I never did anything to formalize it, but in my mind it's the new house's name.

*

In early October 2015, we had another junket planned on the

principle that when the going gets tough, the tough go on vacation. I had a business trip that required a few days in San Francisco. Thereafter, we would head north for the Wine Country and rendezvous with Kathy and Big Jim to tour around Sonoma and Napa, including a visit with my late sister Kathleen and her husband Michael who lived in the lovely town of St. Helena.

We had great weather, stayed in some nice places, and had a lot of laughs. On one morning, however, the girls went shopping and Jim and I went roaming around Calistoga, a historic California town that has been very well preserved. We stopped for lunch in some sandwich place that had picnic tables outside. We had just settled in when the cell phone in my pocket began to ring. It was my office; the Dean of Students at The Nephew's college was looking for me. That can't be good.

The Nephew had been strangely quiet since returning to school for his senior year in late August. He had done almost three years of penance without a car and, since he had been achieving near Dean's List grades, he convinced his trustee to buy him a used one late that summer. I stayed out of the transaction, but had not objected since he seemed to have found a new level of maturity and my hope was he wouldn't blow the car privilege again.

The Dean quickly explained The Nephew's prolonged silence and refusal to return our calls. He had gotten in legal trouble the very night he had returned to campus but kept it to himself. About two weeks later, no doubt for failing to come clean about the first incident, he made another bad choice before making the acquaintance of the cops in the next borough after he had totaled the replacement car in their jurisdiction.

According to the Dean, with two different court cases and multiple charges facing him, The Nephew had gone into a real funk. Despite their counseling efforts, he was refusing to attend classes. We were to return to New York from California on Saturday night, October 10, 2015. The Dean wanted me to pick The Nephew up the next day, clear his things out of the dorm room and take him home with an understanding that, if he straightened himself out and got some help, he could return for the spring semester.

The trip to Pennsylvania that Sunday was the first of many over the next few months. It was a beautiful early fall day, and there couldn't have been a more ideal place for a young man to be than strolling around that campus. But instead of meeting friends, or going to the library, or doing any of the many things college kids do on their day off, The Nephew was doing the walk of shame before curious onlookers, loading his things in my car to go home. It was a pitiful sight, and it's not my nature to pile on, so I limited the many things I could have said to just one: you can come back from this and salvage the situation.

I have perhaps had some bad stretches in my life, but I can't remember any more difficult than the one that began when The Nephew and I arrived home. He resented his well-deserved loss of autonomy. I resented the fact that we were again off to the races with lawyers and recovery programs for the benefit of a sulking guy who showed no sign of either contrition or cooperation.

We were living in Long Beach full-time, but the Village of Rockville Centre had let The Nephew resume his summer employment. Instead of a cushy job tending to the ballfields, however, he received a crack of dawn assignment on the garbage trucks.

This led to a fight every single morning. The Nephew would stay up late at night playing on-line video games against competitors who could be in another country. As I would be returning to the house with Portia from her predawn walk, I could see from a block away that his upstairs room was still dark, and that The Nephew had failed again to set his alarm or pay attention to it. I would drag him out of bed, and yesterday morning's fight would resume and usually continue throughout the twenty minute drive to Rockville Centre. I began counting the days until he would return to school, praying that I wouldn't kill him before then – and that he wouldn't throw the opportunity away again when he got there.

I had found a fine local lawyer to guide The Nephew through his legal troubles. I shuttled him back and forth to Pennsylvania for his court appearances, and to Oceanside a couple of nights a week to attend his program sessions. The Nephew said what the college wanted to hear in his letter seeking readmission, and he returned to school in January.

I don't want to prolong this sad story. The Nephew's legal troubles were all resolved without any permanent damage, but he stayed off the rails for good academically. The college gave him multiple chances: in January, in the spring semester, and even a first summer session, but the administrators properly gave up on a kid who simply refused to go to classes.

When he got the boot from the college the final time, we were in New Hampshire at a wedding and The Nephew went straight to his "real" uncle's house in Baldwin. They came to retrieve his stuff in Long Beach before we got home. He hasn't been back or in contact since.

I don't know what, if anything, Matthew's death had to do with The Nephew's meltdown. It's just another What If? Would things have ended differently with The Nephew, or not ended at all, had our son who called him his brother survived? Who knows?

What I do know is that this was the second demonstration to me that you can do everything you think you should do as a parent and still have a terrible outcome.

*

With ITI going out of business and a big house sitting vacant in Rockville Centre, it wasn't too long before I felt the financial pinch. Half of the office building was now empty. I needed a tenant to pick up the slack. So, I called Big Jim's older brother Bob, a commercial realtor who has also been like a brother to me.

"I need to come over for lunch," Bob said. "You're going to hate being a landlord."

Bob did come that very day. He explained that for almost fifteen years I had only been a glorified maintenance man, whacking weeds, taking out the garbage, changing lightbulbs, and doing whatever was necessary to keep the people employed by our firm and Pat's agency satisfied.

"But what am I going to do, Bob? We love it here."

"So, you sell the building and rent your side back," he responded with great certainty.

I hadn't thought of that move at all. The same night, I called a fellow I knew from my basketball playing days who, with a partner, was buying up commercial parcels in Rockville Centre. I professed my ignorance right away when explaining what was on my mind: I wanted to sell the building but have the law firm stay put under a lease covering its present space.

"You really don't know how this works, do you? It would be ideal for me to have you take a long term lease for the space."

On December 16, 2015, Sixby Realty Company, LLC (or was it "Fiveby" as my wife insisted since there had been six Byrnes but only five shares, the last of which we split?), sold its only asset. A little good luck came our way just in the nick of time. The mortgage had essentially been paid off, so our three surviving kids all received their one-fifth shares in accordance with a fifteen year plan that had actually worked. Patti's and my shares, now a full one each after Matt's death, went to pay off ITI's line of credit and fund the taxes, maintenance, and upkeep on the empty Harvard Avenue house, which we now feared would take a long time to sell. This time, at least for the moment, we had dodged the bullet.

XXVII.

I certainly learned in the cases of Matthew and The Nephew that the condition of a person's car and his driving record are extremely accurate indicators of what's going on in his world. Unless something halts the process, a series of dings signals an eventual total wreck, while parking and speeding tickets may foreshadow more serious criminal charges.

The accident which brought her work with the new agency to an end was not Patti's first "at-fault" one. Even before Matthew had died, she had been involved in a number of fender benders, with increasing frequency. This was uncharacteristic, because she had been a very good driver since she was seventeen, when she would chauffeur me around in the yellow Camaro her father had bought as her high school graduation present – then sold without warning while we were on our honeymoon, no doubt sending me a message of some sort.

I suppose I was ignoring the minor accidents as just another streak of bad luck until Nassau County installed red light cameras at some major intersections. We began receiving tickets at practically two week intervals. I became concerned when I examined the photos of what had happened at the intersection. It did not look like Patti had been going too fast and had just blown through the light, or that she had been trying to beat it. It seemed more like she just had not reacted in time after the light turned yellow, and there was too long a lag between her seeing the signal to stop and actually braking to do so.

I tried to persuade Patti to stop driving, at least until we could get her checked out. This was a very difficult discussion to have, and I met lots of resistance. Our children weighed in, on my side, pointing out that she wasn't working and didn't need to drive any longer. That just opened another wound, because Patti felt diminished because she was no longer doing her part to support the family at a time when the finances were being stretched very thin.

At the suggestion of Theresa, a friend of Patti's from the nail salon, on January 27, 2016 we consulted Chrysti, a Long Beach lawyer who handled Social Security disability applications.

I remember helping Patti out of the car in the snowy parking lot across from the Long Beach train station, crossing Park Avenue and negotiating the slippery sidewalk carefully, then walking behind her as she climbed slowly up the staircase to Chrysti's shared office. It was worth the effort, because this Texas native could not have been more compassionate to the broken woman who sat in front of her. Chrysti listened to the whole sad story, which for the most part I had to tell while Patti sat in a chair next to me crying. As I heard it come out of my mouth, it sounded like a tale I must have made up.

I think the evening's consultation was a turning point for Patti. This perfect stranger gave her sympathy, sound legal advice, and sensible personal advice. Chrysti certainly couldn't lift Patti's depression, but she gave her reason to believe that things could get better. In the lawyer's view, Patti had been disabled since August 24, 2014. Given all of her preexisting medical conditions, The Event was the *coup de grace* to Patti's working career, and Chrysti would set out to prove it. I gathered the necessary documentation, and in short order she did. Social Security's ruling in Patti's favor resulted in automatic Medicare coverage, again in the nick of time since we were beginning to hear rumblings about her nearing "lifetime limits" from the medical insurer.

*

One point Chrysti tried to drive home was how essential it was for Patti to cease driving. The lawyer's description of what could happen in the event of another accident made a far greater impact than any warning from me or the kids.

Patti tried to comply, and for the most part did. One day, however, prompted by winter cabin fever or some other good enough reason to leave the house, she hopped in the car and drove off.

Even Portia knew this was a bad thing for Mommy to do. When she left, the Warrior Princess got anxious and reverted to an old bad habit she hadn't indulged since we had left Rockville Centre: she chewed the new window sill up until Patti came home.

When Patti saw what the worried mastiff had done in her absence, she refrained from joyriding again.

*

Since she had taken over the listing in the summer of 2015, our new realtor, Donna, had been knocking herself out trying to sell the Harvard Avenue house. She and her agents ran multiple open houses, showed it to many couples, and even had an architectural rendering of what a new kitchen and first floor layout of the grand old home could look like. Nothing was working, and the place sat there furnished, but otherwise empty.

I thought it best to try to make the house look lived in, even though it was not. So, in addition to using timers for the first floor lights, I stopped by every day to pick up whatever mail had been left there. As a result, I probably had the most thorough change of address in the history of the U.S. Postal Service. As I paid each bill that arrived, I would dutifully complete the change of address form in the back and have the next one sent to Long Beach.

If you sell your house and move in a reasonable length of time, you probably have to worry that the bills that only come a couple of times a year might be misdirected. Not us. Since the move out took almost three years, I had it whittled down to junk mail arriving in Rockville Centre by the time we finally left.

I kept following this daily ritual to the end, even though it made me sad to walk through the quiet rooms and hallways as I checked to see if anything else had gone wrong since my last inspection.

The only bright part of these visits will sound a little strange. Sometime after we all started living in Long Beach, a large brown rabbit took up residence outside the Rockville Centre dwelling. He became quite familiar with my schedule and would come out of the bushes to greet me, unafraid, when I went up the front steps to get the mail.

I'm not a superstitious guy, or someone who believes in reincarnation, but I would be lying if I said I never considered that

Matt had been disciplined for transgressions in his prior life by being sent back as a large, handsome rabbit.

The postscript to this story is that Paul recently told me that a brown rabbit has taken up residence under the deck he built at the house where he and his wife, Trista, live in Rockville Centre. Maybe the rabbit concluded it was too dangerous to relocate all the way to Long Beach, but he could make it safely from Harvard Avenue to where his brother now lives a few blocks away.

XXVIII.

Before consulting the lawyer in late January 2016, we had seen Patti's long time pain doctor on January 8, 2016.

Dr. Emile knows everything about Patti and has for a long time. He was concerned that her depression was not lifting and noticed that her affect was "off". My father had told me as a kid about the "thousand yard stare" some of his WWII comrades in the Pacific had developed, and I suspect this is what it looked like. When I told Dr. Emile about the driving issues, he promised to call a young neurologist with whom he was friendly, a colleague at NYU Langone. He warned that it would take a few weeks to schedule an appointment with Dr. Martin, but strongly felt this was the way to go.

So, we waited in early 2016, and life went on. Patti had a special day on March 2 when Marymount School, her alma mater, celebrated its 75th anniversary at St. Patrick's Cathedral. Using her rollator, which had mostly replaced the cane, she marched down the center aisle with our granddaughter Grace, then a student in Marymount's lower school.

Valentine's Day was even better. In the remarkable way life has of surprising us, just months after Matthew's death, Paul had met the love of his life, Trista. Not one to overlook any romantic advantage, he had chosen Valentine's Day to "pop the question," and it had worked like a charm.

Less than a week later, however, Patti was back in Winthrop University Hospital. It was essentially a rerun of her hospitalization around the same time the year before. While C. Diff. was suspected, it was never established, and Patti was released on February 24, 2016, again with the catchall diagnosis of gastroenteritis.

Finally, on March 23, 2016, Patti went for electromyography and first met Dr. Martin at NYU's Pearl Barlow Center. A brilliant but exceptionally kind man, he immediately took charge of identifying the source of Patti's cognitive difficulty, aided by his fine nurse practitioner whom I called "Dr. Nikki".

Patti was sent on April 6, 2016 for a neuropsychological evaluation of her cognitive and behavioral functioning. After a joint interview with the head clinician, during which I informed him that my wife had been somewhat "crushed by life" and had sustained a "horrible streak of losses," I left for client meetings for the rest of the day while Patti underwent a battery of tests. Knowing I was stuck, Beba had offered to pick Patti up when the testing was done and take her back to the Villar apartment on the Upper East Side until I could pick her up that evening. When I finally did, Patti was still quite upset, more than anything by the refusal of the assistant administering the tests to let her take a break to get something to eat. When the evaluation was issued in late April, its conclusions clearly indicated that I had not sounded a false alarm and there was definitely something going on.

This triggered a mobilization of medical resources on several fronts, not including audiology, which had already been addressed a few years before when Patti's hearing seemed to disappear overnight. Dr. Nikki arranged for an MRI on June 16, 2016, knowing that the preferred PET scan would be denied by insurance until Patti became Medicare eligible. Dr. Emile referred her to a rheumatologist to replace the late Dr. Bertrand Agus, the wonderful physician who had treated Patti since she was in her early thirties. Dr. Nikki referred us to a Dr. Greg, a psychiatrist specializing in older patients, as well as a social worker who did bereavement counseling. This gentleman in turn referred us to a woman whose brother, like Ann's, had taken his life. As a result, Joanne abandoned her career with a high powered law firm and devoted herself professionally to families like ours who were dealing with the consequences of suicide.

The PET scan was finally done on November 17, 2016. We met with Dr. Martin on December 21, 2016 to review the results.

To my astonishment, Dr. Martin informed me that PTSD, which Patti had plainly experienced the date of The Event, can not only cause or contribute to psychological changes but physiological ones as well. I suppose everyone knows the former is true, but the latter proposition: that a shocking event can actually cause structural damage to your brain? As they used to say in Brooklyn, who knew? Dr. Martin referred us to another neuropsychologist who worked with returning veterans with PTSD to confirm his preliminary diagnosis of frontotemporal lobar degeneration. After consulting with Dr. Greg, he also upped the medication prescribed for Patti to Namzaric, a drug which added Memantine to the Aricept/Donepezil she was already taking.

I remember crying when I first googled FTD to see what they were talking about, but only that one time. As soon as I finished reading, I realized that this latest bit of bad news did not change a thing between Patti and me. We had dealt with much worse already, and we would deal with this as well. I only wish it were caught sooner.

It must be some kind of paradox, like Christ the King cruci-
fied. The more frequently and harder you get your ass kicked, the
less sensitive to it you become. At some point, the disproportion-
ate number of hits just begins to look just silly, and about all you
can do is, as the old advice goes, grin and bear it.

I never seriously suspected when I was young that life could
become an endurance contest, as St. Paul viewed it. If that's what
it is, so be it. I intend to finish as strong as I can.

XXIX.

At the risk of convincing readers I did lose it along the way, let me tell you about the Warrior Princess, our cane corso mastiff Portia. She became part of our family in September 2008, a match made "on the rebound".

I had been scheduled for a colonoscopy in Great Neck on July 25. Patti was going to drive me to the doctor, since I couldn't drive home after the anesthesia. To salvage the day, she promised me lunch at Louie's, a popular seafood restaurant in Port Washington. Then she threw in a big surprise.

"I think it's time for another dog," she said.

"Really?" I replied. Josephine had been gone for about two years, and I had settled in to a less responsible, dogless life.

"Yes. We'll go to the North Shore Animal League after lunch."

I just nodded thinking, *here we go again*.

As had happened with Josephine, we both fell in love with the same animal: a cute little cattle dog. Despite warnings that he would be very active herding us, instead of cattle, and would nip at bare feet every chance he got, we came back Saturday, the next day, to pick Rory up and take him to his new home on the South Shore.

Everyone loved the new pup, and he settled in as part of the family immediately, scampering around the kitchen and television area where we had him confined. By Friday evening, however, he seemed a little bit off. He was lethargic, at least for Rory, and retired to his crate earlier and without the playfulness he usually exhibited. We didn't think anything of it that night and went to bed.

I was the first up in the morning. When I went downstairs to take the dog out, I found Rory collapsed in the back of his crate, covered with feces and vomit. I wrapped him in the little baby receiving blanket we had used to take him home and raced him back to the shelter in Port Washington, coaxing him all the way not to die on us.

As I burst into the waiting area with Rory in my arms, one of the volunteer receptionists literally screamed at me: "What did you do to that animal?" A wave of emotion unlike anything I ever felt before hit me from that unjust accusation. I sat shamefaced in the waiting area for a short while before I was informed what I already knew: Rory was dead.

The poor dog had the parvo virus. He already was doomed when he came home with us. I tried to collect myself on the way home. Everyone was still sleeping when I arrived, and I began rehearsing how to break the news. "Oh, remember Rory, that nice little dog? He's gone." This wasn't going to go well.

It didn't, and a gloom settled over the normally happy house that wouldn't lift. A couple of weeks passed, and I knew I had to do something. Why not replace the dog, but with a big sturdy one that wouldn't die on us? Why not get another mastiff?

Secretly, I started checking internet sites of mastiff rescuers. Next thing I knew, I was speaking on the phone to a lady outside of Boston, who was "handler" for a female cane corso mastiff found running loose in Brooklyn when captured by the ASPCA. She had been sent to a shelter in Pennsylvania and undergone an operation to fix her "cherry eye". The woman sent pictures of the dog, a year plus old, and informed me that several other people were interested.

I finally let everyone else in the family know what was afoot, and filled out the voluminous questionnaires, which couldn't be more searching if you were adopting a child. After the rescue league checked all our references and thoroughly vetted us with our neighbors, we "won" the competition for Portia, her name already, because of our prior mastiff experience – which I suppose convinced these people that we at least knew what we were getting into. We did not. Like addictions, all mastiffs are not equal. Our familiarity with a Neapolitan mastiff, who viewed the world as a friendly place until she got a strong negative vibe and responded in kind, in no way prepared us for a cane corso, full of suspicion regarding persons, places and other dogs – with very limited, mostly inexplicable exceptions.

On a warm early September night, after a long trip from Pennsylvania and multiple drop-offs in New York City of other adoptees, Portia arrived in front of our house in an ASPCA van.

"She's been very carsick the last couple of hours," the lady driving the van informed me.

"Great!" I responded, as Portia squatted to pee on the front lawn before I led her into her new home.

She was very solidly built, for a dog which was barely more than a puppy. In less than forty eight hours, no doubt due to stress, her cherry eye popped again. Portia now resembled Marty Feldman in *Young Frankenstein* and had gone from vaguely scary looking to downright ugly.

Our local veterinarian told us that, if we wanted to fix the eye for good, we should take her to Plainview to the veterinary ophthalmologist who treated the Bronx Zoo animals. Portia almost took the surgeon's arm off when he first examined her with his team of assistants, but after she was muzzled and sedated, he worked his magic.

My rescue dog had already gone from "free" to "expensive". But after her cosmetic surgery, the cherry eye was cured for good and Portia looked like a movie star, at least to the Byrne family.

That was the strange thing. To almost the rest of the world, including Beba and her family, Portia was a frighteningly aggressive dog, except to puppies, all of whom she loved. To those of us who lived within her domain, however, she was an incredibly loyal and protective beast.

Never did I once question whether this dog would have my back in an emergency. When I walked her with her choke collar down Harvard Avenue in the dark, she would lunge at any car that came too close to me. No golden retriever would ever do that. And Portia absolutely worshipped Patti as her "Mommy," although she sometimes "mouthed" her arm a bit too hard with her fang-like teeth, or scratched her leg as Patti sat on a chair while Portia smacked her with her giant paws, desperately seeking attention and affection. Even after many sessions with a trainer, this dog had a lot of bad habits, including chewing the rungs off every wooden chair in the kitchen, but somehow they were always overlooked as Portia just being Portia.

Shortly after Matthew's troubles began, Portia began noticeably losing her energy and strength, like Rory had, retreating to the crate where she slept every night while guarding the kitchen door. I thought she was on the way out until Dr. Kim, our wonderful young vet, determined that the animal had Addison's Disease, affecting her adrenal system, just as President John F. Kennedy had. The monthly medicine, bath – which she began crying and whimpering in anticipation of any morning I removed the choke collar -- and giant bag of food cost more than $300 per month, but she bounced back to her old self, keeping extra close watch on Matthew, whom she considered her boy, in contrast to The Nephew, whom she bit in the ass most mornings when he left in too much of a hurry to catch the bus for Chaminade, and Paul, whom she regarded as my ("Big Man's") assistant.

The dog looked both worried and puzzled throughout Matt's trip downhill, unable to grasp what was going so wrong and why he was acting so differently. After The Event, it seemed as though Portia shared our sorrow, but reacted by redoubling her efforts to protect us from something she could not see but only sense.

When we made the move to Long Beach in July 2015, no one expected Portia to survive the disruption to her world for very long. She surprised us all. She soon settled on a new guard post in the elevated house, across from the front door, so she could keep an eye on both the side staircase leading to the garage and the French doors leading to the backyard and the bay. It was the first time she had an enclosed backyard, and she enjoyed the freedom it provided. She would lounge out in the sun, even on hot sunny days, with her fur warming up so much that when Paul petted her he couldn't understand how she could stand the heat.

I don't know if it were the Addison's Disease or just the short life span of big dogs that caught up to her in the late summer of

2016. Her great strength was vanishing, and this time it would not return. For about two weeks, we had been taking her back and forth to Dr. Kim, who was still hoping for a comeback that both Ann and I doubted. Then, one morning, I knew it was over.

Portia stood staring at the bay, unable to relieve herself, with a dazed look on her face that suggested she was thinking, "What's happening to me?" I made the arrangements, and we all agreed to rendezvous for Portia's last trip to the vet. She would be among friends there; I never knew another dog who loved going to the vet and greeting the people who worked there so much. Even April, her beloved groomer, knelt with the family, crying as we said our goodbyes to this most unusual animal.

There was a lot of sadness as we watched her receive the two injections and close her glazed and unrecognizable eyes, but a great deal of gratitude too. Portia had been determined not to check out on us at our lowest point, and had persevered until we had managed, with great difficulty, to transition to a new stage of life. Like the guard dog she was, she simply refused to die until she knew we would be safe.

I still miss Portia, but we have a great picture of her by the front door she briefly guarded in Long Beach. She is sitting at her old post, waiting and staring out the storm door to the driveway in Rockville Centre. The open back door has a "Welcome Home" poster visible on it, for Ann's return from Los Angeles. The dog had become very vocal in her later years, as though she were trying to speak. Portia probably was trying to warn Ann of the dire situation to which she was returning.

*

Probably six months after Portia died, I received a call from the vet's office. Kathy, one of Portia's many friends there, wanted to speak to me.

"We had something odd occur the other day," she began. "A young man showed up on a rainy day. He seemed like he had been drinking. He asked us how Portia Byrne was making out. We just wanted you to know. We don't give any information out about any of the pets."

"It's okay, Kathy," I responded. "Nothing to worry about. I know who it was."

The Nephew had cut off communication with our family so completely that he still did not know Portia was dead.

*

I've written about Patti at length but the person I actually worried most about after The Event was Ann.

Despite my opposition, she had a wonderful experience in Los Angeles with City Year and returned to New York with the boundless enthusiasm only young people have. She had decided that her life's work would be teaching, and she had managed to gain entry to one of the premier programs in the country to prepare for that noble profession. She was rightly proud of herself, and anxious to get on with her career.

Then Ann walked straight into the horror show I've described. She could not fathom how badly things had deteriorated for Matt since her last trip, barely weeks before for her cousin's wedding, and she became a casualty of her beloved brother's decision to end his life.

As I mentioned, Ann was able to start her program at Teacher's College on time, and continue it as scheduled for two years without interruption. I believe the professors were aware of her situation, and very understanding of what she was enduring.

Her teachers were also quite impressed with Ann's talent as an artist. She went through a tremendous creative spurt after The Event, unbeknownst to us until her graduation when a professor who was a particular fan took us on a tour to see all the fine work Ann had pumped out in various media following Matt's death.

Throughout this period, however, Ann kept unfairly blaming herself for failing to save her brother, as though her inability to catch him and stop him from hanging himself that Sunday ultimately would have made a difference. I don't believe that at all. I think that, at most, a rescue might have postponed but not prevented The Event which, at that point, was bound to happen.

Like me, my other children were not on the scene and are not similarly scarred by what Ann and her mother witnessed. That's not fair, nor is the impatience we have undoubtedly at times displayed with their recovery process because we did not experience the full horror ourselves.

Four years have now passed, however. To her eternal credit, Ann has survived. Her pain will never go away, but she will hopefully become that person she set out to be. She drives her late brother Matthew's Ford Escape, the car he only drove one time. She will probably run it into the ground before giving it up. If there are any reparations due in this life for a wrong unjustly suffered, Ann will someday enjoy all the blessings and happiness this world has to offer. I pray she gets what she deserves.

*

I will no doubt carry on a one-sided philosophical debate with my late son until the day I die. Suicide is the most severe form of self-judgment, by which a person appoints himself judge, jury and executioner because of his perceived flaws. To those left behind, it seems to be an extreme overreaction, or maybe a display of terminal impatience. Because there are really only three possibilities with respect to your life situation: things can get better; things can stay pretty much the same; or things can get worse. Two out of these three alternatives you know you can handle, because you made it this far, as unhappy as you may be with the present circumstances. Why presume that things are going to get worse instead of better?

That's where the disease sneaks in. By sucking your hope dry, it makes today unbearable by convincing you that tomorrow is certain to be even worse. I believe the doctors were correct in concluding that Matthew had mental illness, his unlucky legacy, unleashed and compounded by PTSD and substance abuse. I have no confidence, however, that they were medicating him correctly. The week before Matt died, a friend who knows something about the subject said to me, "They're going to kill him with that stuff." Maybe he was right.

I can only surmise that the fear of drowning Matt developed in Hawaii, by taking away the water he had loved all his life, impelled him to end his life another way. I will never know what thoughts were in his head when he took that last trip to the back-yard. Was he feeling profound sadness and resignation or was he angry and unwilling to wait one minute more before taking vengeance on himself for failure to meet his own expectations? And the most haunting question, although the most irrelevant: at the final moment, did he regret his decision or remain resolute?

I always loved sports, probably because they were supposed to be fair, and I've always sought refuge in them. In my view, life is the greatest sport of them all, even though it is the only sport that doesn't even pretend to be fair. We're forced into the game kicking and screaming because we liked things the way they were, and we don't want to play. There are no prescribed rules, just the ones you decide to live by. There are no standings because the contest ends for all of us the same way. It's not like the World Series, because you simply can't win that last game -- and thank God for our remarkable capacity to overlook our mortality on a daily basis and avoid the paralyzing indifference that would otherwise set in. The only question is how well and hard you played the game of life, and there is no way you should take yourself out of the game until the contest is over.

Matt didn't just kill himself, but all the possibilities and surprises that life can bring. I can prove the mistake he made with the most trivial of examples. My son was such a crazed Yankee fan that, as a kid, he thought Jesse Barfield was a great ballplayer. Would Matt rethink his decision if he knew it would deprive him of the joy of seeing Aaron Judge play baseball? If mental illness were not involved, the question answers itself.

I can perhaps understand his thinking but will never agree

with it. So, the debate will rage on, without conclusion, and without changing anything at all. It's crucial to recognize that we have no control over what happens to us. The only thing we may have some control over is how we react to it.

In the latter stages of recounting this story, I remembered a man I was friendly with, many years ago, whom I'll call The Salesman. He was highly educated but he had been forced out of a technical job due to recession – and his age – and he handled my business for several years. The Salesman was unlike anyone else in his field; he was a total gentleman whose word was his bond, and he had my utmost respect.

At some point, The Salesman simply vanished for a while in totally uncharacteristic fashion. When he finally resurfaced, he was wearing an old school black tie, and I asked what had happened. After finding out that his wife had cheated on him with his best friend, The Salesman's son had gone into a funk and taken his life, leaving the now widowed cheating wife and his children behind.

The Salesman said all the right things to me about having to stay strong for the grandchildren, but he never took the black tie off. Before long, he was dead too. I forget what cause was assigned to it medically, but in the old days they just would have said that The Salesman had died of a broken heart.

Just like I had vowed never to be like The Grieving Father I met at the suicide support group, I swore I wasn't going to end up like the Salesman.

*

The life that his mother, his siblings and I have following Matt's death is not the same one we had before, but it is still very much worth living, as I hoped it would be.

Throughout this book, I tried to avoid boring anyone with the dreary details of a busy lawyer's life which, except for the few days following The Event, continued without interruption. When I was a kid in Catholic school, you were constantly reminded how critical it was to listen carefully and find your "vocation". Thanks largely to Patti, I found mine and, to steal from Robert Frost, it has made all the difference to be a member of a profession where you still don't get scoffed at for making your client's interests your primary concern, rather than making money.

When I was beginning my legal studies, the male professors would warn in sexist fashion that "the Law is a jealous mistress". I was just twenty years old, and probably didn't understand what they meant at first. I figured it out pretty quickly, however, when the demands of the profession began burgeoning and never abated.

If you can indulge my use of the now offensive phrase a moment longer, the mistress is even more jealous after The Event than before. I'm still practicing full-time, but I had to reprioritize my professional life over the last four years, which was probably not a bad idea following a life changing event.

The roster of doctors caring for Patti gives rise to a fairly constant stream of office visits. Since most of the physicians are located in Manhattan, and you have little control over when you get to see them, you can shoot most of a work day on a single appointment. I do my best to schedule more than one appointment at a time, but it always seems like one doctor see patients on Mondays, Wednesdays and Fridays, while the other prefers Tuesdays and Thursdays.

So, we came up with the concept of the "Doctor Date" to make the best of this situation. Between time in the car fighting traffic to Manhattan, the waiting time that varies wildly by office, and the actual visit, you are guaranteed a minimum of four hours plus of togetherness. So, we try to make it special and not an ordeal by working in lunch on the way there, or dinner on the way back. This tactic works pretty well, and sometimes I do think it's like actually dating again.

We have also not abandoned travel, although we've cut way back to maybe two trips to business functions a year, due to the challenges presented by packing, airports, and the general hassle of moving ourselves with luggage and rollator from one place to another. What we find much easier is an ocean cruise, leaving either from New York Harbor or Bayonne. The multinational staffs on cruise ships are incredibly accommodating to disabled passengers, and once you are settled in the cabin, the room moves from port to port without you doing a thing, and you can get off and take a look at the new scenery or stay on board as you see fit.

Time we get to spend with the grandchildren is always a delight. Of course, we now play different roles, but sometimes it feels like we are watching history repeat itself. Sure, it's slightly bittersweet, but it confirms just how blessed our family was for a long time and lets us soundly reject the notion that we just imagined those glorious "good old days".

After fully three years, and a post-contract backout by an impetuous buyer that became quite ugly, we finally sold the Harvard Avenue house. A confident young lawyer, certain that his lawyer wife would love it too, practically committed on his initial visit and made an offer on the house the following morning. Turns out he was Matthew's Chaminade classmate, and recognized Matt's picture in our rogues' gallery that still covered an entire living room wall. The couple has three children under the age of three. We wish them all the luck in the world and will always be indebted to them for finally letting us plant both feet in Long Beach, with a little peace of mind as we look out on the water.

So much has changed in our lives, but maybe Patti's and my relationship hasn't changed much at all. I look in her piercing blue eyes and still see the girl I met when I was sixteen and fell in love with when I was seventeen. While I still sometimes lose patience, I do so less frequently than before, hopefully because I love her more than ever – not just because I'm getting older. She calls me "My Best," and I call her "My Best" in return. I suppose we're both right.

Maybe The Test was really of our marriage. If so, despite some shaky moments, we certainly passed. Things did not go back the way they had been, as I had hoped, and all but our memories of Matthew are gone forever, yet we found strength together we never knew we had. We will definitely make it to the finish line.

XXX.

Like my son, Matthew, my father was one of the good guys who lost his way.

He was a combat veteran of the Pacific theater in World War II. As a kid, I just idolized him, even though I realized he was different from the other dads I knew, even the ones who had also been in "The War". I could never understand why he was rarely happy or, on those infrequent occasions when he was, how he could not sustain it for long.

Dad somehow managed to keep his stuff together for about thirty years after The War. He had already started to behave uncharacteristically when, on Easter Sunday 1976, we gave him his belated birthday present, then told him that Patti was expecting the child who would become Elizabeth. Dad somehow talked Mom into hemming the pants to the new denim leisure suit that night. The next day he got in his car and drove to San Francisco, not to be seen for years.

I did not consider our announcement and his departure unrelated. Becoming a grandfather should be a happy event, but it is tinged with suggestions of mortality that Dad simply wanted no part of it. Like it does, life went on without him.

Some time later, I began to fulfill a promise to a former law school classmate. He had led a pretty sheltered life in Westchester, and sometimes between classes I would regale him with tales of the crazy people I had grown up with in Queens. He thought the stories were great, and he convinced me to write them down. A former English major, he would edit the book, act as my agent to get it published, and the money would start rolling in.

I had been too busy with a demanding judicial clerkship in the federal court for the first two years after graduation, but I began writing in 1978, after I took a job I wound up disliking with a large law firm in lower Manhattan.

The concept of the book, however, had changed dramatically. I didn't think life was so funny anymore. I had no contact with my once beloved father. For foolish reasons, I was on the outs with my two best friends, with whom I later reconciled. I had pretty much lost contact with the other guys from the old neighborhood. Instead of a raunchy and humorous book, now bereft of male companionship, I set out to write *Dust to Dust*, the Great American novel.

And I did. I wrote at night, on weekends, early in the morning, on vacations, literally whenever I could. My pockets were always filled with scraps of paper on which I would scribble an idea, a line of dialogue, or some insight I thought worthwhile. I wrote everywhere: attic, basement – I even wrote a chapter on the bathroom floor of a seedy Best Western outside of Busch Gardens while everyone else lay asleep in the next room.

But my favorite place to write, starting in May 1980, was right at the kitchen table in the house on Wachusett Street. I would get to work there practically each night, after we had bathed and put Beba and Matthew to bed. Picking up where I had left off the night before, I would resume the father-son story that bore more than a little resemblance to my own.

Unwittingly, since I did not know his work at the time, I was writing a Pat Conroy type book, with one huge difference. Instead of being fueled by hatred of a father he understood all too well, my narrative was driven by love of a father I didn't understand at all.

I somehow managed to finish the manuscript in 1984, and my friend dutifully edited it and began trying to place it with publishers. Taking the high road, I resisted a seductive offer from a publishing veteran to dump him and get a "real agent" to market this "beautiful book". In short order, however, my friend became dean of a law school and bailed on the project and me, giving me one of my first solid opportunities to play the "What If Game".

Despite intermittent, half-hearted efforts to do something with it, the manuscript over which I had labored so hard resided in one desk drawer or another for almost thirty years. In the meantime, life went on for Patti and I and our family, as I described it in prior chapters, and it was very sweet.

I don't know if it was because my nearly perfect world had begun falling apart, or because I was feeling that male angst that accompanies an approaching sixtieth birthday, but in late 2010 I became preoccupied with the novel that had never been born. Not having totally lost my mind, I decided to send it for a Kirkus review before taking up the quest again.

The review came back positive, and I re-embarked on the project, a process that would involve at least two full editings and several title changes, as well as innumerable re-writes, additions and deletions performed over the succeeding years when my life was in disarray. Did this effort distract me from trying to save my son, the task on which my full attention should have been focused? Or did all the wrestling with the book's father/son themes in fact keep my priorities in order at a time when it would have been tempting to give up and walk away from the situation?

I do know this: much of what I had written in 1984 and before was eerily prophetic. I won't tell you the whole story – you will have to buy another book for that, but I'll give you a few examples to prove my point:

- I had a youthful fascination not only with the Biblical story of Isaac and Abraham, which the novel uses as an allegory for the relationship between the novel's main character, James, and his father, Dave, but also the Tale of Job. I would have been dismayed to learn in the early 1980's how strongly I would one day identify with Job, including his suspicion that some of his friends and neighbors think that he must have done something truly evil to have triggered all the woe raining down on him and his family.

- In the Prologue of the novel, James returns to the Queens playground of his youth, and finds it totally vandalized. Across one destroyed basketball backboard, the words "LIFE SUCKS" have been spray painted. Perhaps the whole point of the book – as well as my ongoing, one-sided debate with Matt – is to prove that this ultimate nihilistic phrase is not true.

- James the son observes in the narrative that "[y]ou're at the mercy of the people you love. They can always hurt you – or the other people you love – whenever they choose". The truth of that assertion now seems undeniable.

- The final title of the book is *Love's Not Over 'Til It's Over*, *LNOTIO* for short. Perhaps the story's major premise is that, once love truly takes root, it can never be eradicated. As James tries to explain the concept to his father: "Maybe love's like baseball, Pop. Remember what Yogi said? ... It's not over 'til it's over. Maybe it's never over, no matter what." This also rings true to me, with respect to both my father and son, despite all that has happened.

- Finally, and perhaps most importantly for purposes of this chapter, Dave arrives at this frustrated conclusion regarding generational strife: "The same guy who'd been his father turned out to be his son." James the son feels much the same, but from the opposite perspective: *"Fathers and sons are natural enemies. We must be paired off to inflict maximum pain on each other. Maximum disappointment."*

How had the person who had written those lines been so slow to realize that this was not just fiction but happening in real life? My father's undiagnosed condition was PTSD, although it had never been dignified with a name until 1980, the same year Matthew was born. Dad became incapable of deriving pleasure from the simple, universal things people value, like family. He became stubborn and unable to see what was so obvious to me: there was something warped in his once flawless logic. Again, life had mimicked art: "there's some perverse twist in your head keeping you from thinking straight, from feeling normal. And if you keep pretending you don't care, soon enough you won't."

Just like the father character in the book, I finally realized that the same guy who had been my father had turned out to be my son. The little boy who had slept upstairs while I wrote at the kitchen table below inherited the same condition as his grandfather and behaved the same way. Maybe it shouldn't have been any surprise. The firefighters in the rear of an engine or "truck" sit in rows as they nervously ride to a fire, just like soldiers in a landing craft as they approach the island they are invading. My father and son were pretty much made of the same stuff; why should they react differently? Both thought they were tough enough to handle anything that came their way. They were equally mistaken because some stuff is just so bad you can't handle it without sacrificing your humanity. Wouldn't I have wound up just like them had I been placed in comparable situations?

On many occasions, as he deteriorated, I begged Matt to take my warnings seriously. "I've seen this movie before," I assured him. "It doesn't end well." I described the downfall of my beloved alcoholic uncle, killed by a hit in run driver on a rainy November night in 1974 when he stepped into Woodside Avenue after leaving the local tavern.

"You've got to get this under control," I kept telling Matt. "It really is a matter of life or death." I'm afraid that, based on my own past, I underestimated how difficult this would be for him. Although the males in our family tended to be, as Grannie would say, "full of the devil," I expected there would come a point when, motivated by love of a woman or maybe concern for his career, he would throttle down the partying and simply grow up. Matt never laughed at me, but he may have smirked at the time, when he was still able to function and pretend that he did have "it" under control.

He obviously didn't, and his death made me revisit my uncle's some forty years before. My uncle had been at his lowest point, yet I had always assumed he had just been drinking that night, and simply stumbled into the street. Now I wonder whether he did it on purpose, and whether the unlucky driver into whose path he flung himself felt justified when he kept right on going.

All the while Matt's life was escaping from him, I kept working on *LNOTIO*, on and off, first expanding the narrative then ultimately shrinking it to make it more marketable. All was in vain. I must have queried over two hundred agents; some politely expressed their disinterest, while most didn't respond at all. This was rejection on a scale I had never come close to experiencing. I likened it to trying to list your house for sale with over two hundred real estate brokers, and having each one refuse the listing, effectively saying "your house is too ugly to sell!" When does that ever happen? But I was definitely being told over and over that my once "beautiful" book was now too ugly to sell.

Finally, in 2016, my editor Carol convinced me that self-publishing was no longer an exercise in vanity, and I should go directly to the readers to determine the work's merits. I ultimately did and, with very little fanfare, *LNOTIO* became available in the fall of 2017. For over thirty years, the book had never had a dedication, but with the benefit of hindsight that showed me how many of the dots in my life connected, I added one that I thought fit:

"This book is dedicated to Donald T. Byrne,
Matthew E. Byrne, and all fathers and sons
who have ever loved each other."

I had always believed the book deserved to be published; I just never wanted to do it myself, and probably wouldn't have had Matthew survived. It is no best seller, but it has been favorably received. Seems like almost anyone who has actually read it has liked it and, if that person happened to be a Baby Boomer, he or she probably loved it.

In a sense, this book is the nonfiction sequel to *LNOTIO*. It is a story I never would have wanted to write.

XXXI.

You may be rightly curious about this book's title: *In Whom I Am Well Pleased*. What did I mean by that?

I'm no New Testament scholar, but I was always impressed by the two instances I recall when God the Father, just bursting with pride, went off script and bragged to the world: "This is my beloved Son, in whom I am well pleased." It's been phrased in different ways, but the sentiment is quite clear. At least at Jesus's Baptism and the Transfiguration, the Father was so full of love for his Son that he could not keep it to Himself but had to let everyone know.

I still feel the same way about Matt. At one point, I considered changing the title to *In Whom I <u>Was</u> Well Pleased*. Then it struck me that changing the tense would make the title less accurate, not more. After everything, and despite the sorrow and, yes, disappointment, I am still proud to have been Matt's father and grateful that he was my son. As I argued at the CSU family session, how bad could he have been? He was a firefighter and a lifeguard, someone who obviously was concerned with the wellbeing of others. These may have wound up foolhardy career choices for him, but they weren't selfish ones. He certainly could have pursued many safer and more remunerative occupations, which probably would not have killed him within twelve years of his college graduation.

This would have been a very different book had I written it in the immediate wake of The Event, when I was wracked with so many emotions, I couldn't begin to sort them out. I may be kidding myself, but I think I have regained sufficient perspective to honestly relate what happened without whining about our misfortune or excusing the many mistakes that undoubtedly were made by all of us along the way.

Part of me still doesn't believe that it all really happened, but that disbelief has shrunk to a fraction of what it once was, only appearing once in a while. Like the time last year when I answered the phone to a "Hey, DaddyO!" I was stunned; it sounded exactly like Matt, and I actually paused, trying to figure out what to do in case it were him. After a few seconds, I said the only thing I could think of: "Hi. Where have you been?" Of course it was Paul, who initially thought my response was pretty weird until I later explained that, over the intervening years, his voice had come to sound exactly like his brother's.

Other times, the past and the present can get a little jumbled up for me, which isn't altogether new. When Matthew was working as a firefighter, sometimes when I was in Manhattan I would hear the alarm and horns blaring as engines rushed by and nervously wonder if he were responding to that fire or some other emergency. If I saw an engine stopped at the corner, even if it weren't marked "9," I would always look in the open window to see whether one of the guys dressed in the bunker gear was my son. I still do so today, though I know that, even if I were peering into Engine 9 itself, I would never see him. I also have Matt's FDNY uniforms hanging in my closet, where they will remain so long as my own clothes do.

There are other keepsakes of earlier, happier times. Matt's baseball bat and glove also live in that closet, unless I bring them down to a Challenger game, along with my own father's ancient glove which I still treasure as well. I also have the first gift Matt ever bought me, purchased at the St. Agnes School Christmas Fair when he was in kindergarten or first grade. It's just a coffee cup but shows a big penguin with its wing around a little penguin, and the motto: "Happiness is having a father for a best friend." It has a place of honor on the sill of our bedroom window facing the bay, where I can see it each morning. I also start most days by taking a peek at a composite photo of the Byrne children, each shot taken around the age of six months. Their different personalities were already in evidence. It's pretty difficult to question your good fortune when you see the four coconut-headed infants with which Patti and I were blessed, even though the one with the sphinxlike smile is gone.

Other reminders are just plain annoying, and invariably occur after someone is dead. A telephone solicitor asking for Matt to sell him something. Marworth's annual solicitation for donations or, worse yet, its periodic invitations for Matthew to attend a "reunion". Ann tried several times to get them to stop, but this stuff keeps on coming. I just shake my head and wonder how, when you kick someone out of your recovery program, you don't also delete him from your mailing list. I'm a fairly forgiving guy, but I don't think I'll be sending Marworth money any time soon!

Except for occasional relapses triggered by such incidents, I think I have made my peace with The Event and its aftermath. Some people have long and happy lives. Some people, like Matt, have short and fairly tragic ones. Most of us end up somewhere in-between the extremes. I wish with all my might that everything had turned out differently, and I regret my inability to have made that happen. Yet I recognize the similarity of parenting to flipping a coin. It's only wishful thinking to think you can decide on which side it's going to land. You're only guessing and hoping for the right outcome.

Now I am resigned to the way things are, and gratified that, as I pointed out to my mother following Matt's funeral Mass, our family passed The Test: "You're missing the bright side, Ma," I had said, in a typically awkward Byrne attempt to counter sorrow with humor.

"Edward, have you lost your mind?"

"No, Ma. We just took maybe the hardest blow life can deliver right on the chin, but we're still standing!"

I have also taken some comfort from an incredibly unlikely source.

When I was an eighth grader, Herman's Hermits were extremely popular. They weren't in the same league as the Beatles and the Rolling Stones, but Peter Noone, their lead singer, "Herman," was as engaging as any performer in the British Invasion – and he still is. He does a Saturday afternoon show each week on Sirius, and he plays great old songs that you hardly ever hear elsewhere, interspersed with personal stories from "back in the day" that are sometimes hysterical and always full of good cheer.

One Saturday, shortly after The Event, Herman played one of the Hermits' lesser hits: "This Door Swings Both Ways." Like everyone else, as a kid I didn't think too much of the song. It was catchy enough, but I didn't ascribe any meaning to it, much less a deep one. When I heard it so many years later, I realized I had totally underestimated this little song.

As you can now do so easily, I looked up the lyrics to this forgotten gem. Written in the British "Music Hall" tradition, with a "stiff upper lip" message, it captures the dual, bittersweet nature of life, which you cannot fully appreciate until you have experienced both sides of it.

The song's simple lyrics end by repeating a line to this effect:

Maximize your living, if you're not ready to die.

I have taken the advice to heart, and I continue trying to embrace life, not reject it or treat it as if it's been ruined forever. There is no point in getting cheated by just going through the motions. I am not prepared to die so, for the sake of my family, and in honor of my late son, Matthew, I hope to make the most of this gift of life until it is taken from me.

The key word there is "hope". A friend told me some time ago that I must have a great deal of faith. My response was that I had very little faith at all, but plenty of hope and love. Two out of three still isn't bad.

Epilogue

The summer after I finished my freshman year in high school, I went on a school trip with twenty-four other students to Oxford. We stayed in a Jesuit residence, Campion Hall, that was close to the campus. Each weekday morning, two dons would arrive, one after the other, to give us a one hour lecture on English history, followed by the same length session on English literature.

At least in the case of English history, this was an utter waste of time. We American teenagers had no interest whatsoever in which king did what, and we seemed to lack any ability to keep them straight unless they had a nasty nickname or suffered a gruesome fate.

The literature professor, however, was not interested in wasting his time. He assembled such a superior collection of poets that even we swine would take notice of the pearls he had cast before us. Shakespeare, of course. John Donne, maybe the hippest of poets until Jim Morrison, who surpassed him in cool but not quality.

But the poem that struck me most when I was fourteen is set forth below. Despite considering nearly everything a joke at that time, I found it profoundly moving, never thinking that, about four hundred years later, I too would stand in the shoes of the poet, Ben Jonson.

"Farewell, thou child of my right hand, and joy;
My sin was too much hope of thee, lov'd boy.

Seven years tho' wert lent to me, and I thee pay,
Exacted by thy fate, on the just day.
O, could I lose all father now! For why
Will man lament the state he should envy?
To have so soon 'scap'd world's and flesh's rage
And if no other misery, yet age?
Rest in soft peace, and, ask'd, say, "Here doth lie
Ben Jonson his best piece of poetry."
For whose sake henceforth all his vows be such,
As what he loves may never like too much."

The name of the poem is "On My First Son," and he wrote another for his first daughter, who also died prematurely. The poem could have been written about his last son, or his last daughter, or any in-between. Birth order doesn't matter at all. Nor does when or how the child died. Illness. Accident. War. Drug abuse. Suicide.

The cause of the loss may be different, but the feelings of any parent who has looked down at his or her "best piece of poetry" are the same. Sorrow. Regret. Maybe anger. But above all, love and loss.

My neighbor, Claire, who had been busy planning her beautiful daughter's wedding when she was taken on 9/11, said right after The Event, "Now you're like me, a member of the club no one wants to belong to." She was right, and the members of that club have to find a way to go on living with broken hearts. With the grace of God, and the help of each other and the families who share our sadness, we will find a way to do so.

www.ingramcontent.com/pod-product-compliance
Lightning Source LLC
Chambersburg PA
CBHW070018100426
42740CB00013B/2546